makes you want to dive back into one of the most gripping discographies in the music. . . . If you haven't heard Weston's music, really listened to it, then *African Rhythms* is the strongest possible incentive to tune in."—WILL LAYMAN, *Popmatters*

"[*African Rhythms*] is an important addition to the jazz historiography and a long anticipated read for fans of this giant of African American music."—IAN PATTERSON, *All About Jazz*

"*African Rhythms* is just as powerful as [Weston's] music, more so because it pierces the mind with stimulating words that will feed the spirit and may move readers to action."—RON SCOTT, *New York Amsterdam News*

African Rhythms

REFIGURING AMERICAN MUSIC

*A series edited by Ronald Radano and Josh Kun*

*Charles McGovern, contributing editor*

A JOHN HOPE FRANKLIN CENTER BOOK

# AFRICAN RHYTHMS

The Autobiography of Randy Weston

Composed by Randy Weston

Arranged by Willard Jenkins

*Duke University Press*

*Durham and London*

*2010*

Printed in the United States of America on acid-free paper ∞

Designed by C. H. Westmoreland

Typeset in Charis by Tseng Information Systems, Inc.

Library of Congress Cataloging-in-Publication Data appear
on the last printed page of this book.

RANDY WESTON
DEDICATES THIS BOOK TO

*His beloved Mom, Pop, Sister Gladys, his son Azzedin*
*(Niles), and the African Rhythms Family*

WILLARD JENKINS
DEDICATES THIS BOOK TO

*The great ladies of my life:*
*Suzan, Iyesha, and Tiffany; for their continued love,*
*support, and encouragement throughout this project . . .*
*and throughout my life*

*And to the memory of my two loving ancestors who*
*are never far from my thoughts, Annalouise and*
*Willard V. Jenkins Sr.*

# CONTENTS

Willard Jenkins. *Photograph by Ronnie James.*

# ARRANGER'S PREFACE

Writing this book with Randy Weston has been a life-altering experience. How did Randy and I get started down this road? Why an autobiography as opposed to the more typical great-man *biography*? How did we arrive at the "composer-arranger" relationship? The way this journey commenced rather mirrors the ancestral spirit-driven path that Randy Weston has traveled.

Randy Weston's music has long been personally stimulating, rewarding, and revealing, full of images and portrayals both ancient and future, laden with the raw materials that make great music. Ironically—as you will discover later from Randy's recollections of the session he has long considered his "only hit record"—my immersion in his music began in 1972. Certainly I knew him from "Little Niles," "Pam's Waltz," and "Hi-Fly," and as a Monk devotee, but my knowledge before that pivotal point was still relatively limited. As a student at Kent State University I frequently climbed in whatever beater I was driving at the time and headed north on I-271 to nearby Cleveland to a long-gone place called Record Rendezvous downtown on Prospect Avenue, intrepidly surfing the bins for new LPs to continue my jazz education. At the time Creed Taylor's series of recordings for CTI, with a rotating stable of exceptional musicians and striking, glossy gatefold packages with photos by Pete Turner, were laden with the kind of good grooves that were quite amenable to a college-life soundtrack. So when Randy Weston's lone CTI date, *Blue Moses*, showed up in the bins in '72 it quickly made its way to the cash register. With Freddie Hubbard, Grover Washington, Hubert Laws, Billy Cobham, and Airto along for Randy's journey, *Blue Moses* was an irresistible purchase.

Gently applying vinyl disc to turntable, I remember soon being taken with the haunting quality of the tracks "Ganawa—Blue Moses" and "A Night in Medina"—that is, after wearing out the grooves on the rambunctious opener "Ifran." *Blue Moses* was quickly joined in the collection by Randy's even more substantive big-band LP *Tanjah* (1973), with memorable contributions from Candido, Billy Harper, and Jon Faddis, all framed by Melba Liston's arrangements. (Little did I know that Melba had also written the original arrangements for *Blue Moses*, which Creed Taylor scrapped in favor of Don Sebesky's . . . but we'll save that story for later.) Randy Weston moved to the upper echelons of my jazz consciousness.

Ahead to 1995 and a magazine assignment to cover the peerless Montreal Jazz Festival; the creative heart of any Montreal Jazz Festival is its Invitation Series, which engages particularly versatile artists in consecutive evenings of concerts, each with a different configuration or theme. The Invitation Series artists for 1995 were David Murray and Randy Weston, whose offerings were bridged by a duo concert reprising their Black Saint record *The Healers (1993)*, accomplishing the sort of neat and logical handoff that is a hallmark of that great festival. For his concert evenings Randy kicked things off with a superlative trio performance featuring Billy Higgins, Christian McBride, and strings that resulted in the record *Earth Birth* (Verve/Gitanes). That date includes a gorgeous ballad treatment of "Hi-Fly," which I later employed as a radio show theme on WPFW in Washington. The ensuing evenings featured performances by Randy's African Rhythms Sextet, and an evening that drew on material from his *Volcano Blues* (Verve/Gitanes) date, with the Cleveland blues legend Robert Lockwood Jr. sitting in for an ailing Johnny Copeland.

That took us through Friday night; one more evening remained on Weston's Invitation Series. But our travel reservation called for us to split on Saturday afternoon, sadly leaving that tantalizing morsel on the plate. After checking out of our hotel my wife and I had some time to kill before our airport transfer, so we headed over to the festival press office to wile away a few moments. We arrived just in time to hear Randy Weston give a press conference. Afterwards my wife Suzan walked up to Randy to tell him how much she had enjoyed his three concerts, but alas, we were about to leave. In typical Randy fashion, eyebrows raised, with certainty, he admonished, "But you can't leave now, we're going to Africa tonight!" That evening would feature the sextet collaborating with the Gnawa Master Musicians of Morocco, who at that point were unfamiliar to us both. As I stood small-talking with Weston, Suzan dashed away on some unspoken errand.

A few moments later she returned with news that she had rebooked us into our hotel, changed our air reservations to Sunday . . . and by God we were staying for Randy's spiritual trip to North Africa that evening! Needless to say it was an incredible evening in Montreal, and the music of Randy Weston was even more deeply embedded in my playlist. Meanwhile, during a trip to the Pan Jazz Festival in Trinidad, at which we were pleasantly awakened each morning by an insistent saxophonist and flutist practicing diligently in the hotel room next door, we also struck up a lasting friendship with Weston's longtime music director, that same saxophonist-flutist TK (Talib Kibwe) Blue, another catalyst for this project. Little did I realize at the time that the seeds for this book had been sown.

In '98 the perceptive arts administrator Mikki Shepard engaged me to help curate a week of programming for her presenting organization 651 Arts in Brooklyn. On tap were some oral history interviews and panel discussions with some of Brooklyn's black jazz cognoscenti and historic figures, including Randy. The centerpiece was to be a reprise at the Majestic Theatre of Weston's *Uhuru Afrika* (1960), a landmark recording which at the time was long out of print but has since been reissued by Michael Cuscuna of Mosaic Records, an avowed Randy Weston enthusiast. The plan was for me to work with Randy to assemble the surviving personnel from the amazing orchestra that made *Uhuru Afrika* (stay tuned: there's a chapter on that session in the coming pages). The oral history interview session in January at Medgar Evers College marked our first extensive interview. I was immediately struck by the many compelling facets of Weston's life, his warm storytelling skills, and his impressive recall. That same year yielded another energizing encounter between the Gnawa Master Musicians of Morocco and Randy Weston's African Rhythms, this time at the Kennedy Center in Washington.

About a year later I was contracted to write web site content by the National Endowment for the Arts for its Jazz Masters program. (This was before Randy received an NEA Jazz Master fellowship in '01.) As I assembled each Master's biography, discography, bibliography, and videography, I was struck by how few of these great lives had been chronicled in book form. I'd been pondering a book project after writing periodical jazz commentary since 1969. Revelations of the bibliographical disparities of so many of the NEA Jazz Masters somehow hastened persistent thoughts of Randy Weston, though he had yet to be honored by that august program. I spoke with TK Blue to gauge an approach to Weston, memories of our 651 Arts oral history interview still fresh. In '99 I was again engaged by 651 Arts, this time to help curate the concert at Lafayette Church in Brooklyn on September 24 that resulted in Weston's Verve release *Spirit! The Power of Music*, his first performance in the New York area with the Gnawa from Tangier and Marrakech.

Sufficiently encouraged, I broached the subject with Randy in 2000, and he was pleasantly enthusiastic. Weston's busy schedule precluded all but occasional exploratory conversations for several months to lay the groundwork for our project. It was during these conversations that Weston made clear his intent that our book would be his autobiography, as opposed to the more typical jazz biography.

My research clarified that at some point in the project a journey to Africa, preferably with Randy, was a necessity. I had to experience some of the elements of the continent that have so indelibly shaped his existence. We continued to discuss the project and began putting his thoughts down on tape.

In May 2001 I'm sitting at home relaxing on Memorial Day when the telephone rings. At the other end is the now-familiar baritone voice of Randy Weston, who asks, "Are you ready to go to Africa?" "Sure," I played along, "why not." "OK," he said, "we leave on June 7!" Turns out, in what I've come to recognize as typical Randy Weston serendipity, the Moroccan television producer Mustapha Mellouk sought to make a documentary film on Randy's life in Morocco, focusing specifically on his thirty-year kinship with the Gnawa spiritual brotherhood. Having never been to the Motherland, I eagerly adjusted my schedule to join him on this journey. Randy had craftily arranged for me to accompany him, to conduct on-camera interviews with him for the documentary.

What ensued was a remarkable ten-day journey that commenced in Casablanca and then continued to Fes, where I experienced an enchanting evening at the renowned Fes Festival of World Sacred Music, to the Middle Atlas Mountain town of Ifran, where I spent a night in a dorm room at Al Akhawayn University (Randy was recognized at a commencement ceremony the next day, after which we devoured one of the trip's many splendid repasts), and on to a week in the magical city of Marrakech, during which we experienced a mind-blowing Lila, an all-night Gnawa spiritual ceremony—all filmed by the crew. We even took a side trip west to the Atlantic coast for one evening of the amazing Gnawa Festival in teeming Essaouira, running into the visiting musicians Joseph Bowie, Adam Rudolph, Hamid Drake, and Cheikh Tidiane Seck, all there to musically interact with the Gnawa and all delighted to see Randy.

The trip to Essaouira further revealed the adulation that so many Moroccans have for Weston. He's basically a shy man, though one with an outgoing personality. The constant recognition in Essaouira among the hundreds of thousands who gathered there in June for the festival rather overwhelmed him . . . and deeply fascinated me. The morning after we ar-

Randy Weston (left) and Willard Jenkins sitting between two Gnawa
gentlemen in Randy's hotel room in Marrakech.

rived in the town, about three hours west of Marrakech, Randy couldn't
walk five feet in the medina without encountering shouted greetings from
fellow strollers and sidewalk café patrons, or hugs from well-wishers. Every
corner we turned it seemed we were greeted by incessant calls of "Randy,
Randy, Randy." One loving fan cajoled us into an enormous aromatic shop
laden with cedarwood boxes of staggering variety, and insisted on buying
us gifts.

I'd already had tastes of such adulation throughout the trip. One afternoon, as we ambled down one of Marrakech's modern, tree-lined boule-
vards in search of a phone card, the city's distinctive reddish architecture
on either side, a motorcyclist raced up alongside us, jumped off his bike
in heavy traffic, and gave Randy a huge bear hug, joyously exclaiming,
"Thank you, Randy Weston, for what you've done for our culture."

Blessed with the extended opportunity afforded by this trip and an ex-
ceedingly pleasant few days in the lush confines of Riad El-Arsat in the
Marrakech medina, in addition to our on-camera interviews for the proposed Moroccan documentary (which to our knowledge, despite extensive
still and video filming on the trip, curiously has yet to see the light of day),
we began our intensive daily interviewing for this book.

Preparing this book involved conducting scores of taped interviews with important people along Randy's life path. The majority of our sessions occurred at Randy's brownstone on Lafayette Avenue in Brooklyn, the house passed down from his father Frank Edward Weston. A significant number of interviews took place on the road, as I traveled with Randy solo or with his African Rhythms Quintet.

In addition to Morocco, in the intervening years we've traveled to the St. Lucia Jazz Festival in the Caribbean in 2002, where the band performed and recorded a DVD and CD; to a weeklong residency on the island of Guadeloupe, where we experienced the compelling Gwo-ka rhythms; to Randy's old haunts in the Berkshires; to Randy's wife Fatou's abode in Paris and, after a high-speed train trip, to Randy's former digs in the picturesque Alpine town of Annecy, where the master performed an intimate solo concert arranged by his dear friend Colette Giacomotti; to the Tri-C JazzFest Cleveland in 2002, where Randy had a residency (and where I am artistic director); to the Monterey Jazz Festival in 2004, seizing that opportunity to interview Randy's first record producer, Orrin Keepnews; and to the University of Nevada, Reno, in 2006. In Guadeloupe, Cleveland, the Berkshires, and Reno, the gracious Fatou accompanied Randy, and her Senegalese insights and humor added immeasurably to our conversations, as did my soulmate Suzan on several of our travels. The family aspect of this project has been invaluable, especially the gregarious participation of the guys in the African Rhythms Quintet, whom you are also about to meet.

Early on, it became clear that this would not be your conventional jazz book in many respects. Randy and I have each observed that there are relatively few true jazz *autobiographies*, which makes this book all the more unique. It is not a particularly linear book. Randy doesn't dwell on the technical aspects of his craft, unlike the authors of more typical jazz books. And his apprenticeship as a sideman was not extensive. What is central to the book is Randy's stress on what defines his musical expression—what he has referred to on record, in composition, and numerous times in conversation as *the spirits of our ancestors*. Though not a churchgoing man in the traditional sense or an adherent of any one religion, Randy Weston is a deeply spiritual man who believes fervently in the Creator, the ancestral spirits up above, and their ultimate guidance over his life's experiences.

Our interviews were inspired by ongoing research and augmented by the prodigious wealth of materials that Randy has accumulated throughout his journey. He has saved every significant scrap of paper, taped every performance, and kept every article, letter, and memo, and assorted ephemera, from his career. I transcribed all our conversations and provided Randy with the transcripts. He painstakingly made additions, corrections, and suggestions throughout the process, which would often lead us down new streams of discovery and remembrance, and his comments were subsequently edited into the transcriptions. One of the hallmarks of our interviews is that without fail Randy would offhandedly make some new revelation or take us down another path. The freshness of each conversation was a marvel, even when we were covering ground that I thought we had sufficiently traversed.

There were points in the transcripts where Randy would cross off certain references and sweep away dirt that gave him second thoughts. Admittedly this was sometimes to my chagrin, but this is his story. Once I shaped our conversations into chapters, I had Randy's explicit permission to condense and reorder his words. Randy would carefully examine chapter drafts all along the way.

At one point during our collaboration it became clear that our working relationship rather mirrored his relationship with his longtime arranger and confidante Melba Liston (which in turn resembled that between Duke Ellington and Billy Strayhorn), though I don't presume to equate my efforts with hers. That was when we decided on the credits for this book:

Composed by Randy Weston
Arranged by Willard Jenkins

# ACKNOWLEDGMENTS

Randy Weston would like to acknowledge and thank the following, both living and ancestral, who have made major spiritual contributions toward his many years of struggle to continue a sometimes lonely journey to tell the truth about who we are as a people:

Abdeslaam and Khadija Akaaboune and family (Tangier); Ahmed Abdul-Malik; Allal Akouri (Marrakech); Jean-Philippe Allard; Professor Amine Khalid (for the wonderful Tangier tribute to Randy and Abdullah El Gourde); the Archbishop of Canterbury; C. B. Atkins (for the "Uhuru Afrika" record date); Professor Atwell (my second music teacher); Brian Baccus; Bobby Benson (for the inspiration from his music and his club Caban Bamboo, Lagos, Nigeria); Chief Bey; Black Rose; Big Black; Ed Blackwell; Jooney Booth; Cecil Bridgewater; Marie Brown (for the great publishing advice); Ray Bryant; Wole Bucknor; Margaret Busby (thanks for the Black Book Fair); Candido Camero; Wayne Chandler; Moktar Cisse; John Henrik Clarke (master teacher); Suzanne Cloutier (for helping me find Frisco); Ray Copeland (trumpeter and my first arranger); Chano Pozo; Maurice and Vonette Culloz; Ken Dadzie; Dar Ganawa; the Rev. Herbert Daughtry; Asadata Defora (African master musician); Javier de Gambra (Spanish journalist); Cheikh Anta Diop and family; Kenny Drew; Maria Eliot (for her help organizing the festival in Tangier in 1972); Ruth Ellington; Booker Ervin; Frisco (Jocelyn Bingham); Franco Fayenz (Italian journalist); Fela Kuti; Min Xiao Fen; Pablo Ferro; Joe Gaines; Marcus Garvey; Pastor John Gensel; Colette Giacomotti; Sam Gill; Dizzy Gillespie; Frederic Graf; Dexter Gordon; Bill Grauer; Georgia Griggs; Gigi Gryce; John Handy; Jaap Harlaar; Billy Harper; Coleman Hawkins; Langston Hughes; Mahi Ismail; Dr. Willis James; Leon James; Richard Jennings; the Jillala; Dr. Ben A. A. Yosef Johannan; Alma John (TV journalist and activist); Budd Johnson; Mari Jo Johnson; Willie Jones; the Joujouka; Orrin Keepnews; Inyatt Hyatt Khan; Talib Kibwe (TK Blue, my longtime music director and arranger); Hubert Laws; Elma Lewis (the queen of Boston); Melba Liston; Jean Lothrop; Professor Acklyn Lynch; Mandrill; Amina Marix-Evans; Maktar Mbow (director, UNESCO, Paris and Senegal); Papa Oye McKenzie; Genou McMillan; Abdelaziz Menard; Ambassador Mestiri; Rasheedah McNeill; Al Minns; Maurice Montoya; Leroy "Lefty" Morris (for arranging my journey to the Berkshires); Jacque Muyal; Professor Kwabena Nketia (master teacher of African traditional music, Ghana); Yaalengi Ngemi; Gil Noble; Odetta; Babatunde Olatunji; Count Ossie; Cecil Payne; Dr. Sebastien Peter; Pucho and his Latin Soul Brothers; Nadi Qamar; Salah Ragab; A. Philip Randolph; Max Roach; J. A. Rogers; Michel Renette (journalist, Paris-Guadeloupe connection); Doudou N'Diaye Rose; Tuntemeke Sanga; David Sebeko; Shazly (for the Nubian hospitality); Professor Shah (Sufi master, India and Tangier); Mikki Shepard; Arianne Smolderen; Marshall Stearns; Tetsuya and Michiyo Chaki; John Walker; Azzedine Weston; Jitu Weusi; Richard Williams; Andrea Woods . . .

And the following important places: Buddhist Temple (Shizuoka, Japan); Kamigano Shrine; Lush Life; Village Nagh El Mahta in Aswan, Egypt (our marriage village).

Willard Jenkins would like to acknowledge the following, whose support, assistance, and inspiration with this project were essential:

For their invaluable input and insights as our "other voices": the African Rhythms (Alex Blake, TK Blue (Talib Kibwe), Neil Clarke, Benny Powell); Jean Philippe-Allard; Ray Bryant; Regina Carter; Ron Carter; Joellen El-Bashir (Moorland-Spingarn Research Center, Howard University); Min Xao-Fen; Martha Flowers; Sam Gill; Michiko Imata; Richard Jennings; Orrin Keepnews; Yusef Lateef; Gil Melle; Yaa-Lengi Ngemi; Khadija Ouahamane; Charlie Persip; Clark Terry; and the essential Fatoumata Mbengue-Weston.

The readers, for the love and care they gave willingly to the often daunting task of being straightforward with me as they examined chapter drafts: my soulmate Suzan Jenkins; Marie Brown; Sara Donnelly; Janis Lane-Ewart; Robert Fleming; Larry Simpson; Danille Taylor . . .

Thanks also for their invaluable insights, ongoing collegial and professional support, materials, information assistance, and understanding of the importance of this project to Kim Bressant; Gail Boyd; Susan Chandler; Pat Cruz; Penny Von Eschen; David Fraher; Colette Giacomotti; Linda Herring; Eugene Holley; Dermott Hussey; George Jenkins (brotherly love); Cliffie Jones; Robin D. G. Kelley; Maurine Knighton; Brad Laermonth; Howard Mandel; Bill McCullough (thanks, Dad); Middleton O'Malley (thanks for the Storyville); Beth Rutkowski; Mikki Shepard; Arianne Smolderen; Cheryl Weston; Kim Weston; Pam Weston; Sonya Williams; and the WPFW and WWOZ families. And special thanks to our editors, Ken Wissoker and Fred Kameny, and the rest of the crew at Duke University Press for believing in this project.

# INTRODUCTION

I come to be a storyteller; I'm not a jazz musician, I'm really a storyteller through music and I've had some amazing and unique experiences. When it comes to considering these experiences together, my quest is always in the spirit of our ancestors. Whether it's when I hung out as an inexperienced, green piano player with the grandmaster drummer Max Roach, one of my Brooklyn homeboys, or the first time I played for the great Charlie "Yardbird" Parker; whether it was playing in a little Army band during the war trying to dodge bullets, or hanging out with Thelonious Monk and being part of his vast sphere of influence, or being mesmerized by Sufi masters—I'm constantly assembling all these forces to create my message, a message which comes directly through me, passed down from the ancestors and ultimately from the Creator.

In 2006 I passed a milestone of eighty years on the planet, so I've been on this path a long, long time. You know how life is: something that happened to you thirty, forty years ago you don't necessarily carry in your conscious mind; it's always there, buried in the deepest recesses of your mind, but influential nonetheless. Sometimes you can't properly value what transpired at a particular time until many years later; then what I like to think of as your cultural memory kicks in. But the constant theme of my life that came directly from my mom and pop and our neighborhood in Brooklyn . . . was to fight for black people, for the liberation of our minds and spirits. Black people are in a constant struggle on this planet; we are not completely respected for our enormous contributions, we are globally downtrodden and that must change.

In order to enact positive change we must remember the greatness of our ancestors, we must open up our creative minds, open that door that we've sealed as a result of being taken away from our Motherland and enslaved. Additionally, we must celebrate our own diversity as a people, because we are a very great people with unlimited spiritual resources.

I have always worked to be a part of that collective uplifting. I grew up in a truly vibrant time in the twentieth century, when such peerless giants as Paul Robeson, Adam Clayton Powell, Sugar Ray Robinson, Langston Hughes, Joe Louis, Duke Ellington, Billie Holiday, Jimmy Lunceford, Hazel Scott, and other great black masters walked the earth; all very powerful, proud black men and women.

My very existence dictates that even before the importance of music in my life comes pride as a black man; even if I didn't play music I'd still be fighting and striving for black people. Music has been a way for me to convey that struggle; I've been blessed, gifted by the Creator with the power of music. But before the music came tremendous pride, coupled with anger at what racism has done to my people. That foundation of dignity and strength comes from growing up in a segregated, racist society; growing up alongside people who were considered a "minority."

I was endowed with the belief that "I know that no man is better than me," so as a result I grew up spiritual but irate at our collective condition as a people. I use the music as a way to unite all people. I use the music as a vehicle to illustrate that we can develop and have developed a unique language and way of being that you cannot steal, because when we go back to our tradition you can't steal the spirituality of African people. Africa is so deep that no matter how many times I return there I never fail to be educated and further immersed.

I've followed this path naturally. I don't think it was a master plan in my head, but I think it stems from my father's insistence and teachings that I am an African born and living in America; therefore I must make a broader examination of myself. I have to recognize that my ancestors did not begin with my grandfather or my great-grandfather; my ancestors go all the way back to those remarkable people who built ancient civilizations. This music is my way of continuing the struggle of James Reese Europe, Marcus Garvey, Malcolm X, Dr. Martin Luther King, Cheikh Anta Diop . . . all of our great men and women; my quest is to try and continue in their tradition, to use my music to enrich our people.

Growing up in Brooklyn, surrounded by revolutionary Panamanians, Jamaicans, and African Americans . . . we had our own institutions, like the black-owned Paragon Bank, inspired by the Marcus Garvey movement in Brooklyn . . . the list is endless. Out of that incredible Brooklyn environment come Max Roach, Randy Weston . . .

Our people were fighters and in the ensuing years we've acquired a soft underbelly that has made us extremely vulnerable. When people say to me,

"Man, what you're doing is fantastic," I say, "Man, you don't know your history." If you knew what our people were doing in the '20s . . . Ellington and all those people wrote powerful music about black people. And that's what I'm trying to do: write and play music celebrating the spirits of our ancestors, music about the historic greatness of our people, music to uplift us all: black, brown, beige, red, yellow, white . . . God is the real musician. I'm an instrument and the piano is another instrument. Africa taught me that.

# ORIGINS

My dad, Frank Edward Weston, came from a Jamaican family that was descended from the Maroons, a fierce and legendary people who never surrendered to the English during colonization. The Maroons were ferocious fighters—they escaped captivity and preferred freedom in the Blue Mountains over bondage—and that spirit was deep in my dad's blood, but he was actually born and grew up in Panama. My paternal grandmother, who I never knew, had a bakery near the Panama Canal. My dad and his cousin Frisco, the famous entertainer and bon vivant Frisco of Europe who I'll get to later, grew up together as kids. They used to take the train across the canal all the time. According to dad, Frisco was forever the clown, always the actor, the singer, and the dancer . . . obviously a budding showman, even as a child. On this train Frisco would dance and perform for the passengers' amusement, and my father and another young guy would come behind him and collect the money. My dad was a true West Indian man through and through: he had a potent combination of Panama and Jamaica, Spanish and Caribbean.

Dad and Frisco left Panama as teenagers and my father spent the next seven years living in Cuba. Then he came up to Brooklyn, where he eventually met my mother, Vivian Moore, a wise but unassuming woman who was from Meredithville, Virginia. They got together, eventually got married, and they produced me. I was born April 6, 1926, at Peck Memorial Hospital in Brooklyn. My dad used to claim I was just about the first black baby born in that hospital. Remember, segregation was real deep back then. My mother and father separated when I was just three years old, and I went to live with my dad, though my mother and I remained close and were often together. Eventually my dad remarried two more times, but my mother never did. You would think my parents separating would have been a traumatic experience for such a young kid, but to tell you the truth it really wasn't. In retrospect their separation and eventual divorce was probably a good thing. because my dad was such a powerhouse, such a thoroughly

Mom and Pop,
circa 1970s.

domineering man; he was a real strong, totally macho Caribbean brother.
On the other hand, my mother was this quiet, demure southern sister from
Virginia: a very peaceful, spiritual lady who never once asked me for anything in my entire life. Whatever I wanted to do she supported me 100 percent. I don't want to suggest that my father was physically abusive toward
mom, but he was a powerful and all-consuming presence. Luckily my
mother and father always loved each other in such a way that they never
said a disparaging word about each other, at least not around me. That was
a relief because they had such thoroughly different personalities.

My mother was a very small woman who was very tender, but at the
same time she was quite strong and independent in her own sweet way.
She was a domestic worker. When I wrote "African Lady" for my 1960 suite
*Uhuru Afrika* she was my inspiration, she and all those strong sisters like
her who had to toil and scrub folks' floors to make that measly $15 a week,

and they would never complain, never beg; such dignity I can't even begin to describe. Mom was always kinda laid back, but she had a great sense of humor. She and my older sister Gladys always had me cracking up. I found out later, from my sister, that mom used to go dancing at the Savoy Ballroom when she was young, but that part of my mother I never knew, she never talked about that.

My dad was about 6'2", which in those days was really tall. I guess my eventual 6'7" would have been circus material back then! He was a clean-shaven, handsome, dignified man, always dressed sharply and sort of a ladies' man. My dad raised me from the time I was three years old, and my sister Gladys lived with my mother. I would go and stay with mom and Gladys every weekend, at my father's insistence. My dad and I lived at several locations in Brooklyn, mainly in the Bedford-Stuyvesant area. Our first place was on Albany Avenue, where my mother, father, and sister were living when I was born. Then we moved to Pacific Avenue, and then after that we moved over to Putnam Avenue. My mother, who always lived in Brooklyn too after they split, lived on Decatur Street, on Eastern Parkway near Prospect Place for a while, and her last home was on Empire Avenue. Every weekend I'd be with my mother and my sister, and they'd have me in church every Sunday; that was the law. That church experience proved very important to my music later in life.

My dad loved to cook, and I think one of the reasons I'm so big is because he was such a wonderful cook. Between my dad's African-Caribbean style cooking and my mother's down-home Virginia cooking, I was blessed with great food. Man, we were economically poor but we never felt that, we lived like kings and queens. My dad always had his women, a variety of different ladies, but no matter what woman he was seeing or married to, the first thing he insisted upon is that they had better take good care of his only son. He spoiled me like you would not believe; spoiled me with love, not with material things, so I wasn't corrupted in that way. I never had a whole lot of clothes; I would get one new suit a year, at Easter, that was it . . . and I'd better keep that suit looking good for the rest of the year. If I ever got a hole in my sneakers, I'd put paper in those sneakers to cover that hole 'till it was time to get a new pair, and that might not be for a while. We once, thank goodness only temporarily, lived in an apartment with no steam heat and no hot water; we'd have to heat the water on the stove. And remember, I'm not talking about Mississippi or Georgia; I'm talking about wintertime up north in Brooklyn, New York!

But we were so culturally rich and had so much love, so much discipline . . . Like all kids we didn't appreciate it at the time, but getting older we sure recognized the beauty of all that love and discipline. My dad was a very political guy, always reading the newspaper and various books, always quick to share his opinions on things. There was a spiritual side of him that he never talked about, but you could sure sense it. People from the Caribbean islands have this deep connection to Africa and sometimes they tell their children who grew up in the U.S. about that, but they don't always tell you everything. My dad was like that. As a result there was a mystery and magic about this man, to the point that during the time he was dying in the hospital from cancer, at age eighty-seven, I went to see him and he told me something deep; this was after I had traveled a bit as a musician. He said, "You go all around the world talking about freedom." I said, "Yes, sir, that comes from you and your teachings." He said, "Well, since you talk about freedom so much, I want my freedom, get me the hell outta this hospital!" I laughed, but he also told me something else; he said, "You are protected." I never really probed him for what he meant by that, but when I look at my life, I *have* been protected, by some spirit; by some ancestor that has guided me to the right people, to the right places. I've fallen down and been able to right myself, so obviously what he meant by protection was a combination of these things.

Dad always preached about being independent, he always emphasized how black people should strive to own their own businesses, work for themselves, be independent of the white man. That's why he appreciated Marcus Garvey's black empowerment movement so much, because that's what Dad stood for. Dad was a very proud man. Like I said, he was always very sharply dressed and cut an impressive figure. He used to drive his Cadillac wearing beaver hats and spats. Guys were sharp in his day; they knew how to dress, not like so many guys today. But when he'd get in that car, you'd better beware. Dad loved to drive fast; he'd jam his foot on the gas and bam, he was gone. One day while driving in his Cadillac he actually hit this white pedestrian crossing the street, and as he described the scene to me later, this guy flew way up in the air on impact. They had to call an ambulance and take this poor guy to the hospital, he was messed up. So my father ran home, went into the kitchen, and made a big pot of soup, then he went down to the hospital and took this guy some homemade soup. Nowadays he'd be sued for everything he owned. What are you gonna do with a man like that?

He loved to cook and he loved children. Every child in that community was his child. If he saw a kid getting out of line, he'd grab them in a minute and say, "Straighten up" . . . and the kids all listened. And every kid in the neighborhood was like his kid. He didn't care whether you were black, Italian, or Irish, if he saw you doing something wrong he would grab you in a minute and straighten you out. He was very straight ahead, the kind of person who would speak whatever was on his mind; whatever he was thinking he'd tell you to your face. That's the way we grew up. He was all those things. But in essence he gave me Africa; he gave me music . . . so he gave me everything.

My mother was kinda small in stature, with short, dark hair; I remember she had unusually long arms. She was one of those very quiet, unassuming, modest, Sunday go-to-meetin' kinda sisters; just a gentle southern sister from Virginia. After mom and dad broke up, during the week I would stay with my father, but I had to go stay with my mother and sister every weekend, my father would make sure of that. After mom and dad separated I never saw her with another man the rest of her life. I didn't really appreciate how great she was until after she died. She was a church lady through and through; worked hard every day, but she was very independent and very sweet-natured. She wasn't nearly the disciplinarian my father was, so I always looked forward to staying with her those weekends, that was freedom.

My sister Gladys was wonderful. During school days she was my bodyguard. She's five years older than me, and in those days we had some pretty tough people out there in our neighborhood, which was a predominantly black neighborhood of African Americans and African Caribbean people, with a few folks straight from the African continent. My sister protected me, she would whip somebody's butt in a minute; you better not mess with her little brother. Sometimes I'd get in trouble and I'd call her. I'd tell people, "You mess with me, I'll get my sister on you," and the cats would back off. My sister used to tell me how our mother would discipline her, but I never really saw that side of mom. That's when I realized how strong my mother was.

My mother may have been a staunch church lady, but my dad never went to church because he didn't trust certain ministers. He felt like all they were doing was jiving, conning, and ripping off black people. He thought some of them were nothing but fried-chicken-eating frauds that saved the best for themselves and threw the bones to their congregation. Unfortunately this was true sometimes. But my mother was always devoted to the church, she gave me that wonderful spirituality, and despite his personal objections to those ministers, my dad saw the value in it and really wanted me to go to church, so there was no conflict there. My mother worked every day, doing domestic work, taking care of folk's children, washing, cleaning, that kinda thing. She was a real queen in every sense of the word, never complained for a moment.

I got a lot of my spirituality from dad as well. Though he had no use for those ministers and didn't go to church, he would always read the bible and quote the scriptures. My dad came up in that period in time when black people were really active in the struggle for freedom and independence, so he was very aggressive in making sure I had pride in my people. He made sure I knew about Paul Robeson, all the great black artists, and that I knew who our illustrious leaders were; he always made real sure of that. Dad was always in tune with the news and the sports pages.

As a kid I was very shy despite my size; in many ways I was insecure because my dad was such a powerhouse, so fast, so formidable, and he wanted me to be likewise. But it just wasn't in me. I was very nervous growing up because Dad was such a strong presence. He was forever trying to challenge and quiz me on various things. He'd say, "How much is 145 times 10?," or he would put a clock in front of me when I was ten years old or so and if I didn't have the right answer as quickly as he wanted it, he would whoop me. I got a whole lotta whippings, so I grew up very, very insecure because I wasn't fast or a quick learner like he was. My father was a very physical man; he'd kick my butt, either with his hands or it could be a belt, a club, could be anything. At the time that was just how it was, very typical of how kids were raised in my neighborhood. That's particularly how those Caribbean people were, they didn't spare the rod. I may have felt abused and nowadays they'd probably call it that, but at the time they didn't call it abuse, they just thought of it as proper parenting. One time he whooped me so bad I got dramatic and stuck my head outta the window screaming for the police, the fire department, my buddies, the neighbors . . . just about ANYBODY who might help me. "Somebody, please, come rescue me!" But everybody's parents did it. So we didn't call it abuse back then: that was just the way it was. All the guys I grew up with were later very grateful for that kind of upbringing, because the streets were really tough in those days and it was so easy for us kids to get outta line. But despite that rather harsh discipline, at the same time he gave me love, so it was kind of paradoxical.

We really didn't have much in the way of material goods growing up. I used to tell my own children, "we grew up with no TV; no hot water . . . that kinda lack didn't just happen in the South." No matter what our financial situation was, my daddy could take the smallest, most insignificant piece of meat and make a delicious feast out of it. So I really didn't care if I didn't have a lot of things, we made do with what little we had, it was all we knew. We had so much love in our family that we didn't really care about material things.

Our neighborhood—Bedford-Stuyvesant, or Bed-Stuy as it's known—was a really vibrant community at the time, with a wonderful mix of black people from the South, from the Caribbean, and even a few from Africa. There were many Jewish-owned stores in the area, and there were a few Italians and Irish in the neighborhood. You had the black folks in one area, the Irish in another, the Italians in their area, the Germans in their space, and the Jews had their own separate blocks. Sometimes when we'd come in too close contact with each other in school there would be fights between ethnic groups. We had our gangs in the community, though not as violent as gang life today, and these ethnic gangs would control certain territory. If you stumbled into the wrong territory you might get your butt kicked, or at the very least be run outta there unless you knew somebody. But one thing we all pretty much had in common, at least among black folks, was music; and back then there was lots of opportunity to learn music in school. Plus there was music coming out of every window and musicians living all over the neighborhood. There were several ballrooms in the area, including the Sonia Ballroom, and there would be big-band rehearsals there at 11:00 a.m. or 12:00 noon. There were also lots of blues groups playing at various bars in Brooklyn, which at that time in the '30s and '40s had way more bars and clubs than Manhattan.

By the time I got to high school I was only beginning to immerse myself in all this music. My interests were mainly like any normal kid at that age, playing ball, going to the movies, that kind of thing. We'd go to school and study during the week, and if we stayed out of trouble our parents would allow us to go to the movies every Saturday; for about 25 cents we would stay all afternoon. At first I would always have to go to the movies with my sister Gladys, because I was too young to go by myself. When I went to the movies with Gladys she would bring a pot of greens and a fork with her. When we got inside the theater, I'd split from her and go sit with my boys. She'd sit there by herself and eat those aromatic greens with that fork, but nobody better not say nothin' to her.

After my parents broke up, my dad ended up marrying two more times. He had girlfriends in between wives, and no matter who they were he insisted they all had to take good care of me. Our house was always open, and my dad's friends from Jamaica, Barbados, and other island people would come over and play cards. He was so exceptionally generous with his friends and even with total strangers, I've never known anybody else like him in that respect. If he saw somebody out in the street down on their luck, they could be unkempt with raggedy clothes, needin' a bath or whatever. He'd bring them into our apartment, draw them a hot bath, and give them a suit of clothes. Granted, sometimes they would rip him off, steal his watch or something, but he'd just shrug it off and say "It's OK, don't make no difference to me, you give and you get back." That's the kind of person he was.

Unfortunately my dad's two other marriages didn't last. One wife was a woman from North Carolina named Cherry, she was really beautiful. Being from the old school, what my Dad would do is get in his big Buick and drive down South, which is how he met Cherry. Somehow he figured that women from the South made better wives. Unfortunately Cherry died prematurely. Another woman he married was an actress and singer named Clarisse. She had a talent agency on 125th Street in Harlem. My dad wanted both me and Clarisse to work with him in his restaurant business. But she wasn't into that kind of work; she wanted to be with show folks, so they broke up. Neither of those marriages lasted very long. There was one woman who stuck around him for a while, but they never got married. Her name was Mildred Pettigrew. She was from Virginia, and man, could she ever cook! At my dad's restaurant, which I'll get into later, he would do the Caribbean-style cooking and she would take care of the Southern-style cooking. Dad would insist that all of these women take care of me. If they didn't take care of me, they were in trouble with him.

As far as my extended family goes, I never saw my grandparents on either my mother or my father's side. I had one uncle on my father's side, but he was very quiet, very shy. He was one of those henpecked husbands, which my father couldn't stand, and he was always angry with him because of it. My cousin June Masters, on my father's side, ran a bed and breakfast in Jamaica. Her mother was a pharmacist who came from Jamaica; June and I have stayed in touch through the years. My cousin Frisco, on my father's side, was the most powerful relative of all. His given name was Jocelyn Bingham. He and my father grew up together and left Panama around the same time. Frisco was an all-around entertainer, kinda like an earlier Sammy Davis Jr. type.

After Frisco and my father left Panama, Frisco eventually migrated to San Francisco and performed there, which is where he got his name. Frisco later took work on a freighter and traveled to China and other foreign ports; he learned to speak six or seven languages along the way. He eventually wound up in London, where he owned the very first black nightclub in town. Later he owned the first bebop club in Paris. Frisco was very popular and eventually was decorated by the French. He knew everybody from Louis Armstrong and Joe Louis to Bricktop and Kwame Nkrumah. I found out just a couple of years ago that he was in the first talking film in England, singing two songs. A director from the Italian television network RAI once told me that Frisco was the first man to bring jazz to Italy; so he was a real black entertainment pioneer in Europe, in league with people like Josephine Baker and Bricktop, but not as celebrated. I still have his 1927 Selmer saxophone, a classical drum that he brought from Italy, and some photographs of him. This guy was incredible.

## Finding Frisco

Allow me to jump ahead a bit here. I finally met Frisco when he was about eighty-three or eighty-four years old, in 1968. At the time I met Frisco I was very good friends with a woman named Suzanne Cloutier, who played opposite Orson Welles in *Othello*. She was married to the actor Peter Ustinov. I met Suzanne in Paris but ironically we later discovered that we went to the same doctor in New York. Suzanne and Peter were going through some marital changes when we met. She had met Frisco and become very close to him. When I met Frisco his son was managing a little club in Paris called the Living Room. Back during the Second World War my father and Frisco corresponded with each other through letters. My father would occasionally send him food, cigarettes, chocolates, things they couldn't get in England because of the blitz. There was a lot of rationing going on at the time. Then somehow they lost contact with each other after the war.

The first time I went to Paris, in 1968, my father said, "Why don't you see if you can find Frisco, I've lost contact with him. I know he's in Paris, he ended up marrying a French woman and they live in a big villa right outside Paris." Suzanne had asked me to bring her some vitamins from this

Dad's cousin Frisco
(Jocelyn Bingham),
circa 1948.

doctor we shared in New York. She had a villa in Paris and she invited me to stay there when I visited, with her and her two children. Suzanne was tight friends with an Iranian woman who worked as an advance travel person for the Shah of Iran. One night this Iranian woman was over at Suzanne's place and I said, "Let's go hear some jazz, at a club called the Living Room," not knowing at the time that Frisco's son managed this nightclub. I had been there before on this trip and had sat in with the house band. On this particular night a musician named Art Williams invited me to sit in. So I'm playing the piano and the spirit was good that night. It was so good that the actress Ava Gardner, who was in the club that evening with some friends, came up to me after the set to tell me how much she loved my playing. She kissed my hand, and that was quite a thrill, because of all the Hollywood actresses of that time, she was my favorite.

After the set Suzanne asked the pianist Art Williams about Frisco. Art said, "Frisco's son owns this place." Overhearing that, I jumped up, and Art said, "Yeah, in fact there's his son right over there." I ran over to Frisco's son, introduced myself, and asked him if his father was still alive, which he was. I told him about my father and said, "Aw, man, I really want to see Frisco." His son said he'd arrange it, to come back the following night and he'd have his father there. So the next night I went back and there's Frisco, as always quite dapper and debonair, with a fresh carnation in his lapel, a real distinguished-looking gent with jet-black complexion and silver gray hair. I got so excited I called my father in New York immediately and said, "Pop, I've found him, I've found Frisco!" I put dad on the phone and these two cousins, who hadn't talked in years, were thrilled to speak with each other.

Later I brought my father over to Paris, and Maurice Culoz, the jazz critic, and his wife Vonette took us all to dinner with Frisco. These two cousins argued all night long. Frisco was one of the most famous men in Europe; he had nightclubs, the royalty all knew him. When the American ambassador to France, Ambassador Bolling, retired later that year, they had a reception for him at the embassy. Suzanne, Frisco, and I went to the reception together and everybody was grabbing Frisco all night long. He was the most famous relative in the family.

## Enterprising Dad

My dad always believed in business, in being self-reliant, so he eventually opened a barbershop on Pacific Street and Kingston Avenue in 1940. Since he was Panamanian and spoke fluent Spanish, a lot of the barbers he hired were guys who had just arrived from Puerto Rico and Cuba, guys who really knew how to cut hair beautifully. We lived right across the street from the barber shop. I remember when Japan bombed Pearl Harbor, the Americans were so shook up they panicked, and since they needed all the workers they could get for the war effort, for the first time they allowed blacks to work in the defense plants. They stepped up production and building of armaments to fight Japan. Before that, all black folks were allowed to do was sweep floors and be servants, they weren't even allowed to drive a truck; and I'm talking about New York, not Mississippi or Georgia. All of a sudden all of dad's barbers left and went to work in the defense plants where they could make some steady money.

When they left the barbershop my father felt he had no choice; he put on a barber coat and tried cutting hair himself. He was messin' up folks' heads royally until he finally learned to do it right. He must have messed up about twenty-five heads. I used to laugh, because the customers would look at their haircuts in the mirror after he'd messed them up, and before they could even start complaining my dad would say, "What are you talking about, you got a great haircut, and you look good, man!" He was so strong that they dare not talk back. He did that until he really learned how to cut hair. As a teenager he'd have me helping out in the shop; that was back in the days of conkolene, the chemical they used to process black men's hair. So I used to conk the young guy's hair and sometimes I'd forget to put the Vaseline on them, which was a sort of balm, and their heads would be burnin' up from that harsh chemical. It was a wild scene in that shop; before they split, the Puerto Rican barbers were drinking the hair tonic to get a buzz, and everybody was taking and playing numbers to get by.

Numbers, or what they called back then the policy game, was illegal, so sometimes the police would be sitting out in front of the barbershop in their squad cars watching to see who was doing what, who was going in and coming out. Guys were collecting numbers outta the barbershop. One day my dad was cutting somebody's hair, and I'm in the shop shining shoes. These two detectives are sitting outside the shop in a plain car. My dad had apparently had enough of this surveillance, so he starts fussing, "What them guys doing out there . . . watching this shop like that." At one point he put down his scissors and comb, strode across the street, and confronted these two detectives, cussing them out the whole time. I couldn't believe it, but the detectives actually drove off. I never saw my dad fight physically, but his voice was so powerful that his tone alone was enough to shake folks up. So I guess those detectives got an earful.

After that, during the Second World War, Dad opened up a restaurant called Trios because he loved to cook. It was the kind of place they called a luncheonette back then, which also sold newspapers, candy, cigarettes, and things like that. Guys would come in sometime and ask to buy some cigarette papers. Boy, oh boy, why'd they do that? He knew they wanted the papers to roll some marijuana. He'd lay into them: "Whatcha' wanna do that for . . . you smokin' that shit!" But everybody in the neighborhood loved him. He treated everybody's child like they were his child, and he was hospitable to a fault. Even as an adult I might call him and say, "Pop, I'm with so-and-so, his wife and daughter, and we're hungry." He'd say,

"Come on over," Even up until he was eighty-four years old he'd get out of bed, go downstairs, and cook: fish, chicken, bake biscuits, pie, everything . . . Then he'd feed you and while you're eating he'd be watching you, trying to figure out what kind of person you are. After your stomach was full, that's when he'd pounce. He might say, "So, you're a"—asking about whatever profession you were—"what about so and so." That was my dad, a real character.

## 2

# GROWING UP IN BROOKLYN

My dad was very much a follower of Marcus Garvey and his self-determination movement. Dad was never much of an organization person, he wasn't really a joiner, but he did patronize the Paragon Bank, the black bank I mentioned earlier which grew from Garvey's movement. And dad certainly supported, practiced, and preached black self-determination all his life, so though dad wasn't formally part of his organization Garvey was speaking his language. Dad was unusual for his time in the level of pride he had for his African heritage. He had books around the house by serious black scholars like J. A. Rogers, Leo Hansbury, and others, and he would encourage us to read their work. He also had many maps and portraits of African kings on the walls, and was forever talking to me about Africa. He would take me to various meetings of black folks; some things I didn't even understand myself at the time because I was too young to understand. But he was planting the seeds for what I would become as far as developing my consciousness of the plight of Africans all over the world.

Other elements crept into my consciousness growing up that made me aware of our condition. Like many other young kids growing up in the 1930s and '40s, I would go to the movies on Saturdays to see the latest Tarzan or the cowboy movies with Tom Mix and those guys. I was seeing a lot of things, particularly in those Tarzan movies, that would sure make you ashamed of Africa, with their nonsense, gibberish languages, and the subservient behavior they'd ascribe to the Africans in those movies. With the negative and white supremacist images in those films, you couldn't blame black folks for not wanting to make a connection with Africa at all; you'd be ashamed too. Luckily my dad was just the opposite; he'd be talking about the great African civilizations all the time, about having pride in being black. He used to always stress to me that I was an African born in America. This was a very revolutionary identification to make at the time, but that's how he thought and what he taught me. Thinking of yourself that way, as an African born in America, especially in those days, gave you a different mind-set, because if you're a black person in America, without that kind of positive indoctrination you'd be thinking that our history starts with slavery. You would think that our history starts with the white man coming to Africa and "civilizing" Africa. But my dad insisted, "Son, it's just the reverse. Between the ancient Egyptians, the ancient Ethiopians, the great university of Fes, the Moors in Spain . . . we civilized *them*!"

As a child I was conflicted between what I was hearing at home and what I was learning out in the world; because number one, you go to school and get your history lessons, and they don't teach you anything about Africa. Whatever they teach you, it's that the white man came to Africa, brought Christianity and freedom to those supposedly primitive Africans. So I had this terrible conflict growing up as a child. But I was more fortunate than most, because Africa was already being embedded in me at home. At the same time, in the Bed-Stuy community where I grew up, not just my mother and dad but that whole community of black people had their black heroes, people like Joe Louis. Whenever Joe Louis would fight and win, all the black folks would come out in the streets and celebrate. If Joe Louis lost, everybody was sad and depressed. So there was a general community sense of black pride to a certain degree.

Growing up in those neighborhoods at that time, we were so culturally rich and had so much love, so much discipline . . . we didn't really appreciate it at the time, but as we got older we recognized that our elders were incredible. My dad was very political, always reading to broaden himself. His appetite for pride in his African heritage was contagious; so I got a righteous indoctrination in our African heritage from a very young age, right in my home.

There were two sides to my dad: this very aggressive and boisterous guy, then the other side was this spiritual man who read the bible every day and had all these images of Africa and books about black folks around the house to help me counteract the racism in the school teachings, and all the other negative images that could make you ashamed of being black. Between the "Our Gang" comedies, Steppin' Fetchit, Tarzan, and all those other harmful images, that stuff could play on our young minds very significantly. Dad worked hard to counteract all that.

But this kind of indoctrination wasn't just going on in my house. Other guys around the neighborhood who I came up with were really influential, guys like the great drummer-bandleader Max Roach; semi-pro basketball player Lefty Morris (who was a pivotal figure later in my life); our "international advisor" Freddy Braithwaite (whose son is one of the original rappers named Fab Five Freddie), who was always dapper and quick to inform us about things like Mao's philosophies; the wonderful sculptor Jimmy Gittins, who sculpted a beautiful Malcolm X piece . . . These were guys who were maybe three or four years older than me; that seems like a big gap when you're young, but we all had similar home training. We all had the same sense of identifying with our people, of knowing who the black greats were, so it wasn't just my parents. There were a lot of guys growing up around me whose parents had come up from the Caribbean with a lot of pride—guys like the drummer Al Harewood and his brother Eustace, who was also a drummer.

I had a rich parental mix in my life: an African American southern-born mother and Caribbean-born father, which was not very unusual in my neighborhood. But despite the culturally mixed backgrounds around the neighborhood we were all in tune with each other; we young people had both parents directing us; guiding us . . . it was a neighborhood thing. My dad stood out because he was so strong and good-looking, but he was also a neighborhood businessman, so people would always come to the barbershop or the restaurant to see him, to hear what he had to say. And such businesses—particularly the barbershop or beauty shop—have always been special places for African Americans, where a mixture of neighborhood gossip and news of the world, especially where it concerned black folk, was discussed, argued over, and rehashed. The barber in those days was often like a combination philosopher and town crier in the black community. So my dad was kind of a well-known neighborhood sage, a real man of the people.

J. A. Rogers was an anthropological photojournalist and a key contributor to Alain Locke's book *The New Negro*, and my father loved his books. I distinctly remember one of them, a book called *From Superman to Man*. The good thing about Rogers's books, and what I gravitated to as a child, was the fact that they were filled with depictions of ancient Africans. Rogers's books were my first real contact with Africa. He detailed our African history, let us know that we're an African people, which backed up what my father used to preach. And that was important because as I said, when we left the house—say, to go to the movies—we entered another world, with Tarzan, Tom Mix, John Wayne, whatever.

Our neighborhood was very important in forming my African-centric outlook. I grew up in a neighborhood with black decision makers, black newspapers, black banks . . . These were all necessitated because the white man didn't want us around, as though our money wasn't good; he wanted us to stay where we were; segregation ruled. So we had this thoroughly black scene. My father and so many others, especially people from the Caribbean, were really followers of not just Marcus Garvey but the other black leadership of the time. For example there was Father Divine, who had restaurants where you could eat the best foods for 5 or 10 cents. You had all these various sects and cults, but at the same time there were some very dynamic black leaders. A lot of them, no matter what they took in, they usually always gave something back to the people.

## The Influence of Music

Besides Joe Louis, a lot of our neighborhood heroes were the musicians. The importance of Duke Ellington, Ella Fitzgerald, Count Basie, and such giants was not just about their music, but the fact that their music was something for which we could claim ownership; it was definitely black music. We felt we could make music better than anybody else. We knew it was our music, black music, but we didn't make a big political thing about it in a sense. I was blessed with a combination of the black church, the blues, and the calypso from our Caribbean side; plus hanging out at the Palladium and hearing music from our Afro-Caribbean side. We grew up in a very rich, very culture-conscious area, and all of our parents insisted that we take music lessons. I think they had two things in mind: number one, music was in their blood; number two, music was a way of keeping us off the streets, because the streets of New York were pretty mean in those days. If you left your block and ventured onto another block, there was liable to be some rough guys on that block who felt like they owned the block and they would challenge you, they'd want to know who you were, who you gonna see, what was your business on their block. And if you didn't have the right answers you got your butt kicked.

Our musical interests weren't just about listening to those giants on the radio, or on the Victrola at home. My mother and father liked to go to practically any kind of concert; they were ready for just about any style of music. This was true throughout their lives. For example, in the mid-'60s, when South African pianist Abdullah Ibrahim first came to New York, my daddy was with me . . . same thing with Miriam Makeba when she first debuted in New York. Unlike today, that generation just loved music, period, it wasn't so much about *styles* of music, they just loved *good* music; could be Cuban, could be calypso, jazz, blues, opera . . . we grew up very healthy that way, with a lotta music in the house. Consequently everybody's kids had to take piano lessons, or violin, or trumpet lessons; it was a discipline our parents insisted upon.

We didn't really have any musicians in our family. I had one cousin, named Robert Moore, from my mother's family. He would always walk around the house with his string bass. I don't think he was much of a bass player, certainly no professional, but he would take me around to places to hear music and he'd always make me play piano for folks as a youngster. There was another guy in the family, a cousin somewhere down the line—a Panamanian named Vincent Poulson who played trumpet in Latin bands, but I only met him once. So it wasn't as though there were a lot of musicians in my family for inspiration.

But as I said, music was a constant thing in my parents' homes. They had records by everybody from Marian Anderson to the Ink Spots; including Cuban music, the Southernaires from the black church, Ellington, Lil Green . . . It was all black music and our parents covered the whole gamut. That's how we grew up, listening to all kinds of music, in both my mother and my father's homes. And music was all over the community, not just in our home. Maybe segregation had a lot to do with it too, because at that time we couldn't go to the hotels, or the big nightclubs, and the white restaurants wouldn't serve us. So out of that exclusion we created a whole way of life; this was true in black neighborhoods all over the United States, not just in Brooklyn; and that emphasis on music was keenly important to us youngsters growing up.

If it wasn't records it was the radio going all the time. I remember on Saturdays there was a radio show on WNEW called "Make Believe Ballroom," hosted by a guy named Martin Block. Saturdays was when he would play jazz music. I used to turn up that radio full volume and everybody in the streets outside our place could hear Count Basie, Duke Ellington, Billie Holiday . . . blasting from our radio; but nobody made a big deal of it. It was a regular thing and the neighbors didn't seem to mind. There was a lot of big-band music on the radio in those days; everybody from Glenn Miller to Benny Goodman, Jimmy Lunceford, Les Hite, Andy Kirk's orchestra, a combination of all of that. My parents were cool with me blasting the radio, they were into everything. There was just music everywhere: jukeboxes, big-band rehearsals around the neighborhood, kids taking music lessons. In those days it was extremely important for kids to be involved in the arts.

When I was twelve my parents arranged for me to take dance lessons. They used to have these agencies around New York that would get kids at a young age and promise their parents they'd make them a star. Ironically the place I went to for dance lessons was called Starr-Allen in Manhattan, but they didn't have much star-making effect on my two left feet! One of my dance lesson classmates was a kid named Scoby Stroman, who later became a fine drummer and dancer and worked in my band for a while. Our parents insisted that we have arts education, so they would put us in these kinds of places, not necessarily for us to become professional dancers; if so, they were outta luck in my case, because I never could dance. A lot of poor people wanted to educate their children in the arts because that was one area where we had a lot of successful black folks to aspire to, so they would put their kids in these various schools—agencies, they called them. Kids would learn to tap dance and a combination of things.

My dad told me many years later that when he was in Panama working as a kid he overheard some pianist playing inside a restaurant as he was walking past, and he made a habit of going past this place because he loved to hear this guy play the piano. So perhaps the seed was planted in his mind then; in the back of his mind he wanted his son to be a piano player. As I said, music or some kind of arts lessons were a requirement for all the youngsters in our neighborhood like me, as a way of keeping us disciplined. I didn't start piano lessons until I was fourteen.

Dad found this piano teacher for me and I'll never forget her. Mrs. Chapman was her name; that poor woman spent three years trying to teach me to play the piano, at 50 cents per lesson for one hour a week. She was a real old-school teacher. She would smack my hands with a ruler if I made a mistake, but she wasn't malicious. Otherwise she was a sweet, patient lady, and she did her best, but I just wasn't in tune with the European music she was trying to indoctrinate me in. She would have me playing scales, scales, and more scales; Bach, Handel, those early books of simple songs, but more in the European classical area. Black music . . . that was on the side . . . "The devil's music," as some church folk used to call it, and maybe she felt that way too, though she never expressed it that way. But she was steadfastly indoctrinating me in European music . . . or so she thought.

Those piano lessons were doubly hard for me because I really wanted to be outside playing ball with my friends. Since I was so tall I guess I had

Mrs. Lucy Chapman,
Randy's first piano teacher
*Courtesy of Steve Bowser.*

visions of being a ballplayer. Our culture was so *swinging* that I couldn't identify with that standard European music, which seemed so stiff to me as a kid. After three years Mrs. Chapman threw up her hands and told my father, "Mr. Weston, you'd best save your money, your son will never play the piano!" But my dad wasn't about to give up that easily. He got me another teacher, a guy named Professor Atwell. This guy was a little bit hipper than Mrs. Chapman, he knew popular songs, so he continued my lessons and eventually I learned a couple of tunes. Ironically, the first popular song I learned was from Al Harewood, the drummer who grew up in my neighborhood at the same time. I was so happy I could play a little popular song! And Atwell was real laid back; he wasn't a strict disciplinarian like Mrs. Chapman, which worked better for me.

Around the neighborhood a lot of the young people were totally into jazz at the time. We'd go around saying stuff like "Hey, man, did you hear the latest song, you gotta get this!" Even when we were playing handball and stickball in the streets all the kids were talking about "Hey, man, you gotta hear so-and-so, the new one by Basie, man, this is bad!" Around the time I was taking piano lessons from Professor Atwell, Jimmy Nottingham, the trumpet player who later played with Basie, Charlie Barnet, Dizzy Gillespie, and a lot of people, lived in the neighborhood. Jimmy and I went to school together and we used to practice together sometimes. But I guess we were pretty sad players back then. The neighbors would take a broom and bang on the ceiling or on the floor for us to "stop making that noise."

When I reached high school age my dad wanted me to go to Boys High School in Brooklyn because they had very high academic standards. Max Roach went to Boys High; so did saxophonist Cecil Payne, pianist Duke Jordan, trumpeter Ray Copeland, a lot of the great musicians; also a lot of the track stars, football players . . . it was a very fantastic and renowned school. However I had fallen in love with music and I really wanted to go to Music and Arts High School in Manhattan, but my dad wouldn't let me go. I wasn't in a position to decide what I wanted to do at that age, and you know, my father was very domineering. But I would get bored with the academic side at Boys High because I was so obsessed with music. My friend bassist and oud player Ahmad Abdul-Malik, whose parents were Sudanese and who later worked with me and with Monk, went to Music and Arts. He was learning not only to play and tune instruments there but also learning instrument making. I had other friends at Music and Arts, guys like piano player Gil Coggins, who made one of Miles Davis's first recordings, and an alto sax player named Eddie Steed who was a very close friend of mine.

Ironically—and this is kind of bizarre, but I always say there's a spiritual meaning behind everything that's happened—I would cut class at Boys High and go over to Music and Arts on the subway just to hang out with the guys; the teachers would actually allow me to come into the classrooms over there. When I came back to Boys High for the last few weeks of school, the music teacher Mrs. Bernstein was a very nice lady and ironically they made me president of the music class, even though I'd been cutting class all that time.

My size was always a consideration. I was six foot tall at age twelve, wearing a size 12 shoe. Naturally this gave me something of a complex, since kids would tease me all the time. I was going through a lotta changes in my life at that time, but music was my constant refuge. I never had the confidence to really be anybody, to really think I was ever going to be a musician; I was too timid, too slow. While the other guys were dancing with the girls, I could never dance. My social life was practically nonexistent, at least where the girls were concerned, because I couldn't dance. When we'd go to the high school dances I would just sit in the corner. Thank God all the would-be jazz musicians got the reputation of sitting in the corner; but for me it was a convenient defense mechanism simply because I couldn't dance. It wasn't about being cool and standoffish.

Not having much confidence, I had no real relationships with the girls all through school. My social life was mostly with the guys; I liked them, but the girls were off to the side. The guys would be hanging out at my father's restaurant, listening to the jukebox. Everybody would come by and we would discuss everything from communism in China to politics and racism, to whatever various musicians were doing.

I graduated from high school wearing my father's suit at commencement because we didn't have much money in those days to buy a new suit. Dad's suit was obviously too big for me; after all, he was 6'2" and robust, and I was pretty skinny in those days, but I had to wear it. They bought me some size 12 wingtips to go with dad's suit, which really made me self-conscious. I used to walk down the street in those wingtips and I imagined everybody in the world was staring at my big feet . . . and those wingtips were white. So you can imagine me graduating in my father's suit, wearing these huge white wingtips. I'll never forget those shoes, because after graduation I was so embarrassed by the bright whiteness of those shoes that I had them dyed black, but I was still too embarrassed to wear them; it seemed like everybody was watching my big feet. My real refuge in life, the way to overcome my shyness, was immersion in the music.

About the time I finished high school I was really only hanging out with either other musicians or aspiring musicians like me. There were black musicians' clubs, or hangout spots, at that time; there was one in Harlem and one in Brooklyn on Schenectady Avenue near Fulton Street. These were wonderful places, they were like clubhouses where the elder musicians hung out back in the days before black musicians could join the regular musicians' union. These were guys who didn't necessarily have big names per se, they had played with the big orchestras years ago—Fess Williams, Buddy Johnson, Andy Kirk, and those kinds of bands. A few of the bandleaders hung out at the Brooklyn clubhouse, guys like Buddy Riser, the older generation of musicians. These clubs were a combination of things. I would almost call them cultural centers, places of black culture, where black youth who were aspiring to be musicians hang out with experienced black musicians.

These places would have a blackboard listing various events and opportunities, a pool table, telephone, and a table where the elders would sit playing cards and chewing the fat. These were places for musicians where we young brothers could be in touch with the elders. This was really a place where we could listen to their wisdom, even get some counseling. For example, you might be sitting at the card table with some elder musicians and mention that you've got a gig at so-and-so club. You might want to know if you were being paid fairly; you'd tell them the amount and they might say, "Next time you get *four* dollars instead of two dollars." They talked to us about life, about music. It was a combination of things. We learned many valuable lessons being with these elder musicians.

The individual homes of the musicians were also places of culture, places to learn; like Max Roach, Ray Abrams, or Duke Jordan's homes. We younger guys were welcomed into their houses all the time. I met Dizzy Gillespie, Miles Davis, Leo Parker at Max's house; George Russell was living at Max's house when he wrote "Cubana Be, Cubana Bop" for Dizzy Gillespie's Afro-Cuban orchestra.

My house was open to the musicians as well. I lived right across the street from the great piano player Eddie Heywood, who had such a big hit with "Begin the Beguine" and later with "Canadian Sunset." The individual houses of the musicians were places which kept the culture circulating. During the beginning of the Second World War the government put a 20 percent tax on dancehalls, which had the effect of killing a lot of the great dancehalls like the Savoy Ballroom in Harlem, the Brooklyn Palace, and the Sonia Ballroom. They all closed down. But black folks loved to dance, so before that period, and even after the dancehalls closed, during the so-called bebop period, I went to dances to hear people like Charlie Parker, Billy Eckstine, and his big band. I even went to dances where Art Blakey and Max Roach would have battles of the bands, at a place in downtown Manhattan called Chateau Gardens. At Brooklyn dances folks would bring their own food and drink and we'd dance to bebop. But the wartime was gradually changing the scene.

# 3

# THE SCENE SHIFTS
# TO THE PACIFIC

Shortly after high school, because Hitler and Hirohito—Germany and Japan—were really kicking butt and were threatening to take over the world, the U.S. began to escalate the military draft to get more soldiers in action. Back in those days a man in uniform was sure popular with the girls, but even still I had decided that scene just wasn't for me. By this time I'd become obsessed with following the music and playing the music. The draft rules said that at eighteen years of age you had to join the armed forces almost automatically, unless you were lucky enough to get some kind of special deferment, either through illness or some affliction. In 1944, not long after high school graduation and after I turned eighteen, I got my draft notice. I didn't want anything to do with military of any kind.

The musicians I was hanging out with at the time suggested all kinds of schemes to beat the draft. One way was to use Benzedrine. The trick was to get some Benzedrine from the drugstore, put it in a warm Coca-Cola bottle, shake it up, and drink it. Supposedly when you did this, your heart would start racing off the charts and the service would reject you automatically during the physical. So a group of guys and I, who were all the same age and facing the same dilemma, stayed up all night drinking this nasty concoction. That stuff damn near killed me before I even made it to the physical exam. At that time young draftees in the New York area had to report to Grand Central Plaza, which had this huge staging area for the service physicals. Man, you would see some of the ugliest bodies you ever wanted to see in that place, because everybody going through this process had to strip completely naked. So imagine this huge place with lines upon lines of thousands of naked eighteen-year-olds of every conceivable shape, race, size, and color.

The process was completely dehumanizing. They'd check out your different body parts, examine your medical and other history and whatnot. Most of the draftees had two ways out—or so we thought—either drink this concoction or pretend to be a homosexual. Those were the two most prevalent means of beating the draft. By the time I moved up the line and got to meet with the doctor, he was writing things down and looking at the chart with the results of my other tests, including my heart check, and he's saying "No, man, you can't go to the Army," because of my heart rate, which must have been really racing with all that foul concoction I'd drank the night before, or at least that's what I imagined.

When I got to the final checkpoint in the process the last guy examining me looked at me and asked, "How tall are you?" I piped up, "I'm 6'7"," thinking this was one time it sure was great to be tall, because those were the days when the war was fought in the trenches and they wouldn't take you if you were too short or too tall. The military thinking was that if you were too short in the trenches you'd be too far down and couldn't shoot effectively, and if you were too tall your head would be sticking out of the trenches and the enemy could blow your brains out. So they wouldn't take you at my height . . . or so I suspected. Under my breath I said to myself, "Fantastic!" I went back home and thought everything was cool.

About three months later another letter came from the government ordering me to report for another military exam. But this time I figure I'm cool because after all, I'm 6'7", way too tall for the Army. Armed with that confidence in my height, I went through all the tests straight, no nasty Benzedrine concoction for me this time. When I got to the last guy in the process he asks, "How tall are you?" I stood up as tall as I could and said, "I'm 6'7"." He said, "You're not 6'7". This paper says you checked in at this height," as he showed me the sheet that clearly said I wasn't quite 6'7". I was incensed. I ran through all those naked bodies right up to the last guy, the guy who had measured my height. He said, "No man, you're not 6'7", you're 6'5"!"

Wait a minute—in high school they had listed me as 6'7" when I was playing basketball, but I learned that was just a game they played to try and intimidate other schools' teams with their big guys. So I really wasn't lying: I had really believed I was 6'7", because that's how they listed me on the basketball team roster. I pleaded with this guy, saying, "Man, you made a mistake, will you please measure me again." I stretched every bone in my body and this guy said, "You're 6'5½"." I knew I was busted right then and there.

I was inducted into the Army and they sent me to Fort Dix, New Jersey, for six weeks of basic training. There were a few musicians at Fort Dix, including the drummer Charlie Smith, who used to play with Billy Taylor. Charlie stayed in the stockade the whole time because he refused to soldier, then finally they discharged him. There was an alto player named Henry McIntosh there, a wonderful player in the tradition of Ernie Henry. He was a very sensitive kind of guy and for one reason or another they wound up discharging him too.

Fort Dix was so close to New York City that I would always get weekend passes and come home to Brooklyn. After seeing my mom and dad I'd head right to 52nd Street, because that's where all the jazz musicians were in those wartime days. One memorable evening I went to see Billie Holiday at the Onyx Club, and while I'm hanging out at the bar by the door all of a sudden Queen Billie herself walks in, all decked out in a fur coat and the usual gardenia in her hair, cradling that little dog of hers in her arms. With my uniform on I guess I must have looked trustworthy, because she looked right at me and said, "Would you hold my dog?" I said, "Yeah, certainly, of course, your majesty!" So I held her dog the entire set. She sang "Strange Fruit" that night and it really brought tears to my eyes. The only two women who could make me cry with their singing were Billie and Mahalia Jackson. When she finished and came offstage she thanked me for holding her dog, but of course I was much too shy to say, "Hey, baby, what's your phone number?"

Right after that I got another letter from the government ordering me to report to Fort Monmouth, also in Jersey, at a certain time, with all my deployment orders. I was real upset because I had never left home; I had been babied all my life. My dad got all emotional too, because I was his only son. But I had to go, so I just resigned myself. When we arrived at the place where they assign you, there were something like a thousand men all together, all assigned to the Army signal corps of heavy construction battalion.

Out of all the guys in this battalion, which was all black, of course, because the Army was still segregated back then, only a few of us were from the North. The rest were from the South and some of them couldn't read or write. There were no white troops, only white officers. We were given a choice of three categories: Company A, Company B, or Headquarters. This organization was the signal corps of heavy construction, which meant we were going to climb telephone poles and string the contact wire, all with a carbine strapped to our backs.

After we were dispersed we're all in the barracks lying on our beds waiting for our assignments, talking among ourselves, all these different characters in one room. Soon the officer came in with our individual assignments; my assignment was either Company A or Company B, but I ignored it completely—or so I tried. Then the officer called out those assigned to headquarters, which was for the so-called intelligentsia: the captain, the lieutenant, the company clerk, the mess sergeant, and all those guys. He's steadily calling off names for the headquarters assignments and he obviously didn't call my name; it had already been called. So I just layed low.

Finally after two days the guy comes back and says, "Soldier, what's your name?" I said, "They didn't call my name, I'm supposed to be at headquarters, but I didn't hear my name called." How on earth could anyone imagine me—all 6′7″, uh, 6′5½″—climbing that pole? I would have been dead after the first climb; this attempted gamesmanship was about survival, baby! So the guy says, "OK, you come over to the office." Remember, I'm from the North and so were some of the officers and clerks, so I thought I was in like Flynn.

When I got to headquarters they said, "We don't see your name, but you get on line and you go with the other soldiers and get your gas mask." I walk in this line right up to this big counter and there's this brother there, the supply sergeant, and he takes one look at me and says, "Come here, soldier, what are you doing?" He said, "Come over here and help me unpack these boxes." I thought to myself, "Great man," and that was that; I thought I was set. I got tight with this dude, opening up these boxes and accounting for the supplies. I was also studying signal corps nomenclature so I totally knew my way around, knew all the ins and outs. I was studying every guy, all the laundry, studying all this stuff, learning it backwards and forwards. I also thought I was a smart guy getting over because the clerk I was working for was a brother from the South, and he couldn't write very well.

One day the supply sergeant said, "You're pretty intelligent, you get a promotion and you can be my company clerk, you won't have to deal with that other shit." I said, "Great!" This brother was from Florida, he kinda looked like Gigi Gryce, a great alto sax player and composer who played with me years later and was a major influence in other special ways which I'll explain later. I was furiously studying all this Army stuff and finally I got my two stripes as a corporal. In the meantime we got our orders saying it was time to go overseas, with the 84th Signal Corps Heavy Construction Battalion.

It's time to go overseas and we were getting antsy because they don't tell you exactly where you'll be going. We knew we were going but we didn't know where. We did know we were going to Asia because they put us on the train all the way west to Spokane, Washington. Other than that we didn't know anything, all we knew was that we were going to war. Before we shipped out our two main officers in charge were the head man, Captain Beardmore, and our lieutenant, Lt. Danzig. Both of these guys were from the North and Danzig was the supply lieutenant. Then there was my main man the staff sergeant and myself.

In the midst of all this stuff going on, some of the guys in the supply area in charge of crating up supplies would, instead of putting the real goods in those crates, they were putting rocks in there. They would sell the real goods on the black market and put rocks in the boxes, seal them up, and send them overseas; if you can imagine this kind of chicanery going on at wartime. All these guys—the lieutenant, the sergeant, and all these cats— were dealing in this black market stuff big time, all but innocent me, fresh-faced corporal that I was, I didn't know anything about this. According to general procedure when you're getting ready to ship out overseas every-body's gotta crate up all the supplies, the guns, and other equipment, but instead these cats were putting nothing but rocks in the boxes. Well, even-tually they got busted, and since I was the only one who knew anything about the operation, I became the supply sergeant by default. The rest of the supply guys got busted and put in the stockade.

After that long train trip west we spent two days in Spokane, a place I'll never forget because that was my first time coming in contact with prosti-tution, and the ladies there were quite active. One guy I was tight with was the kind of guy who would sleepwalk around the barracks. He'd be sleep-walking and kick the hardest pole in the place—in his sleep—and wake up screaming; we had guys like that. So one night this guy thinks he has just gotta get a woman, he wanted some goodies, some poontang as they used to refer to it in those days. There would be a long line of soldiers at the whorehouse, all waiting for one woman, and all getting ready to ship out the next day. By the time this sleepwalking guy got to the front of the line and got his turn, all his sexual anxieties apparently came out and we even-tually had to go in there and physically pull him off this woman because she was screaming bloody murder, he was just pounding her. We had to pull him out!

The next morning we got on the boat and of course it was segregated;

the white soldiers were on the best part of the boat, the Latinos were on another part, and we were on another part; there was complete segregation. We traveled twenty-five miserable days across the Pacific Ocean, with lights out every day because the Japanese had submarines patrolling the waters. Since I was staff sergeant I could move around a little bit, but I had to stay more or less in my own area most of the time. I used to check out the Navy guys, who were also on the ship, and I was impressed that the naval officers were always sharp. They'd have the best food, with servants and all that type of stuff, which made me wonder what that was all about; why the big difference between them and the Army?

We were part of a convoy and we had to meet another convoy in the Philippines; then from the Philippines we'd go straight to Okinawa, Japan. It was a wretched trip, and I must have had an attack of arthritis because my ankles swelled up like balloons. They put me in the sick bay, put ice on my ankles, and I stayed there a couple of days. When we finally got to Okinawa everybody had to climb down the ladder with their knapsack strapped to their backs, their rifles, and all their belongings. When the boat landed, my ankles were still swollen, so I was the only soldier to come down in a cargo net. What a comical sight that must have been. Funny thing, but within a few hours of arriving in Okinawa the swelling disappeared and my ankles came back to normal.

In the Army when you achieved a certain number of points you could be discharged, no matter what your rank was. We had a white colonel named Col. Heaney. I'll never forget this dude. He brought us to Okinawa, realized he had enough points, and split, left us high and dry. He left us right there on the beach in Okinawa . . . if you can imagine a thousand soldiers with no papers. Unbelievably, it was a month before Washington even realized we were there. We had to steal food from the U.S. quartermaster to feed ourselves. Some of the guys had to climb under barbed wire—not me, I was too big—but members of our outfit had to climb under this barbed wire to steal food from the quartermaster for our unit until we got the OK from Washington that we were supposed to be there, which took a month. I've gotta believe this could only have happened to a black unit.

Meanwhile the Creator must have had another plan for me. My sister's husband, my brother-in-law Teddy Jones (who was a bass player), was stationed twelve kilometers away from where we were on the beach in Okinawa. He was with the 12th battalion Seabees on the island. There were two ways to get to where he was—how I found out I don't remember, but we used to write each other so maybe that was how. One way was to go through what used to be a jungle. I say used to be because Okinawa had been damn near completely destroyed by flame throwers, you could smell death in the air 24/7. You'd be moving around and would spot an arm or a leg or whatever body parts lying around; it was a very disturbing experience being on that island.

The American soldiers had used flame throwers to get the Japanese out of their caves because the Japanese were determined to fight to the death; so all the fauna on the island was burned. The only way to get through was through the burnt foliage. You'd have to go over a small bridge until you got to where the Seabees were. The Seabees were the engineers who built the bridges, roads, and whatnot, so they had everything: fresh fruit, beer, vegetables, meat, everything. I went over there and my brother-in-law loaded me up. The white soldiers had to go the long way around to get to where the Seabees were. If they went through that burnt foliage the snipers would pick them off, because there was absolutely no cover there; only the brothers could go through there, because surprisingly the Japanese snipers wouldn't mess with the brothers.

When I think about those times I think to myself, "Boy, you were young and crazy." But I went through there regularly because my brother-in-law had told me about how the Japanese snipers wouldn't mess with the brothers. That was an incredible experience. Because of Teddy I had fresh fruit, fresh vegetables, beer, and great supplies.

Our papers eventually came through, so we were able to establish a base. We erected our tents and we no longer had to sleep on the beach and eat only K-rations. We were over there for the purpose of running communication poles, stringing wire, and fighting at the same time; this was totally ridiculous—we're up there stringing wire with carbines on our backs. Fortunately I didn't climb the poles, I got out of that and ended up being the supply sergeant. As I said, the Creator must have been looking out for me, because I was really supposed to climb those poles, but I knew I would break my ass, there was no way I was gonna climb a telephone pole.

There was one particularly racist officer, a guy from Kentucky. When we were at Fort Dix and we would have parades and inspections, he would always harass us and tell us that no matter what we blacks achieved in the service, at the end of our stint when we went back home we would still have to sit in the back of the bus. Most of these guys were from the South, so they had lived that stuff more than those of us from the North. The only black lieutenant was the medical officer. In Okinawa the officers had the best guns, they drank the best sake. When you're at war, in strange places, a lot of seemingly innocent people die, get killed by their own people. As it turned out the brothers from the South eventually took care of this lieutenant from Kentucky. They called that fragging during the Vietnam war.

Once we became "official" and got our papers, Washington supplied us with all the food we needed. But on the other hand the Okinawan people were starving. It was a sad scene. The supply sergeant is an interesting position to have in such a situation. The supply sergeant and the mess sergeant are two of the most important people in the unit. Not even the general can tell the supply sergeant what to do under certain circumstances; same way with the mess sergeant, who handles all the food. They have unique power, so the generals have to go through proper channels to tell them what to do. There would be tons of food for us and we would have all this extra food; by contrast the Okinawan people were starving. At night we would sneak out and leave cases of food outside our tents for them to take and go back up into the mountains where they lived. Even the Japanese snipers would come down and take the food, which was probably another reason they never bothered the brothers.

We suffered two horrendous typhoons, two incredible typhoons like I have never experienced before or since. The winds were so powerful they literally cut ships in half. These typhoons were so overwhelming that the next day I swear we saw a piece of broom straw that had gone completely through steel without being broken. That was the power of those winds. We were lucky, we were young and crazy. But all the tents and houses got blown away, so we had to climb up in the mountains for refuge. We had to go inside these caves because the wind was too strong; it was blowing 175 miles an hour at some points.

I spent my year on Okinawa, got all my points to leave, and when it was time for me to go back to the States the war was over, but they were still fighting on Okinawa because the Japanese snipers were still holding out. I was responsible for everything and had to account for it before I could go back to the States. I had to open all the cases, and there were rocks inside some of the cases so it took me quite a while. But in the end I accounted for most of the stuff, though some had been lost to the typhoon. Those two typhoons saved my butt, because I was able to blame them for a lot of the supplies not showing up because guys had stolen the stuff and put rocks in the boxes.

Besides Charlie Smith and Henry McIntosh, who I mentioned earlier, there were other jazz musicians around while I was in the service. I met the saxophonists Bill Barron and Ernie Henry when I came back from Okinawa; they were stationed in Missouri. My homie from Brooklyn, the baritone saxman Cecil Payne, was in the European Army Orchestra, and they came to Okinawa to perform while I was out there. One of the funniest sights I saw was Cecil Payne playing the sax in the band while wearing an Army helmet. I met two really strong musicians from Chicago, a guy named William Barbie who played trumpet and alto sax, and a red-haired trumpet player named Red Sanders; but I lost track of those guys.

I didn't get opportunities to play much piano in the service. We had a few little groups that would play casually, nothing special. I'd get together with the guys from Chicago and we'd try to play someplace if they had a piano, especially when we were at Fort Dix. But in Okinawa and later when I was stationed in Missouri it was difficult, because there were no pianos there.

## 4

# POSTWAR

## Escaping the Panic

After the war I returned home to Brooklyn, and by this time I was thoroughly immersed in the music—both playing and listening, though I was still a bit reticent about envisioning myself as a professional musician. And the idea of devoting my entire life as a musician really wasn't a consideration, at least not yet. My dad had his small restaurant on Sumner Avenue, a street which ironically, considering his support of Garvey's principles, is now known as Marcus Garvey Boulevard. Being the entrepreneur that he was, dad wanted to expand and he wanted me to assist him, so he moved to a brownstone at 330-A Lafayette Avenue and opened another small restaurant. I took over managing the old place on Sumner Avenue, which was known as Trios. It was what was referred to back then as a luncheonette or what they now call a deli; not exactly a full-service restaurant as we think of them—we didn't have any waiters. But we stayed open twenty-four hours, seven days a week, which just illustrates what an industrious, ambitious man my father was.

Back then Brooklyn was full of great as well as plenty of aspiring jazz musicians, and since I knew many of them, Trios became a place where musicians would hang out. Also, all the local brothers and sisters who loved the music hung out at Trios, so we had a little neighborhood scene in Bed-Stuy. We had about six tables and a long bar in the place, but we didn't serve alcohol. We served everything from southern cooking to my Dad's Caribbean cooking, ice cream, cigarettes, tobacco, candy, newspapers, that kind of thing. My dad originally started the place out just selling hot dogs and hamburgers and expanded. It became a real place to hang out, not only because of the people who frequented the place but—and this was the major attraction for the musicians and the music-loving crowd—we also had the hippest jukebox in the area.

At the time I considered myself merely a student of the music, not a real musician, more of a dabbler, a semi-pro of sorts. Frankly I was a bit intimidated because the '40s on into the early '50s were a time when many of the real monsters of the piano were around, and for a young guy like myself who hadn't quite gotten his confidence up, it was a rather competitive atmosphere. I'd go out to hear Art Tatum, Erroll Garner, Eddie Heywood, Hank Jones . . . all the bad cats on piano. One time I was standing at the bar at a joint I used to frequent called the White Rose Bar at 6th Avenue and 52nd Street in Manhattan during the real high point of 52nd Street. Not only were the drinks cheap at the White Rose, but they also had free sandwiches, an irresistible combination for a young guy with a tight wallet. All the cats would go there to hang out at intermission from their gigs at other joints on 52nd Street, which was really jumping back then.

On this particular night I'm just standing there at the bar eyeing one of my real idols, Coleman Hawkins, and eavesdropping on a conversation between him and another sax master, Ben Webster. As a young guy when you're around guys of that caliber you really want to know what they're talking about, because you figure whatever these giants are talking about is gonna be some heavy stuff! I'm listening and I overhear Ben Webster tell Coleman Hawkins, "You better watch out, 'cause there's a bad young cat on tenor who just came on the scene named Don Byas." So even though he was such a promising young saxophonist and potential rival, Hawk checked him out and soon hired Don Byas for his band. I guess Hawk said if this guy Byas is that good I'd better get him in my band and keep an eye on him. For one week on 52nd Street it was Coleman Hawkins, Don Byas, and a rhythm section, I think he had Sir Charles Thompson on piano. And this was just an example of the caliber of all these different groups playing on 52nd Street; and nobody sounded like anybody else, they were all such originals.

As far as my own playing went, I was strictly an apprentice at that point. When those greats from the '30s, '40s, '50s were in their heyday at that time, I was in the restaurant business: that was my profession. I was working hard, seven days a week, sixteen hours a day, so being a full-time musician was the furthest thing from my mind. I'd try to make a few gigs on Saturday night, maybe play a dance or a little club in Brooklyn, played a few weddings, perhaps backing up a singer someplace; that was about it, pretty much what they call "casual" gigs. I was deep into the restaurant business, that was occupying most of my time, and besides that I really didn't think I had the kind of talent to make it with all these giants I was hanging around. I was something of a frustrated musician. I wanted to play music but at the same time I had no confidence that I was in a class to be able to deal with these masters, who seemed to be in such abundance back then.

Like I said, there were a lotta giants around Brooklyn back then, many of them living in my neighborhood. I mentioned Eddie Heywood, who lived directly across the street. Max Roach's house was two blocks away. George Russell was living in Max Roach's house at the time. Miles Davis, who was the same age as me, had just come up from East St. Louis and he was a young struggling musician who didn't have any money at the time, so he lived in a small place in the neighborhood on Kingston Avenue with his wife and young children.

I used to hang out at Max Roach's house on Monroe Street all the time. Max's house was a magnet for the new generation of musicians who emerged in the late 1940s, what the writers and fans called the bebop musicians. Miles would always be there at Max's house as well because he was working with Charlie Parker at the time and Max was the drummer in that band; Duke Jordan, who was also living in Brooklyn, was the pianist, and Tommy Potter was the bassist. So Charlie Parker's rhythm section was all Brooklyn guys.

I remember a really nice moment with some of these guys. In 1947, when the great trumpeter Freddie Webster, who was a big influence on Miles, died so prematurely, George Russell, Miles Davis, Max, and me all got in my father's car and we drove out to Coney Island by the ocean. While we strolled reminiscing on Freddie, Miles took out his trumpet right there on the beach and played a beautiful tribute to Freddie Webster that I'll never forget.

That whole area of Brooklyn was very rich in culture and loaded with artists. Cecil Payne's father had a tailor shop adjoining my dad's barber shop. The saxophonist Ernie Henry was also living in the neighborhood. The bassist Leonard Gaskin, another Brooklynite, was playing with Erroll Garner at the time. These guys like Ray Abrams, Cecil, Ernie, and Leonard were my peers, but I really didn't feel like I had the kind of talent that they did. To me they were great, great musicians, a lot of them unrecognized. When I did start playing in earnest I started by doing my own thing, playing my own music, not so much the standards of the day. One time I was over at Max's house and Charlie Parker walked in. I had started writing my own tunes by this time and Max immediately put me on the spot. He said, "Randy, play some of your music for Bird." I was in total shock. As far as what Max wanted me to play for Bird, it had to be something I wrote early on, like "Under Blunder," one of my earliest compositions. I actually wrote that piece after being stuck in the subway in the tunnel under the East River on my way to Manhattan. The idea of playing something for Bird scared me to death. This man was already a legend. But after I finished playing Bird said, "Yeah, yeah Randy that was nice."

My second encounter with Bird came when I tried to arrange a gig for him in Brooklyn. Back in those days, the late '40s, we had a loose-knit social organization in Brooklyn, with guys like Freddie Braithwaite and Jimmy Gittins, guys who were maybe three or four years older than me. They were totally into the music, because at that time the musicians and the people who loved the music were one, there was no separation between the musicians and the folks. We had a club in Brooklyn called the 78 Club, on Herkimer Place between Nostrand and Bedford Avenues, owned by a brother named Scottie. That was where Cecil Payne and a lot of the guys used to play. Max was also involved with this group of guys. Though he was a very prominent musician even then, Max was always straight ahead, very revolutionary, very militant . . . always ahead of his time, not only about his music but also in his efforts on behalf of black people. We were all very conscious of our situation as black people and we all had this fighting spirit inside of us. But back to the organization, our whole idea was to arrange for Charlie Parker to play at this 78 Club on a particular night.

Bird's A&R guy from the record company, and a man who produced a lot of his records at the time, was Teddy Reig, who also happened to be from Brooklyn. That particular evening of the gig Reig brought Bird to the 78 Club and we could see immediately that Bird was drunk, completely drugged out or whatever, he was out of it, and we all felt Teddy was behind this in order to sabotage our concert. Bird was absolutely in no shape to play, and we were so angry that we just about threw this guy Teddy Reig down the stairs. But cooler heads prevailed and that didn't happen. That sure was a wasted opportunity.

My next memory of Charlie Parker was much sweeter. After that embarrassing experience at Max Roach's house, me and Maurice Brown, a young drummer who studied with Max Roach, went down to a club called the Royal Roost which was on Broadway in Manhattan. This was the joint that was famous for Symphony Sid's live radio broadcasts, the "all night, all frantic one," and the place where Bird recorded so many live sides. That night we went there to hear Tadd Dameron, who had Charlie Rouse and

Fats Navarro in the band. The Roost was one of those downstairs places, like so many jazz clubs at the time. So we went down the stairs and the first thing we saw was Charlie Parker standing at the bar holding court with some people.

You always knew Charlie Parker was around because he was so gregarious, always the center of attention. He was the only musician I've ever known who always had his instrument by his side; you never saw him without that saxophone. Even if he went to the supermarket he had that saxophone with him; he slept with that thing, and sometimes he even carried it around in a paper bag. So we're coming down the stairs at the Roost and he spots us and starts beckoning. I'm looking all around to see who he's calling because I had assumed he surely didn't remember me, I'm just a young, inconspicuous guy; it was impossible that this great man would remember me. So I kept looking around to see who he was calling and Maurice said, "Hey man, he's talking to you!"

As you came down the stairs at the Royal Roost the bar was on the left side of the room and the stage was on the right side. Bird says, "Hey, Randy, what you doin'?" I said, "Hey, Bird, we came to hear Tadd." He got off the bar and said, "Come with me." I had no idea where this was leading, but if Charlie Parker tells you to come on, you come on, you don't ask no questions. So we climbed the stairs, went out to the street, and he called a taxi; we jumped in the taxi with Bird, and he still hadn't said anything about what's happening or where we're going. But remember, this is Bird we're talking about and we were just thrilled to be in his company.

Next thing you know we're on 52nd Street at the 3 Deuces. There was a quartet playing there at the time, but I forget exactly who it was. Bird walked over to the bandstand—right in the middle of a song—and told the piano player and the drummer to get up off their instruments—mid-tune. Man, you know that's usually a sure way to get killed, to go and interrupt a musician when he's onstage playing. But Bird was so spiritually powerful that these musicians acted like Buddha had just arrived, and they dutifully got up from their instruments. Bird told me to sit at the piano and Maurice Brown to sit at the drums. He took out his horn, and we must have played between a half-hour and forty-five minutes nonstop, just like that. Then just as quickly as we started he stopped, packed up his horn, and split without saying another word. I was in such a daze I don't even remember exactly what we played.

Me and Maurice were floating, we were in heaven, we'd played with the master. I still don't remember what we played; I guess we did things like "Now's the Time," "Lady Bird," "Ow," and tunes like that which were in Bird's book at that time. But that was my one and only opportunity to play with Charlie Parker. That was a moment I'll never forget.

## Coping with the Panic

Bird was a true victim of his times. And working the kind of hours many of these musicians were accustomed to, some felt the need for some kind of boost, some kind of stimulant to supposedly keep the creative juices flowing and enable you to work those late hours. Because when you go up on that stage and get involved in that arduous creative process, sometimes you have to somehow remove yourself from what's really going on in everyday life; you have to get away from the ambulance sirens, the blah-blah-blah, and the other atmospherics and try to concentrate on this new music, or whatever. In order to do that many musicians seemed to fit into certain categories: some drank beer, some liked bourbon, scotch, or some other alcohol; some musicians liked to smoke reefer; some even liked cocaine. You had this variation between alcohol, marijuana, and cocaine; those were the only stimulants we knew anything about at that time.

Heroin really wasn't much of a factor in the late '40s, at least not on a widespread basis. We knew nothing about heroin; it didn't exist as far as my crowd of musicians and friends were concerned. One day I was working in the restaurant and a group of musicians were hanging out as usual. I kept the jukebox full of creative music; we had everything in there from Stravinsky to Bird, all the latest stuff. So the musicians used to hang out to hear the music and catch up on the latest news.

Two women walked into the restaurant, two beautiful sisters, one of whom I knew well, she wasn't a girlfriend of mine but I knew her. In those days folks would always be sharply dressed; some people used to put on a suit just to go to the corner for a pack of cigarettes, that's just how folks were in those days, in the late '40s, early '50s. I was behind the counter, and these two sharply dressed women strolled in and sat down to have something to eat. Meanwhile the guys were chattering about whatever young people of that day talked about. Things weren't real good after the Second World War, because at the end of the war we were promised certain freedoms as black people, but we came back from the war to face the same old tired prejudice, the same racism was going on; and remember, this was back before black people could actually even vote, that was the prevailing condition of the times. A lot of our conversations focused on these conditions.

So these two sisters were sitting there at a table and they reached into their purses and pulled out these small packets of powder and gave them to the guys. In essence they were saying, "Check this out, it gets you high, its cheap, and it don't smell strong like reefer." During those days I remember how some guys might go to prison for three or four years just for possessing one joint, which sounds ridiculous now in the twenty-first century, but that's how sick the laws were back then. Obviously something that left no odor the way marijuana did was bound to have a certain appeal. These chicks said, "This stuff is good and it's very cheap." Cocaine back then was like champagne, you got a hold of some of that maybe once a year, it was so expensive that it really wasn't very prevalent. But this drug heroin was cheap.

Most of us weren't hip to this heroin, had never heard of it, and this thing wound up spreading like a cancer. It spread rapidly among the musicians, it spread among the people, it spread among almost all of us involved in that scene, the young people of that particular time, including myself. Luckily I was always repelled by needles, so I never stuck anything in my arm and wasn't mainlining, but I was snorting this stuff, as were a lot of the guys I hung out with. However, that wasn't the real problem; this drug panic was coupled with a turn for the worse in how our people were abusing each other, due in part to systemic segregation and racism. Many of us had fought for our country in the war, only to return home to the same old Jim Crow.

Our restaurant Trios was located in between a bar on the corner and a liquor store, a lethal combination. Guys in the neighborhood were working hard jobs for the man, carrying coal, toting blocks of ice, real backbreaking work like that, which were the only kinds of jobs available to black people at that time. Naturally after working so hard these folks would go into the bars on Friday and Saturday nights, hoot it up and get tanked, to seek some relief from that drudgery. Those scenes could quickly get explosive when people got liquored up. Then somebody would get riled up and pull out a knife or somebody else might pull a gun; there was beginning to be a lot of what they now call black-on-black crime, and it was real hard to be around that in your own neighborhood.

Years later it came out that this heroin epidemic was being spread by organized crime. As far as stimulants, before that time organized crime had only dealt with alcohol during Prohibition, but now they had these young guys and girls saying, "Yeah, let's do some heroin," like it was some kind of hip thing to do. When you look at it in retrospect it was natural they'd try to give it to the artists first, because it was the artists who often influenced the people. Folks looked up to the artists and emulated their dress and their behavior, so if a Charlie Parker got hooked up with heroin, it must be great; some musicians thought, "I can play like Charlie Parker and be like him" with heroin, or so the myth went.

Heroin and black folks abusing each other began to spread like wildfire. A lot of my friends died, and some of them wound up in prison. It was a very depressing period for me; besides the drugs there were black folks beating up blacks, blacks shooting other blacks . . . I'd see this with my own eyes and it made me very upset. My early training centered on black unity; I could never understand why we'd turn against each other. My business started deteriorating as a result of all this nonsense, also fueled by my own dabbling with heroin. A lot of my guys died, a lot of guys got sick, and this wonderful group of young musicians and friends of the music that we grew up with, who had such dignity and pride . . . all of a sudden heroin turned people into thieves and idiots and it was really the devil that entered into our community. I was getting increasingly depressed and nearly despondent, I wanted to get out of there so bad.

As I've always said, sometimes in life things happen that are so right you just cannot explain them; some call that grace. One day I ran into a guy named Lefty Morris, who at the time was playing semi-pro basketball up in the Berkshires in Lenox, Massachusetts, on a team called the Lenox Merchants. I used to play ball locally and I knew him from the courts. This man was built like Atlas, with a fantastic body. Lefty and I would often talk about spirituality, about the liberation of our people. I told this guy Lefty how bad I was feeling, how I couldn't take much more of seeing black folks shooting and stabbing each other and how depressed all this stuff was making me.

"That's not the way we grew up, man," I told him. "Sure, we had our little gangs, but at the same time we had some kind of pride as a people." At the time I was down to 180 pounds and at 6′7″—yep, I did finally grow to 6′7″ while I was in the service—I was looking like a pencil, not very healthy. Lefty said, "Randy, why don't you go up to the Berkshires, its really beautiful up there. Go up there and look for this woman named Mrs. Barton, who owns an employment agency, she'll give you a job. Spend the summer, she'll get you a job, you'll get plenty of fresh air, drink fresh milk, eat fresh vegetables, and get yourself healthy again." I told my mom and pop that I had to get out of Brooklyn because I was aiming for something higher than this mess, I didn't want to die like this. So I closed the restaurant, bought a bus ticket, and went up to the Berkshires.

When I arrived I went to see this woman Mrs. Barton, an older white woman with beautiful silver hair. I said, "My name is Randy Weston. I'm looking for a job." She said, "Randy, I don't have anything right now, but since you came all the way up here, there's a colored woman named Gerty, I want you to go see her." In those days there were these various houses, owned by black women, that would rent rooms to black men or black women who were working domestically in the area because we couldn't stay in the segregated white hotels.

Mrs. Barton said, "You go and stay at Gerty's, meanwhile I'll find you a job; it may take me a few days, but you stay there and when I get you a job you pay her and you give me my commission." So I went to this sister Gerty's house; she was a very nice older sister and she even cooked for me. Soon after, Mrs. Barton called me with a job in a place on Lake Buel, which is right around Great Barrington, Massachusetts. The guy who owned this particular resort happened to be a high school teacher in Brooklyn; it was just he and his daughter living there. He gave me a job cutting down trees, cleaning floors, doing all kinds of handy work.

Right away I saw that all of these resorts in the Berkshires area had beautiful pianos. Tanglewood was in the area and the Boston Symphony Orchestra was in residence there for seven weeks a year. As a result they brought students in from all over the world, not to mention the audience which came there in the summers and stayed in the resorts; so the whole area was very conducive to music, which excited me right away, even though I still hadn't yet decided I wanted to be a professional musician.

As my daily routine developed I would work all day in the resort and play their piano at night, when there were fewer people around . . . or so I thought. But inevitably some of the people who worked there as well as the guests began to notice my practicing the piano at night. They would stop me in the hallway or around the grounds and tell me how much they enjoyed my playing. Some would quietly eavesdrop on my nightly practice sessions, eventually telling me, "You play nice, play some more." Obviously this was rather flattering and quite encouraging as well. I guess I needed that kind of support.

Being up in the Berkshires was beginning to have a rejuvenating effect on me; I was finally away from all that madness in New York. I was starting to get healthy, drinking lots of milk, eating plenty of fresh fruit, enjoying the fresh air and the sheer tranquility of nature of this beautiful scene. I was able to stop using drugs entirely, in part because I didn't develop a full-blown habit like some of the guys who were using needles. That first handyman job lasted maybe three weeks or so, and when it ended I sure didn't want to go back to New York, so I went over to see Mrs. Barton, hoping she could find me some more work. She said, "Well, I'll see if I can find you another job." Pretty quickly she found me another job at a place called Seven Hills, a resort in Lenox, Massachusetts.

When I reported for work at Seven Hills they assigned me to work in the kitchen under this black chef. This guy was a real skilled chef, who had formerly worked at the Waldorf-Astoria. He was a real hard man, a very strict taskmaster and disciplinarian. He started by training me to be a breakfast chef. I had to learn how to feed 150 people: eggs over easy or upside down, oatmeal, cream of wheat . . . and how to do all this stuff with a squad of waiters running around the kitchen. Man, this was more than I was used to, with that fast pace. Needless to say I did my share of messing up, and this chef would cuss me out, call me all kinds of idiot . . .

But I had to take it from this guy, grin and bear it, because I needed this job and I sure didn't want to leave this beautiful place for that New York rat race. And once again they had very nice pianos at Seven Hills. I happily resumed my routine of working all day and practicing the piano at night, and the people there were very encouraging of my playing. All the guests at Seven Hills were there for the music at Tanglewood and elsewhere in the area, so they were already quite music-oriented.

When my job at Seven Hills ended I moved over to another place called Windsor Mountain, also in Lenox. Many of my fellow workers there were from Central Europe, people who had escaped Hitler during the Holocaust. Some of these people hadn't been able to escape the Nazis and they still had concentration camp tattoos on their arms; these were Jews from Germany and Poland, all up in the Berkshires working at this place. The owner of Windsor Mountain was a very strict German woman, a very formidable, strong woman named Mrs. Oustaban who didn't tolerate any foolishness. I was a dishwasher there and I also helped out the bell staff by assisting the old people with their luggage.

The guests and residents were all artists: violinists, singers, pianists . . . classical artists. One day some of them who had been hearing me practice at night came to me and said, "Randy, we're going to have a concert next weekend and we'd like you to play." This was very interesting, but I had to politely decline, telling them that I don't play Bach, Mozart, or Beethoven, the stuff I thought they were into; I wasn't a classical pianist. But they insisted. They said, "No, no, we want you to play what we hear you play when you practice at night." Man, was I shocked!

I still didn't have much confidence in myself as a musician. I really wasn't composing anything at the time; I guess what they heard me play was some standards, things like "How High the Moon," "All the Things You Are" . . . the kinds of things that Bird and Diz were using the chord structures to write new tunes, things like that. But I finally got up my nerve and consented to play this concert because these people had been so pleasant and encouraging to me.

So I played the concert, playing the usual stuff I had been practicing at night, the bebop standards and things. The response was really great. They said, "You're fantastic!" This really threw me for a loop, because I thought these people were all the heavies, people who knew the music of Bach, Beethoven, and the classical masters. What did I know about that stuff? I was starting to feel kinda good about myself as a result of this.

One afternoon I'm working away in the kitchen, alongside two young women, one from Czechoslovakia, one from Hungary, named Vera and Hella. We were chatting and they said, "Randy, we hear there's some jazz at this resort called the Music Inn, and it's about three miles away. Would you like to go over there with us this evening?" Jazz up here in the Berkshires? I said, "Yeah, wonderful." I was surprised and delighted, but I really didn't know what to expect since I thought that all this place was about was European classical music.

Since none of us had a car or a ride to this Music Inn, we had to walk the three miles through the woods, in the dark, if you could imagine a 6'7" black man striding through the woods with these two European women. What a sight that must have been. When we finally arrived the program was already under way. This enlightened man, who I later learned was named Marshall Stearns, was giving a very interesting lecture to an audience of about a hundred people. Right when we got there he was playing a record of Benny Goodman's version of Jelly Roll Morton's tune "King Porter Stomp" and contrasting it with Fletcher Henderson's arrangement of the same tune. Hmm, this is interesting, I thought to myself . . . Who's

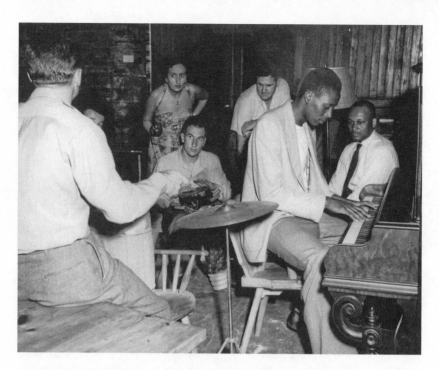

The Randy Weston Trio, with Jim Tite, drums, and Sam Gill (hidden), bass, performing at Music Inn. Watching is the famed calypsonian MacBeth (wearing tie). *Photographer unknown, courtesy of the Estate of Stephanie Barber.*

this cat? This really wasn't a classroom situation per se and the audience wasn't students, they were people who had come to this particular resort for music. They would go over to Tanglewood and catch the orchestral performances at night, or sometimes they had jazz concerts, or perhaps they would go to nearby Jacob's Pillow for classical dance performances. This whole area was stimulating for me, a haven for people involved in music and other arts. Stearns's audience was a combination of vacationers, editors, critics, all kinds of people like that.

The more I listened to his lecture the more I became intrigued by Stearns's approach to jazz history. He would start out talking about West Africa being the origins of this music. I had never before heard or read any other jazz critic or educator doing this, making the clear connections of jazz origins to Africa. Everybody else told that same old "up the river from New

Orleans" story, leaving Africa completely out of the picture. I said, "Who *is* this guy?" I *had* to know him.

The manager of the Music Inn was a guy named Jim Tite, who played a little on the drums. After Stearns concluded his lecture someone introduced me to Tite and told him I was a piano player. I said, "Yeah, I play piano." He said, "Great, I'm a drummer and you should come by and hang out, maybe we can jam a little." He played drums in an older, Gene Krupa style, but he could play a little bit. The couple who actually owned the Music Inn were Phil and Stephanie Barber. They were New York theater people who had decided to buy this property in the Berkshires and dedicate it to music and music education. Somehow they hooked up with Marshall Stearns and engaged him to present a series of history of jazz lectures. How Marshall Stearns came up with his pan-African concept I have no idea, because this was way before the civil rights movement, we're talking about the 1950s. Eventually his collection started the Institute of Jazz Studies at Rutgers University in Newark, and now there's a beautiful documentary film about this place Music Inn, produced by Gunther Schuller's son George.

Besides his own lectures Marshall Stearns had established a guest lecture series at the Music Inn. He would bring all these heavy people to the place to not only perform in the Berkshires but also do lectures during the day. For example, Mahalia Jackson and her piano accompanist Mildred Falls came up and performed a concert and during the day they gave a talk about gospel music. I was thoroughly into these Music Inn programs and all of a sudden I'm meeting all these heavy black people. I met Babatunde Olatunji from Nigeria, the great dancer Geoffrey Holder, the singer and actor Brock Peters, the Cuban master drummer Candido . . . I spent time with Langston Hughes up there, a man who would later become very important at a key point in my life; Dan Burleigh, who was a journalist with the old Pittsburgh Courier and who also played some piano, created the "skiffle" style, and wrote the original book on jive, came to the Music Inn for Marshall's lecture series; the actress Butterfly McQueen from *Gone with the Wind* . . . I was fascinated hearing Dr. Willis James of Spelman College talk about field cry hollers and how slaves communicated during slavery. The Berkshires was opening up a whole new world to me.

Marshall Stearns had put together this pan-African concept and invited all these people to the Music Inn to speak and perform. That's where I first became acquainted with the Savoy Ballroom dancers Al Minns and Leon James, whose paths would later cross mine on an important journey. Stephanie Barber heard me play the piano and said, "Why don't you come over here and be a breakfast chef at the Music Inn." Thinking that

Marshall Stearns (back partially turned, with glasses) conducting
one of his roundtable discussions at Music Inn, with Dr. Willis James
to his left. *Photographer unknown, courtesy of the Institute of
Jazz Studies.*

would put me even closer to Marshall's programs, I took her up on the offer
and I wound up being the breakfast chef there, learning how to deal with
the seven frying pans and all that stuff, working with a little French chef.
Then I would play piano at night. Eventually I stopped cooking and started
working there with my very first trio. It was a couple of summers before I
became a full-time musician there. Stephanie Barber couldn't believe that
you could dance to what they called modern jazz; she wanted me to play
for the dancers. I ended up recruiting my Brooklyn homies Sam Gill on
bass and Willie Jones on drums to come up, and we would play for people
to dance. Stephanie was amazed that they had modern jazz for people to
dance.

## Sam Gill, bassist in Randy's Music Inn trio
*(retired principal bassist, Denver Symphony)*

*Sam Gill:* When Randy went up to the Berkshires and was in a position where he could hire a trio, he contacted me, and I was quite honored and surprised. It was a godsend when he brought me and Willie Jones to Music Inn. We played up there for about four or five years as a trio in the summer. Randy knew I played classical music, had gone to Juilliard and studied it a lot, but he was always showing me the beauties of jazz and how jazz should be taken seriously. Randy talked about how important this music was to our culture before everybody else. He made me take jazz much more seriously, through his instruction, his ideas, and philosophy.

In those days Randy's music was not the conventional jazz that we were used to hearing. Back then every other piano player was sounding like Bud Powell, which was harmonically just regular, hymn-type chords. But Randy was influenced by Thelonious Monk. He was one of the only musicians at that time that could understand Thelonious, because Thelonious's music was highly complex. Randy had the rare ability to interpret what Monk was doing, which is what made Randy outstanding among his peers. In the Brooklyn community he was one of our most outstanding young musicians coming along because he had the ability, the talent, and the outlook to understand Monk, who none of the rest of us could understand at that time.

The classical musicians who were in residence up in the Berkshires during that time also heard something different in Randy. There was one man I remember, an Italian composer, who used to come to hear us every night and just marvel at Randy. He would say, "That reminds me of Ravel." Leonard Bernstein would come in and do piano portraits of different people. Randy was doing a lot of that too; I don't know if he picked it up from Bernstein or if Bernstein picked it up from Randy. Bernstein was quite the character, he used to carry a cane and wear a cape like Mandrake or something. There were other classical musicians who used to come hear us. In our off evenings we would go to hear the Boston Symphony—Randy, Willie Jones, and myself.

Eventually I wound up playing piano for Marshall Stearns's history of jazz lectures. I was a young guy who could play piano a little bit like Thelonious

Monk. Stearns's lectures would go from West Africa to the Caribbean to the black church, up through the '20s, '30s, Ma Rainey, the '40s, all the way up to what they call modern jazz. The person he would always end up with was Bud Powell, but he had never heard Monk for some reason—and Monk had actually mentored Bud, so Marshall was missing a real important link.

When I played Monk for Marshall, he said, "What's that?" I said, "Man, that's the newest thing." He said to me, "Let's do the history of jazz together; you put together a quartet, we'll get the two dancers from the Savoy Ballroom to deal with the dance aspect of the music, and we'll tour the universities." In turn I was missing some links myself; I hadn't yet really learned or absorbed the older styles of piano, like ragtime, stride, boogie-woogie, those classic styles of jazz piano. But Marshall pulled my coat to the older styles and I introduced him to this new Thelonious Monk style. He got me to listen to Fats Waller, James P. Johnson, Jimmy Yancey, Meade Lux Lewis, Albert Ammons, Eubie Blake, all those great masters. Eventually he had me play different passages and styles to illustrate points he was making in his lectures, so we established a real strong working relationship and friendship.

Marshall would do the speaking and I would demonstrate the various styles he talked about on the piano. Our history of jazz programs would go something like this: We would go from West Africa to the Caribbean, to the 1920s; I'd play stuff like "When the Saints Go Marching In" to illustrate New Orleans style. We would cover Ma Rainey and the blues, up through the 1930s and the big bands; and for that period we would have the two Savoy Ballroom dancers Al Minns and Leon James to illustrate the various swing dance styles. And by the end of the program I was playing Monk and Bud Powell, what at that point was considered modern jazz.

We would use a couple of different units, with people like Cecil Payne on saxophones, Ahmed Abdul-Malik on bass, the drummer could be Scoby Stroman sometimes; personnel would vary, depending upon where we were performing the program. The unique thing about Marshall Stearns was how he would trace the music's roots back to Africa; that always impressed me about him. We would show that this music people called jazz is African culture in America. Most historians didn't want to deal with that at the time; they wanted to say jazz began in New Orleans. Jazz did not begin in New Orleans; jazz roots go back thousands of years, coming out of the ancient African civilizations. Our program was very successful in illustrating these connections. After Marshall got sick I would do the speaking and musical demonstration, and sometimes Langston Hughes would perform Marshall's speaking role in the program, but we'll get back to him in a minute.

Fast forwarding a bit, in 1958 Marshall Stearns got us some engagements and we started doing our history of jazz programs at universities across the country, from New York to California to the University of Minnesota. We were the first ones to do the history of jazz in the school systems. After a period of time Marshall had a heart attack and could no longer do the programs, so he said, "Randy, you do the programs because you know what it's all about and when you do it it's even more natural than when I do it."

For ten summers I went up to the Berkshires to play in those resorts. During the rest of the year I was back in Brooklyn, running my dad's restaurant and making local gigs. During my summers in the Berkshires I always kept a sign-in book by the piano for patrons to sign so I would have their mailing addresses for later, so that when I played in New York during the rest of the year I would keep in touch and invite them to hear me play. I got opportunities to work in some of the prominent New York clubs, like the Five Spot and the Half Note; I was beginning to develop the Randy Weston Trio.

Meanwhile I had gotten married to a woman named Mildred Mosley in 1949, but she never went up to the Berkshires with me, she was back in New York working instead. Eventually we had three children, Pamela, Niles, and Kim, and I would bring them up to the Berkshires for the summer, which enabled them to get out of the city, get some fresh air and enjoy the beauty of the land up there. Mildred would come up every now and then, but basically I had the kids by myself. One good thing about the Berkshires is they had sisters who worked in the big hotels and they would look after the kids if I needed that. Elmo Hope's wife Bertha, who was a wonderful pianist herself, was one of the sisters up there, so I got to know her, and Elmo would come up sometime. Charlie Persip's family is from up there and I got to know them very well, so we were surrounded by friends, a nice family environment.

Just to get the kids out of New York for the summers was great. And in my case I was so grateful because that Berkshires experience enabled me to rid myself of drugs and be far from that other madness. Not to mention how the place was like a music paradise, with the opera, the Boston Symphony, people like Leonard Bernstein and Lukas Foss in residence, jazz at the Music Inn, plus all the people coming in to do the lecture series. Those ten summers in the Berkshires were a real cleansing experience for me, and I was able to further develop myself as a player and finally gain the confidence to where I was able to reconcile myself to making music my profession, which didn't really happen until I was twenty-nine; but there I go jumping the gun again.

## 5

Rhythm is the secret . . . the beginning and the end.
African rhythms have found their way into the hearts of many.
Many are feeding their souls and curing their wounds
with its glory.—PAPA OYEH MACKENZIE, Ghanaian percussionist

# POST-BERKSHIRES

## Succumbing to the Irresistible Lure

As a developing musician I really didn't spend too much time on the road working as a sideman, but one particularly memorable gig was with the old rhythm-and-blues crooner Bullmoose Jackson. He had a big hit with "I Love You, Yes I Do." The late 1940s, early 1950s were still a time when all the artists would come to New York, including the big jazz and blues bands, and lay over during their down time. Sometimes these bands were laid off for a few days or even weeks, so a lot of the sidemen would pick up local musicians like me and we would play at places around Manhattan and Brooklyn. There was a saxophone player, a guy with a pretty strong personality, named Frank "Floorshow" Culley. They called him Floorshow because he was one of those honking, bar-walking saxophonists who would hold one note for a long time and walk the bar and make all those kinds of crowd-pleasing, showbiz moves. I wound up making a gig with him somewhere locally during one of his layoffs from the road.

Eventually Floorshow got a gig with Bullmoose Jackson as the band's straw boss, the guy responsible for hiring and paying the musicians and making all those kinds of arrangements. In 1949 Floorshow was hiring a band to go on the road with Bullmoose, and he liked the way I played and wanted me in the band. Although I was twenty-three at the time, I was still an inexperienced young man living with his father who wasn't exactly used to leaving home other than for my travels in the service. Floorshow came to my father to convince him why I should travel with him and Bullmoose

Jackson. This guy Floorshow was quite the talker and he quickly got my father's attention. Finally my dad said OK, because Floorshow was such a good con man who could talk his way into anything, or so it seemed. We had a rehearsal up in Harlem to prepare the road show and one of the guys they'd hired was the drummer Connie Kay, who I didn't know at the time and who later played for over forty years in the Modern Jazz Quartet. A guy named Wallace was on trumpet, Fats Morris played trombone, and on bass Floorshow had a Cherokee Indian they called Count. This guy Count couldn't really play the bass, he would just pull the strings, but he was a good chauffeur and since this was a road gig, competent bass player or not, he was in the band.

This tour was a really big deal for me because other than the service it was not only my first time leaving home but also my first time going down south on the blues circuit. The pay was $25 a day, which sounded like a lot of money at first—remember this was 1949. Out of that $25 you had to pay your room rent and buy your meals; but for me I was still living at home and this looked like a golden opportunity to travel. It was the same for Connie Kay, and he and I quickly became tight friends. We were similar in height and worked great together on the bandstand as a rhythm section, overcoming the bass player's obvious shortcomings.

The tour started in the fall and one of our first memorable gigs was in Washington, D.C. This was during a period when battles of the bands were quite common and very popular. In D.C. the battle was Bullmoose Jackson versus Ruth Brown's band, which had Willis "Gatortail" Jackson on sax. Willis was like Floorshow, one of those entertaining bar walkers who would hold that one continuous note while removing his clothes and stuff like that. But Willis Jackson was a better saxophone player than Floorshow, who was just one of those guerillas, all show and bluster, little substance. The first time I saw those cats lying down on the floor battling, playing one note and meanwhile taking off their shirts and ties, was something I had never seen before and it was pretty corny to me. But the audience ate it up. This was some real black showbiz of the day. Ruth's band probably won that battle because Bullmoose was more of a crooner, with a sweet and tender voice, a very romantic kind of singing, not exactly a hardcore blues shouter or a dynamic crowd pleaser like Ruth. Bullmoose sang the blues all right, but Ruth and Willis were more dynamic performers.

We played the whole black circuit on this tour, from the Eastern Seaboard down to Ft. Lauderdale, Florida, and over to Mobile (Alabama), New

Orleans, Houston, and Oklahoma City; those were the stops that stood out in my mind. I also remember playing in places in North Carolina where there was hay on the floor, with folks dancing on the hay. We played in joints where the piano had maybe two working octaves and the bandstand was so tiny that the piano couldn't fit onstage and I'd have to sit in the audience to play. But it was a learning experience and we quickly learned that although that $25 a day sounded like great pay in the beginning to a young inexperienced guy like me, after we paid for our rooms and our meals we had hardly any money left. Floorshow was also an incurable gambler who would take our payroll and gamble with it, leaving us short sometimes. So we never had any real money.

This was way before civil rights, so we were staying in all-black hotels. Another memorable gig was in Mobile, Alabama, where we played in a place that had never had a black band before. When we arrived there was a state trooper posted outside this ballroom where we were to play. Floorshow's advance publicity photo had preceded the band and it pictured him with his saxophone up in the air; he fancied himself as an acrobat of the sax and he would often jump in the air while holding that one note. The state trooper at the door asked us, "Which one of you guys is this guy?," pointing at the photo. We all said, "That's Floorshow," because he was a real pain in the ass that was always making us crazy so we wanted to get even. The trooper looked hard and said, "We better see you do this tonight," pointing straight at Floorshow, "or we'll take your ass to prison!" Welcome to Mobile! Right away we knew this could be a hot night in Alabama.

We got to the gig and right at the start of the show Bullmoose is singing these syrupy romantic ballads and his usual blues. All of a sudden these overly excited white women started rushing the stage—and remember, this is Ku Klux Klan country. Needless to say, this shook us up, and we kept trying to tell Bullmoose to change the tempo, change the songs, or do something to lower that heat. There were actually women sitting on top of the piano. Thankfully nothing happened, but we did a whole lot of sweating that night, and it wasn't from the room temperature.

Another memorable tour stop was in Oklahoma City, where it was freezing cold with a whole lotta snow on the ground. But I got a golden opportunity to see Louis Armstrong, who was also in Oklahoma City, staying at the same hotel as our band. I got a chance to meet him and shake his hand. Floorshow, who had his wife traveling with the band, was so cheap he didn't even want to feed her. We'd drive all night from one place to the next gig and when we'd get to our destination he'd tell his wife he had to go park the car. Instead he'd go to a restaurant and eat enough for ten people. Then he'd go back to his room and when his wife complained that she was hungry he'd say, "What's the matter with you, you eat too much!" He was that kind of dude.

One time he got mad and almost tried to kill us in Oklahoma. He had tried to run some kind of game with the band's money and we were all mad at him; so there was a little war brewing and we were about to mutiny on his ass. Meanwhile we've gotta travel to the next gig. Still grumbling, we get in the car for the drive and he's got his wife sitting in the middle, I'm crammed into the passenger's side, and the rest of the band is in the back. We're driving on ice, and because the band was fussing at him about the money he deliberately put his pedal to the metal, driving as fast as he could, I guess to try and scare us out of being so mad at him. But that didn't work; it just made us madder.

When we got to Texas there was a great band in Houston led by Lowell Fulsom and featuring Ray Charles, who was quite young and none of us had ever heard of him at that point. Wherever we went there was a band waiting to do battle with us. When we walked into that Houston club Lowell Fulsom had the whole band standing on tables playing, with Ray Charles onstage all by himself playing the blues. Needless to say, we got our butts thoroughly whipped that night, they really put a hurtin' on us, and we snuck out of Texas with our tails between our legs.

When we got back to New York in early '51 it was around the time that Atlantic Records was recording the first rhythm-and-blues records. Floorshow did a record date for Atlantic called "Cole Slaw." At the time Atlantic also had a young singing group called the Clovers and they needed a rhythm section to play with them. Since we'd been Floorshow's rhythm section on "Cole Slaw" for Atlantic we ended up making the Clovers' first record, "Don't You Know I Love You," on February 22, 1951.

As I said, I didn't really do as much sideman work as most of my peers at the time, because I had my own musical concept in mind. It started off with the waltzes I wrote. When I was up in the Berkshires and I started to compose, people said to me, "What you're doing is different than what everybody else is doing." The power of Duke Ellington and Thelonious Monk, who were both composers who more or less played only their own material, was a heavy influence on me. I admired that kind of self-sufficiency and wanted to emulate them. Even in the early days I was considered a composer first and a pianist second, which is why on my early recordings most of the solos are by the other musicians in the band. That whole band leadership urge also stemmed from the influence of my do-for-self preaching father, who pounded into me, "Do your own business, don't work for nobody, work for yourself."

## Influences

My biggest musical influences were some powerful musicians. Like all young musicians I tried to play like certain artists when I started playing the piano seriously. I was pretty successful at imitating Count Basie; he was my first influence. I was fascinated by his sense of rhythm and space and how he could say so much with so few notes. He was a master of that and that's a very difficult thing to master. I'd have to say he was my very first influence.

My next influence was Nat "King" Cole, because when I heard him I'd never heard a piano played with such beauty and taste. Every single note from him was just sheer beauty. That's also one of the qualities I like in John Lewis's playing, not that they play alike necessarily, but with both Nat and John each note is a pearl. People generally don't recognize Nat Cole's influence on my playing when they hear it, but I sure hear it and feel it. Nat's greatest influence on me was in his choice of notes. When I wrote and recorded the tune "Earth Birth" I could hear Nat's influence in the ballad section of that tune.

My next influence would be Art Tatum. When I first heard Tatum he shattered me and frightened me at the same time, he was so awesome. I never consciously thought I was playing anything like Art Tatum, but when I play I hear Art Tatum, maybe four or five notes of his runs. He's there because he taught me by his example to be daring and he was such a rhythmic and harmonic genius.

Perhaps my biggest influence would be Thelonious Monk. I heard Monk through Coleman Hawkins. Hawk was my idol; when he recorded his big hit version of "Body and Soul" in 1939 I ran out and bought three copies: one to play around the house and I wrapped the other two up and hid them for safekeeping. I used to try to play the piano like Coleman Hawkins played the saxophone. When I heard Monk play the piano I didn't get him at first, but he eventually opened the door for me, showed me the direction for our music, where we maintain all the traditions of African music and we create from there instead of leaving there and going in another direction. But I must admit it took a minute for Monk's playing to affect me.

The first time I heard Monk was on a Coleman Hawkins gig on 52nd Street. I went to hear Hawk and didn't recognize his piano player. As they played their set I remember thinking to myself, "Who's this cat on piano, I can play more piano than this guy!" I didn't understand what he was doing because he was playing so differently from anyone else. I heard something unusual in this guy but I couldn't quite put my finger on what it was. I was intrigued so I went back to hear Hawk again with this same guy on piano, and when I heard him the second time I felt Monk put the magic back into the music; music became universal for me. Monk did some other things with the music, he was so beautiful. "Misterioso," the title of one of his songs, explains perfectly what he did with music. When I heard Monk that second time something clicked and I realized just how advanced he was. I just had to go and meet him because I was looking for something different on the piano at this time and his concept was so original it truly touched me.

Ahmed Abdul-Malik, the great bassist whose father was Sudanese and who ironically later played with both Monk and me, turned me on to a lot of music. When we were kids he introduced me to the instruments of North Africa and the Middle East, such as the kanoun and the oud. These were instruments where you could play eighth-tones, play in between the standard notes on the western scale. Malik and I used to experiment in local bands as kids . . . trying to play the notes between the cracks. Guys just weren't into that at the time and we used to get thrown out of local bands for trying to be different. I was already searching for something different. Malik would take me down to the Arab neighborhood around Atlantic Avenue in downtown Brooklyn to hear North African musicians. He spoke fluent Arabic so we had no trouble communicating.

I would try to play those notes on the piano, but when I heard Monk he was already doing that. I heard something in him that truly excited me, really opened me up. I thought to myself, "Hey, that's the way to go!" Eventually I asked Monk if I could come to his house and talk with him about piano and he said, "Sure" and gave me his address. The first time I went to Monk's house I was there nearly seven hours, and all he said was to listen to all kinds of music. The second time I went over there Monk sat down at the piano and played for about three straight hours without saying a word.

I just sat there and marveled at his invention. When he finished he just said, "See you later." I asked if I could come back sometime and he said, "Sure," and that was that. My first lesson from Thelonious Monk! I'm convinced Monk came out of the ancient times because when he played the piano it was no longer a piano, it became for me another instrument entirely. When I heard Monk play the piano it stretched my imagination for what I could do on the instrument; suddenly the possibilities seemed endless.

Monk's house was on West 63rd Street, behind where Lincoln Center is today, ironically in an area known as San Juan Hill. I would go over there and we'd talk, and I'd listen to him play the piano. These were real piano lessons, though not in the conventional sense. I heard some absolutely amazing piano over there. And I went to some of Monk's band rehearsals and also brought him to Brooklyn on occasion. Monk would have no money in his pocket and I'd sit there with him and he'd say, "C'mon, let's take a walk." But before Monk would go into the street he'd put on a shirt, tie, his beret, with his shoes shining and everything. And when we would walk the streets together everybody would hail Monk like the emperor was walking through the streets. Back in those days dress was extremely important. A musician wouldn't even go out to buy a pack of cigarettes unless he had on a shirt and tie.

This was before Monk was generally accepted among the musicians; many thought he was too far out. But I was convinced of his genius and tried to convince others. Since then they've become convinced of Monk's greatness. I'm very proud that I was so close to Monk and could recognize that indescribable originality in his playing before the jazz establishment finally got around to it. Monk was a master composer, a master pianist, and he brought the mystery back into the music; he had a kind of magic, a wonderful way of saying you can play music beautifully by going this way, certainly not with his words but through his playing example. In Monk's playing I heard something that no European could possibly capture.

When you'd watch Monk play the piano, Monk was doing a whole ballet, he wasn't just playing the piano; if you watch the way he moves on the piano it's a whole movement that's pure Africa, the kind of spontaneous creativity you'll find in all African traditional music. And humor, which you can find in abundance in Monk's music, is a very important part of African music. What we don't realize, despite the fact that we left the continent of Africa hundreds of years ago, is that we approach life and the music just as our ancestors did; Africa never left us. When I heard Thelonious

Monk play the piano he opened the door, showed me the direction for our music, where we maintain all the traditions of African music and we create from there instead of leaving there and going in another direction. Monk brought the mystery back into music, a kind of magic, a wonderful way of saying you can play music beautifully by going this way.

Monk's biggest influence, Duke Ellington, is an unquestioned master of masters. Duke was able to be in his time and ahead of his time simultaneously, which is not easy. Duke Ellington was writing about black people back in the '20s and '30s. He wrote "Black, Brown and Beige" in 1943. Ellington is like a prophet. Every time I touch the piano there's some Ellington coming out of my music, because he covered the whole scope of universal culture. I started writing music about Africa in 1954, and my main influences in that respect were Duke Ellington and Dizzy Gillespie, because they put an emphasis on our people and that made a tremendous impact upon me. Duke Ellington was a poet, he was always creating new things, always creating wonderful sounds out of the piano with a lot of depth, and he was very committed to his people. Ellington was a true keeper of the history of black people.

As far as influences go, people whose examples helped mold me, if you were to ask *who is Randy Weston*, it would be like making a stew. You throw in some Ellington, some Basie, some Monk, some Tatum, and some Nat Cole; throw in Africa, throw in some Coleman Hawkins, Dizzy Gillespie, and Chano Pozo. You put all of those ingredients in the pot, stir it up, and you have Randy Weston. They all gave me so much according to how they approached music and what they did with it. Yet and still it wasn't until about 1959 that I became thoroughly convinced that a career as a musician was the path I should follow. But unlike a lot of musicians I actually got my first recording opportunity even *before* I made that decision.

## First Record Date

My first recording session opportunity as a leader happened because I was playing in the Berkshires a lot at that incredible place the Music Inn. I was playing solo piano there initially because Stephanie Barber, the proprietor of the Music Inn, was so skeptical about whether her patrons would dance to modern jazz. She and I had several good-natured arguments about that. So to prove a point I brought up my guys from Brooklyn, the bassist Sam Gill and the drummer Willie Jones, and we started playing the gig as a trio.

Stephanie had this beautiful resort with all kinds of intellectual stimulation around, including wonderful and spirited discussions on music during the day. But at night the patrons wanted to relax and dance. So we proved to her that we could play for dancing.

In the meantime a guy named Bill Grauer came up there on vacation. He owned a small record company called Riverside Records, along with another guy named Orrin Keepnews; but Grauer was the head guy. At the time they were also producing a magazine called the *Record Changer*, which dealt with some of the older jazz styles from the '20s, '30s, and early '40s. In fact I think they were called "moldy figs" or something like that, for recording those older styles. But in reality they were more advanced than that in their musical thinking. Grauer heard me play at Music Inn, called his partner Orrin Keepnews, and they decided to try and record me as their first live artist. Prior to that they had been recording beautiful piano rolls of Fats Waller, Jelly Roll Morton, Jimmy Yancey . . . a lot of the older guys in those classic piano styles; then they would make LPs from these piano rolls. They also recorded sound effects records, like the sounds of sports cars. In fact I believe that's how they started their company.

Grauer and Keepnews decided that I would be their first new recording artist. They wanted to record me playing solo piano, but I was reluctant because I just didn't have the confidence in my playing to record solo piano. We argued back and forth since I wanted to record the trio with Sam and Willie. Finally we compromised on a duo recording of piano and bass with Sam Gill. They also requested that I record songs of a popular American composer of my choice. I always liked Cole Porter's music, so we ended up doing all Cole Porter for my first recording, *Randy Weston Plays Cole Porter in a Modern Mood*. On April 27, 1954, we went into the studio and recorded the date all in one day.

I was scared to death because it was my first recording. I grew up in what I like to think of as the golden age of the piano. I used to go and listen to Willie "the Lion" Smith, Luckey Roberts, Eubie Blake, and all those classic cats. From the more modern side I was into Thelonious Monk, Herbie Nichols, Bud Powell, and Erroll Garner . . . Those people were all active at the time, so it was a powerful period of the piano. And besides those giants I knew pianists in Brooklyn who were incredible and who never recorded. With all these masters around I didn't have the confidence that I was ever going to be a professional pianist, let alone record, so I was really nervous. That first session was important not only because it was my first record but also because from that date it helped me five years later to decide to commit myself fully to being a professional musician. As I said, I really didn't decide to totally immerse myself in a career in music until 1959, but that first recording certainly sent me on my way.

I was also very encouraged by the response to that first record. The people really seemed to like it and the critics liked it as well. Back in those days there was hardly any record promotion, and certainly not from a small company like Riverside. But *DownBeat* magazine gave it a very good, four-star review. The critics seemed to like the record a lot. In fact I've always felt the critics' response to my work has been reasonable.

For my follow-up Riverside record I was able to get Art Blakey on drums for a trio date. I loved Monk and Art Blakey very much; the two of them would be together a lot, and I would just hang out and listen to them. Art Blakey was always the perfect drummer for Monk's music. Blakey's drumming had that lovely—I call it sanctified—swing; Art Blakey would just swing you to death. He was around Brooklyn a lot in those days, and back in the late '40s he formed an all-Muslim big band called the Jazz Messengers, primarily in Brooklyn. As a result of the good reviews I got for my first record, and because Art Blakey had a name, Riverside decided to let me make a trio record, which we made in January 1955 in Hackensack, New Jersey, at Rudy Van Gelder's first studio. It was very easy integrating Blakey with Sam Gill and me because it was just a matter of swing.

One tune we recorded was "Pam's Waltz," which was the first waltz I wrote. Art had a reputation for being a very strong, forceful drummer with the sticks, with his patented rolls and all that stuff, but he could be sensitive as well. For some of the record he used the brushes and played some beautiful rhythms with the brushes on "Pam's Waltz." Rudy Van Gelder's studio was much warmer than the East Side studio we used for the first record. Fortunately I wasn't as nervous this time, because it was my second outing. But for every recording there's a certain amount of nervousness involved and I think it's very healthy as long as it's not excessive. Every concert, every recording is a new trip.

My third record was *With These Hands*, which we made in March of '56. On that date I was given the opportunity to add a horn, and for that I wanted Cecil Payne, who I grew up with in Brooklyn. Cecil was one of my idols, and wherever he played I would go to hear him because I just love his sound on the baritone saxophone. One of the most beautiful things on that date is Cecil Payne's interpretation of "The Man I Love," as well as what he played on "I Can't Get Started," and my tune "Little Niles." He certainly proved his great musicianship on that record. The drummer was Wilbert

Hogan, who was playing with Lionel Hampton's band at the time. In those days if you played with Lionel Hampton or Count Basie, or any of those big bands, you were great. Wilbert lived in Brooklyn and we were very close; he was a tremendous drummer. On bass I had Ahmed Abdul-Malik, who I could never forget because he had the biggest sound on string bass, a huge sound. He and I used to practice together and, as I said, he would always play notes between the notes; so I was always trying to find notes between the notes on the piano. Cecil Payne, Malik, and I were like family.

My original contract with Riverside Records had options. Since Monk and I were very close and Riverside wanted to sign Monk, they wanted me to help them sign Monk, which eventually they did. And they also started recording other great artists. After the first three records, whatever it was that I wanted to record at the time they weren't able to do, and it was the end of my contract.

I even worked at Riverside as a clerk for a time, cataloguing records and other things that helped me know a bit more about the business side of making records. They had put out some incredible LPs on African traditional music, besides those classic jazz piano rolls. At the time Marshall Stearns wanted me to work with him on his History of Jazz programs to demonstrate the various styles, but he wanted me to learn the older styles of piano. When you're young you always want to play the "latest thing," so when Bud and Monk came out that was the latest thing and I was really into their music. Those other, classic things sounded outdated, but I came to find out its all modern music. Riverside had that great collection, which also included Jimmy Yancey, Meade Lux Lewis, Albert Ammons, and some of the other older cats. Riverside didn't have a clerk at the time, they were operating on a shoestring. So I wound up being their clerk, doing some typing and other work for them at the Riverside office on 49th Street. That job didn't last too long, but it gave me an opportunity to listen to the older piano styles, plus all those piano rolls enabled me to build up a nice collection of Riverside things they were doing before I came along.

## Orrin Keepnews, Randy Weston's first record producer

*Orrin Keepnews*: I first met Randy Weston in the summer of 1953, back when he was also the assistant chef at the Music Inn. I didn't go to the Music Inn at the time, but my partner at Riverside, Bill Grauer, did in the summer of 1953. That was actually the first year of Riverside Records, and we weren't even thinking of ourselves for anything except reissues of classic jazz. Bill went up to the Berkshires and he heard Randy and got very excited about him. As the years progressed I didn't have reason to have that much faith in the musical tastes of my partner, and we ended up agreeing that he would take care of business and I would take care of the music side. But when I did finally get to hear Randy he was damned impressive, so the suggestion was made that we sign him.

At the time we wanted to put ourselves into the current, contemporary jazz scene and not just be a reissue or classic operation. Here was this guy Randy who sounded damned interesting, looked damned interesting, seemed to be an easy human being to work with, and we felt that as a first artist what we desperately needed was a new artist, not someone who had recorded for Blue Note or some other label. With Randy it seemed sort of pre-ordained; we were trying to develop an attitude of being in the living scene, and here was this man who seemed just right to put us there. Even though I was still a couple of years away from having a relationship with Monk, clearly Randy was a disciple of Monk, somebody influenced by Monk. I wasn't looking at that as any kind of selling point because I didn't know anything about selling points, but it was another reason I was attracted to Randy.

Because we hardly had any money we wanted Randy to record a solo piano album and he said no, he didn't want to do a solo album, so we compromised on Sam Gill recording with him. As far as the tunes, the idea was, let's make it easy: we don't know what our audience is anyway, so let's take it easy and let's record standards rather than way-out, original bebop compositions. With the Cole Porter idea the thing was if you do an entire album of the same composer it appears like a very deliberate thing, it's a theme, it's not just that we threw together a bunch of tunes because we couldn't think of anything to do. Cole Porter was Randy's best solution to the one-composer rule that we threw at him.

As for Randy's playing, what attracted me were the same characteristics that I found initially so attractive in Thelonious. Randy at that point, even more so than later, was clearly influenced by Monk; you heard a lot of Monk in Randy's playing. What had initially been so attractive to me about Monk was the fact that I was able to hear in Monk's playing where he was coming from. I was able to hear the traditionalists, I was able to hear the stride piano, and so I heard a reflection of that in Randy's playing. I don't think I would have been able to relate musically to Bud Powell at that point, I wasn't equipped to hear that. Given my background as a fan of traditional jazz, I was better equipped to hear Monk or Randy than any number of other modern players.

By the time we recorded Randy's second record I had gotten a little bit more realistic, a little bit more knowledgeable about the world that I was trying to live in, and frankly a little bit more aware of the artists on the scene. And among other things I was aware of was that Randy was a very impressive composer. Both his tunes "Zulu" and "Pam's Waltz" debuted on that record, which was more about Randy's repertoire, which was the most sensible and proper way to deal with an artist in that way. If there is a good generalization in the record business it is to leave the artist alone as much as possible. When Randy said he could get Art Blakey to play on the date we didn't try to talk him out of that.

That second record was my first date at Van Gelder's studio, which made me feel like "Here I am, really in the professional jazz world." The album was done in one day, so it was customary and necessary that you built your payments on that part of the union provision regarding how much recorded time you're able to get out of a session. A session in those days was three hours of time in the studio or up to fifteen minutes on an LP side. This was for an album somewhere between thirty-five and forty minutes. The way that worked was fifteen minutes is a session and each additional five minutes before you get to another session is another one-third of another session. I gave Mr. Blakey a check for two times scale plus two overtimes. He looked at the check and said, "You don't have to be that chintzy, I mean I don't mind working for scale but the least you could do is give me three sessions for an album." I don't remember whether I gave him another check or whatever, but I immediately made an extra payment and Art and I had a good relationship for the rest of his life.

Union scale for a sideman in those days was $41.25, and the leader's was double that. If you wanted to be a real round-number guy you're making an album and the leader was going to get $250 and the sidemen are going to get $125. So with very little capital investment—and we had very little capital investment—you could make a trio record and your musician costs are going to be $500. Plus your studio costs were a good deal less than they are now, and you didn't have any re-mixing to do in those days because this was in the days before stereo, this was all straight to one-track. The economic factors were a very important consideration in creating this context for Randy.

I think what you'll see in the differences between the beginning and the end of my working relationship with Randy is . . . he undergoes changes obviously, he goes from being a guy that's asked to do this for the first time on the basis of some noodling around he did on his summer job in the Berkshires, he's gone from there to being a professional musician, so he has grown. But to that extent I have grown to be a more helpful and understanding producer, which wasn't hard to do because I was starting from zero.

Then we did the live date at the Café Bohemia with Cecil Payne. Live recording at that point was very much in its infancy. It was actually a very simple procedure: You took a portable tape machine and you set yourself up in a club. You would stake out a table or two in the back of the club and you miked your musicians as closely as you could in a studio. That Bohemia date was actually a strange choice, because a very arrogant and unpleasant man ran that club. When you walked into the club there was a long bar in a quite narrow space, because there was not that much passageway from the bar back into the seating area. Miles played there a lot and the MJQ played there, and it was very much of a musician's hangout. It would be maybe two or three deep at the bar on a Saturday night, and I can remember this feisty little guy coming through, knocking us out of the way to clear a path for the sit-down customers to come in. I don't think anybody thought of it particularly as a musician-friendly club. There are lots of examples of the fact that just because you hire musicians does not necessarily mean that you have their best interests at heart. This guy wasn't quite Morris Levy but he was not by any means a musician-friendly person. So we made those three records with Randy and after that it was a mutual parting of the ways. We really weren't moving him forward career-wise, and we agreed that he might be better off trying to find somebody else to advance his career.

I've been profoundly disappointed in the jazz public, and in jazz writers, at the reaction to Randy Weston. I consider this man now, as I always have, to be a major talent. You're going to have a hard time finding somebody who doesn't like him as a person. He has this great combination of being basically a shy man, but still with an outgoing personality. He's all of those kinds of factors that you think would make somebody be more inclined to want to work for him rather than against him. And he sure as hell can play and has always been a most interesting writer. I've always been concerned at what has been an inadequate response to this man. He's led a very interesting life and had a very interesting career which to a very large extent is of his own making; he has gone out there and done all these unusual and unprecedented things. Randy has never stopped being enthusiastic, inventive, and creative.

I guess this lack of recognition of true artistry happens in a business like ours where people who aren't particularly qualified in the first place make an awful lot of decisions. I do not have a high regard for the status of jazz criticism, especially to the extent that a considerable number of listeners who may think of themselves as intelligent and independent allow themselves to be shaped by a lot of these unqualified experts. Randy never was a critic's darling, he is not an easy musician to appreciate because he's playing difficult music, he's playing music with depth to it, with certain idiosyncrasies. It would have helped if Randy had gotten serious critical attention. But at least we're fishing in the right part of the lake.

Music is an expression of the heart which resonates commonality within all people. It is a process which enhances consciousness and unifies and uplifts both the artist and its listeners. To communicate in this universal language the artist must be a giver, a speaker of truth. He must trust his inner self and devote himself to his work in an ongoing struggle to share its knowledge and his art. The artist is a channel through which energy and light flows. His music is a reflection of himself—his spirituality, his life experience, his never-ending growth as an artist—and is supported by the rhythmic flow of energy which is a gift of nature. For this expression to keep time with the flow of life there can be no room for greed or competition which will only cripple the artist's ability to communicate, to touch his listeners.

In order to set people free with his music, he must know inner freedom. He must strive to sustain contact with the absolute and he must always be a giver through his art—a giver of life and love.—KWAKU DADDEY, Ghanaian percussionist

## ENTER MELBA LISTON

The live recording date at Café Bohemia, which was my last record for the Riverside label, was kind of a funny date. I used to work the Café Bohemia with my trio, playing opposite Miles Davis's band with Cannonball and Coltrane, sometimes Red Garland, other times my Jamaican cousin Wynton Kelly, with Philly Joe Jones and Paul Chambers in the rhythm section. At the time I had a manager named Louise Sundrie. We had met up in the Berkshires and she was a very aggressive woman, but aggressive in a fairly diplomatic way. She managed to get us into Café Bohemia working as a trio. The guy who hired the artists at the Bohemia was Ed Smalls. He wanted us to do a live recording there, but the trick was that he tried to insist that we record one of his songs. Frankly I really didn't like the tune he was pushing.

Luckily something happened and he wasn't able to be at the live recording session, so I avoided recording his piece.

Café Bohemia was really crowded that night and the top of the piano wasn't exactly attached very securely. We had a freak accident when a patron bumped the piano and the top fell off and hit Cecil Payne's baritone sax, but fortunately he could still play it. The rest of the band was Ahmed Abdul-Malik on bass and Al Dreares on drums. That date was also significant because we recorded Sam Gill's tune "Solemn Meditations," which wound up being my first theme song.

After my Riverside contract ended with the Café Bohemia date in October 1956, it wasn't long before a new recording opportunity came along. Less than a month later, on November 21, I went back into the studio to record *The Modern Art of Jazz* record. The label was Dawn, a record company organized by a slickster named Chuck Darwin. He was one of those guys you find in the record business who are all too typical: the big smile, the warm personality, and the total lack of artistic sincerity; they hug you one moment and profess their undying love for you and your music, the next moment they're dipping into your pocket. He put out a good series of records, including some Zoot Sims and Al Cohn dates and a couple of records by a band called Les Modes that was led by Charlie Rouse and Julius Watkins.

By this time I was feeling more secure in my playing and more secure about my writing. For *The Modern Art of Jazz* I wanted to create a real Brooklyn atmosphere, use some of my guys from the neighborhood. So I brought Cecil Payne back and added Ahmed Abdul-Malik on bass, Ray Copeland on trumpet, and Wilbert Hogan on drums. Ray and I had grown up together, gone to Brooklyn Boys High School, and I knew his father, who was a detective with the police department. Ray, Malik, Cecil, and I had all played together on many occasions and had grown up playing in big bands together. I also got Ray to do the arrangements, because at the time he was playing first trumpet for the Radio City Music Hall Orchestra, so he was making a name for himself and had become a good arranger; but despite his growing reputation he was a regular Brooklyn guy just like the rest of us. When we recorded Monk's tune "Well You Needn't" something happened to Cecil Payne's baritone again, so he played alto, which was actually his original instrument. All in all it was a really nice date, with a very tribal feeling among the Brooklyn guys. But that was strictly a one-shot recording date for Chuck Darwin's label.

For my next record idea I had to once again go fishing for another record label. I met a woman named Kay Norton, a very intense blonde woman who was vice-president of United Artists Records; and a woman record company executive was pretty unusual in those days. But I could see how she rose to that position because she was just as slick as the guys who ran record companies. Later on she ended up managing Benny Golson's and Art Farmer's group, the Jazztet. For this particular record date I had a real concept in mind. My first song for children was "Pam's Waltz," written for my daughter Pamela. That's how I started writing songs for children—not actually children's songs, but songs about different children.

I used to watch children closely, my own and others, and they're so free that they would inspire me. So for this first record for United Artists I wanted to do seven waltzes for children. "Pam's Waltz" and "Little Niles," which I wrote for my son Niles (who later became Azzedin) were tunes I had written up in the Berkshires. "Little Niles" actually became the album title, but I'm jumping the gun. By this time I had met Melba Liston and this record became our first collaboration.

Kay Norton was interested in this concept of songs about children so we started working on the music. The first piece on the record is "Earth Birth," about the first child arriving on the planet, the child opening up his eyes and seeing the planet for the first time. The second piece is "Little Susan," and I found out many years later that Little Susan, whose father Bill was a guy I knew, is now the wife of Arturo O'Farrill, the pianist and bandleader, and she's a concert pianist. This was during the days when certain fans who knew and supported the music would hang out with the musicians, which this guy Bill did with the musicians in Quincy Jones's band among others. Susan was a cute little girl and her parents were from the islands, so she inspired me to write something a bit Caribbean. The next waltz is "Nice Ice," about little children ice skating. "Babe's Blues" is about children listening and dancing to the blues. "Let's Climb the Hill" is about the children I used to see in the park going up the hills and coming back down with such joy.

This recording was a great example of the genius of Melba Liston. We had Jamil Nasser on bass, Johnny Griffin on tenor sax, Ray Copeland and Idrees Sulieman on trumpet, Charlie Persip on drums, and Melba Liston herself played trombone. Despite the fact that she was a wonderful trombone player with a big, full sound, Melba was quite shy about playing her instrument, and I had to talk her into taking a trombone solo on the record.

Maybe shy is the wrong word to describe Melba, but she was a rather withdrawn woman. Despite that Melba was a tough taskmaster in the studio, in her own quiet way. She didn't say a lot but it seemed she was always very particular about trumpet players; she would always fight with the trumpet players, though I remember she really loved Ernie Royal, because he would play it just as she wrote it. Maybe it was all her years sitting in the trombone section in big bands right in front of those screaming trumpets. But somehow Ray and Idrees wound up fighting with her, because they thought she wrote a wrong note for them. Each of the musicians is featured on a different tune: Johnny Griffin on "Nice Ice," Jamil on "Babe's Blues," Ray Copeland on "Little Niles." That carried on across the record.

## Meeting Melba

That "Little Niles" record was a milestone for me because it marked my first collaboration with Melba Liston, the first of many. She became absolutely essential to my work. One night in 1957 I went down to Birdland to hear Dizzy Gillespie's big band. That band had been a powerful influence on me during the late '40s, early '50s when Dizzy employed Chano Pozo and developed that Afro-Cuban sound. So wherever Dizzy was performing I wanted to be there. On this particular night as I walked down the stairs at Birdland, the band was already swinging hard, as usual; that sound would bring a smile to anybody's face. As I walked in and saw who was on the bandstand with Dizzy that night I immediately focused on this beautiful sister in the trombone section; she was the only woman in the band, so you really couldn't miss her. And with that natural hairstyle she wore and Melba's beauty, it felt like instant love. Then the band played the ballad "My Reverie," which turned out to be Melba's arrangement and her featured trombone solo spot.

She had this big, gorgeous sound on the trombone, and coupled with that incredible arrangement . . . I was hooked. I simply had to meet this sister! After the set I made a beeline for the bandstand to shake this woman's hand, and when we clasped hands there really was something electric in our contact, I was blown away immediately. By this time she had moved to New York from California and was living up in Harlem near Mary Lou Williams, whose house was a known hangout for musicians wanting to really learn this music and get next to her genius, including Thelonious Monk.

So Melba and I exchanged telephone numbers. There was just something about this sister that I needed to know her better.

I had become interested in composing in three-quarter and six-eight time from my exposure to the legendary calypsonian MacBeth. He was one of the many great black artists who performed in the Berkshires while I was up there, and one night he laid down this great tune in waltz time. My mind started turning, because this waltz time really spoke to me. Almost immediately I started writing these seven waltzes for children. Eventually Melba and I got together and she invited me to her little place. I immediately laid this idea of recording these seven waltzes for children on her and asked her if she would write the arrangements, remembering how great her arrangement was of "My Reverie" for Dizzy's band. She agreed, and that's how this long and fruitful partnership began. Our relationship was thoroughly unique, kind of like Billy Strayhorn and Duke Ellington's arranger-composer relationship.

Melba had the incredible ability of making musicians sound better through what she wrote for them. That's the mark of a great arranger. She wrote for Duke Ellington, Count Basie, Quincy Jones, Gloria Lynne, the Supremes, Bob Marley, Motown hits . . . a long list of great artists. The Bob Marley relationship is probably quite surprising to most people, but she taught at the Jamaica Institute of Music and the University of the West Indies for five years, as head of the Afro American Department, and while based in Jamaica she came in contact with many of the reggae artists, including Marley. She was simply a genius who had a very original way of writing arrangements. Most arrangement writing is along horizontal lines, but Melba wrote the parts in an oblique direction.

It was always about love between us but it was more love of music and people. She found out many, many years after we met, toward the end of her life, that her father had been one of the trustees of Marcus Garvey's organization—so we had a kind of spiritual tie through the advanced thinking and care for the plight of black people that we both got from our fathers. She certainly had the revolutionary spirit; she wore her hair natural and was never interested in straightening her hair. Melba had great pride in herself and her people, and it came out clearly in her music. So when we made the *Uhuru Afrika* recording we talked about it extensively in the planning stages. It was a natural thing for her to express the greatness of her people through music, just like it was for me, because we were constantly involved in the struggle of black people. Back then black artists were more involved in the struggle than they are today, much more involved.

## Working Relationship

With each of my compositions that Melba arranged I would start out by telling her the story behind the piece. Then she would go to the piano and start doing her voicings. I would go to the piano and just play, just improvise, and say, "OK, Melba, with this particular piece I can hear the trombone"—for example "Earth Birth" from the *Little Niles* record. As I said, Melba never liked to take solos. She was a fantastic trombone soloist with an enormous sound, but I had to literally fight with her to get her to take a solo, especially on our first recording together. When it came time to record "Earth Birth," I was adamant that she take that solo because that's how I heard it in my head when I wrote it.

When I wrote "Earth Birth" I sat at the piano and played it for Melba; I played the introduction because all the arrangements are based upon piano arrangements. I put that introduction on tape as a piano solo and gave it to her. Then I came back at a certain time so she could ask me any questions she might have. She said, "OK, are you sure you want this tune to feature a trombone solo?" I said, "Yes, you have to do this," and her solo was really beautiful, one of the highlights of that record. But not surprisingly that turned out to be the only time she ever actually *played* on one of the many recording sessions and concerts she arranged for me. That was really a pity, not to mention the fact that she only made one record under her own name, but she was such a wonderful arranger that her greatness is secure in that department.

Melba was so skillful and so creative that she would often change the arrangement several times, sometimes at the actual recording session. You might try rushing Melba to get the music ahead of time so you could practice it and be ready, but she was such a perfectionist that you never knew when she would make last-minute changes, so you had to be flexible with that. I was used to how she worked, but that sometimes led to frustrated musicians. As I said, she had particular battles with trumpet players who always seemed to want to change what she had written, to better suit their playing—or so they thought. She was really a composer-arranger, and even when you'd try to find out what she was up to before the session, much of the time you'd never really know what was up until you got to the studio. But her writing was always exceptional and always fit exactly what I needed.

Melba was a very quiet and private person. Perhaps being a woman, and a black woman at that, working in this music almost exclusively alongside men, that could not have been easy for her. You know how musicians are, or men are, period. I don't know that she ever overcame those gender issues that face women working in a man's world. She just kinda rode with the waves, accepted certain ridiculous conditions as reality, and just tried to make her art as best she could—which was awfully well.

We did a lot of things together besides recordings, like concerts with my big band at Town Hall and the Village Gate . . . We developed a strong bond and yes, we had a romance for a time, but our relationship was much deeper than that. Later on she got married to a schoolteacher. But that didn't work out ultimately. A lot of the great women in our business marry guys who seem to want to compete with them, and that's what Melba's ex-husband was all about. So their relationship didn't last very long, he was just one of those kind of dudes. Her love was music, that's the only thing she really wanted to do was music, and she kept saying that over and over.

When I think about Melba, and about so many other women in the jazz business, like Sarah Vaughan, like Billie Holiday and others, it seems that some of these great women artists have frequently been attracted to macho men, men who seem strong because these sisters apparently felt a need to have a strong man to protect them in this tough business where professionally they're constantly dealing with nothing but other men. Because wherever they go there are going to be some guys approaching them, so they want their own men to be strong and protective. But sadly some of those men who seem so strong on the surface to these women are also macho and beat these women or abuse them and do all kinda wrong stuff to them. It must be extremely difficult for a woman musician, particularly a woman traveling with a big band with just the guys. I don't know if Melba ever really got over that experience.

Before we made the *Uhuru Afrika* record session—which is an entire story unto itself—we did the *Destry Rides Again* recording of tunes from the Broadway show, which itself was sort of a tradeoff I'll explain later. After *Destry* in 1959 we made the *Live at the Five Spot* record, for which Melba wrote all the arrangements. That was an incredible experience. Melba was plagued by health problems for a long time, and this period was no exception unfortunately, but she soldiered on as always. United Artists still wasn't ready for the *Uhuru Afrika* project, so I came up with an idea to do a small live date, and the Five Spot was a very popular club at the time. I insisted that Melba do the arrangements. But she got sick while out in California visiting her family and she was hospitalized.

The wonderful trumpet player Kenny Dorham was living in Brooklyn at that particular time. He had been playing with Max Roach's group and he was also in a boxing club because he and Miles Davis used to box a little bit, so Kenny and I used to work out together. My dad still had his restaurant, and it was always a place where the guys liked to come and hang out, including Kenny. So I was very tight with Kenny and I was very happy when he agreed to do this Five Spot date with me. As I mentioned earlier, my first idol in this music was Coleman Hawkins, and I wanted him to make the record as well. It wasn't difficult getting him to agree to do it, which was a thrill; it was just a matter of his availability. I got Roy Haynes to play the drums, and I loved Roy because he was on the scene a lot at that time. Clifford Jarvis was another drummer I was interested in: he was only seventeen years old then.

At the time I was living on 13th Street in Manhattan. I had this incredible apartment and I had finally gotten custody of my son Niles from my ex-wife. He was eleven years old and she put him out—I guess she just couldn't handle this very active eleven-year-old boy—so she just said, "You take him, just take him." So at eleven years old it was just Niles and I together. I also had Clifford Jarvis staying at my house and these two young dudes just about drove me crazy, but fortunately I was young myself so I could deal with it. I had written a piece called "Lisa Lovely" and I wanted to use two drummers on that piece, so I had Clifford Jarvis play on that with Roy Haynes; Clifford took the first solo and Roy took the second solo. I also had Wilbur Little, another wonderful player who did some playing later on with my band, on bass.

Melba wrote the arrangements despite being sick in the hospital in California. She sent them by mail and, typical Melba, they arrived on the day of the recording, so there was no time to rehearse. On the night of the performance that we were to record Coleman Hawkins came walking into the club and had everybody's heads turning with a stunning nineteen-year-old blonde. Hawk walked into the club like "The king is here." Then I passed out the music, Hawk and Kenny looked it over, we talked about it briefly, and then we did two sets, with no rehearsal. These were top-shelf professionals, so it came off beautifully. My God, Hawk, I just loved his sound, and Kenny Dorham played so beautifully; it was a wonderful date.

Skipping ahead a bit, Melba and I continued to work through various projects during the '60s until I split for Africa. Then in the early 1970s we were chosen to do a big-band concert at the Newport Jazz Festival, which had by that time shifted to New York, and the concert was scheduled for Central Park. We were constantly looking for ways to combine our music with other aspects of our black culture. With my Jamaican roots from my father's side I was always aware of what was going on down there with music and family. I wanted to bring up the Rastafarian musicians to play with our big band, plus the great Jamaican guitarist Ernest Ranglin. Since I still had family down there on my father's side I took Melba down for a visit in 1973. There wasn't much work at that time for creative musicians with rock being so big in the 1970s; we seemed to be losing the young people completely to this new popular music.

I took Melba down to Jamaica to meet a guy who was director of the National Dance Theatre Company of Jamaica named Rex Nettleford, who was also a professor at the University of the West Indies. He used to bring his dance company to New York to perform once a year. The idea was to try and get Melba a teaching position there at the University of the West Indies. When we got there I wanted to connect with this guy Count Ossie, an original Rasta who came before Bob Marley and all those cats. I wanted to bring these guys up to perform with the big band on that Newport concert at Central Park. But unfortunately the government wouldn't give Count Ossie and his guys any visas because these guys smoked too much ganja, so we ended up just taking Ernest Ranglin back for the concert and he performed with the big band. Then we went back to Jamaica after the concert and Melba stayed five years, teaching all kinds of music at the university. She made arrangements for a lot of Jamaican artists, especially the reggae musicians, including Bob Marley. And she taught a lot of young Caribbean musicians the techniques of our music.

After that Melba and I did a lot of things together. One of the most memorable sessions we made was for the *Spirits of Our Ancestors* record for Verve, through our relationship with Jean Phillipe Allard in Paris. Jean Phillipe gave me the OK to do a date with the personnel I wanted: Billy Harper, Dewey Redman, Pharoah Sanders, Idrees Sulaiman, Idris Muhammad, Big Black, Talib Kibwe, Benny Powell, Alex Blake, Azzedin Weston, and Jamil

Nasser . . . all the heavy, spiritual brothers, with Brian Baccus co-producing. By this time Melba had suffered a stroke and she was confined to a wheelchair.

When the idea for the *Spirits of Our Ancestors* record date came to me, I just went to see Melba and said, "I have an opportunity to do this record and you *must* do the arrangements; stroke or no stroke you have to do this!" Remarkably, with the help of her aunt, Melba learned to write music through a computer—her aunt Thelma was a computer specialist. Melba could no longer play the trombone, but she could still write music. Our ancestors gave her the spirit to do that date and several record dates after that. It was a fantastic record session and was so good that the one disc we were supposed to record became a two-disc set: the music just grew as we went along.

## Jean-Philippe Allard, producer, Verve Records

*Jean-Philippe Allard*: I learned a lot from Randy. On the *Spirits of Our Ancestors* record date (1991), when Dizzy Gillespie came to the session, I learned a lot with all those different great musicians in the studio, and to have Dizzy in the studio was really something special. I could see how a giant like Dizzy could inspire everybody immediately. And of course that record was also made with the arrangements of Melba Liston.

Melba and Randy's working relationship was a little mysterious for me because it was really personal between them and Melba had difficulty communicating at that time, so for her it was not easy. She was mainly smiling or crying; I think she was crying because she was happy. Randy is a natural chief, a boss . . . in the band there's no doubt he's the boss. But when Melba was in the studio she became the boss and that was amazing to see because she was in a wheelchair and she couldn't walk or anything . . . But she was the boss, which was interesting also because she was a woman in a world of men. I think she had respect from everybody.

One of the featured pieces on that record was "African Sunrise," which I had been commissioned to write and subsequently play at the Chicago Jazz Festival and which was to feature Dizzy Gillespie. Dizzy was just supposed

Melba Liston, circa 1990s. *Photograph by Cheung Ching Ming.*

to come into the studio and dub in his solo on "African Sunrise." Our mutual friend Jacques Muyal brought Dizzy to the studio. Dizzy was actually on his way to catch a plane to California. But he took out his horn and played on a rehearsal take of "African Sunrise." He was so moved by Melba's arrangement—and Melba was right there in the studio with us, in her wheelchair—that he took out his trumpet and played. We wanted to do another take, but before I knew it Dizzy was packing up his horn and leaving for the airport. When we played back the rehearsal take with Diz, it was perfect. So we used that rehearsal take on the record. To see Dizzy and Melba back working together in the studio that day was really special.

Later, in '93, Melba arranged my *Volcano Blues* date, an all-blues record, with the great bluesman Johnny Copeland; she also arranged the *Saga* record date in 1995 and later that year the live date with stringed orchestra *Earth Birth* at the Montreal Jazz Festival, and *Khepera* in 1998. It was always the same method, with Melba using the computer to write as her aunt had assisted her with. To prepare for *Khepera* I took her up to the Berkshires, up to the country to spend some concentrated time together without the usual distractions and immerse ourselves in getting that music together.

Her aunt Thelma came along to take care of her. As I've always said, the Creator brings people together for a reason, and with Melba and me it was a truly special relationship that was heaven-sent. But I'd have to say the absolute crowning achievement of our working relationship was when we did the *Uhuru Afrika* record.

African music is the music of life and it only imitates life itself through songs of nature and man. It is the original in as much as it springs from the life of people and songs that relate to the people. It is innovative in that it changes as peoples change. To a great extent it is a music of experimentation because the natural flow of life is an experiment. —JOHN HENRIK CLARKE

# UHURU AFRIKA

## Freedom Africa

As I've always stressed in interviews and whenever I've spoken in public, my whole life I have been reading about and immersing myself in Africa. I have been forever fascinated by and deeply interested in the history of Africa, the current problems of Africa, the triumphs of the African people, the political situation in Africa . . . and that interest came long before I made my first trip there. I was always in tune with Africa and I was always upset about the separation of our people, the separation of those people who are considered part of the African diaspora from the Motherland itself. The terrible effect of colonialism was to separate our people, and it was always very painful for me because I've always seen the similarities in people of African descent, not the differences. My dad always said that black people would never be free as a people until Africa is free; that's the only time we will be collectively strong, when Africa is strong. But as long as Africa was weak, we would continue to be weak; he stressed that all the time, and that's why we must help to rebuild Africa, because we're all black people of the world and we owe that to our Motherland.

I wanted to create a large-scale suite to illustrate that the African people are a global people and that what we do and who we are comes from our collective experience, from our African cultural memory. And no matter where we are . . . whether we're in the Fiji Islands, whether we're in Brazil, or Cuba, Europe, or the United States, we all come from the same African family, going all the way back to the very first civilization. I wanted this suite to be performed by African people not only from different parts of the world but also from different areas of music. This idea had been in my head for years, and finally in the late '50s it started coming together. I once met a great Somali poet named Musa and he told me something that really stuck with me: "The first thing that changes is the music," he said, "the music changes and everything else follows the music. Where does the music come from? The music comes from the universe, the music comes from our ancestors; we don't know where." The music that we tend to take as ours is really coming from the Creator, and it comes at certain points and through certain artists to give people inspiration, to set a tone for certain serious things that are happening and going to transpire in world history.

The late 1950s and early 1960s were a very interesting period because everybody was so full of fire. The civil rights movement was blooming, the black student movement in the South was growing, Paul Robeson, Malcolm X, Martin Luther King Jr. were showing the way and making great strides toward raising our consciousness, and it was truly an incredible period. There was all this movement of energy toward the freedom and liberation of black people. It was also a time when several African nations, such as Ghana, were declaring their independence from colonization. I wanted to write a suite dedicated to Mother Africa. My father taught me at a very young age that I was an African born in America, that I have to understand African history. So I decided to name this major work *Uhuru Afrika*, which is Swahili for freedom Africa.

This was also a time when several other musicians and I were very active in trying to develop the African American Musicians Society; Melba Liston was one of our vice-presidents. We were going through a lot of changes as far as racism, and a lot of crazy things were going on for black musicians. The alto saxophonist Gigi Gryce was right there as one of our leaders; he was one guy who kept us on course as far as the business of music was concerned. When I remember Gigi Gryce, I think of one bit of sage advice he always stressed: "Never sell a song." Too many musicians have sold their music for little or nothing, often for some kind of instant gratification that certainly won't sustain them into the future. Musicians would sell their songs for practically nothing and someone else would reap the long-term benefits, especially if that song was popular. I remember the song I wrote for my son, "Little Niles." I never really thought it was that great, yet there were people who made me play that song all the time; one was Gigi Gryce, and "Little Niles" became a standard, which has enabled me to collect royalties ever since. Gigi had a lot of courage and I knew I wanted him to be part of the *Uhuru Afrika* project for sure. This was definitely a period of organizing and increased consciousness among black musicians, and Gigi was at the vanguard of that self-determination movement.

This work *Uhuru Afrika* had been in my mind for a while, so I started gathering my resources because I knew this would be an important and laborious undertaking. After Melba Liston and I collaborated so successfully on those seven waltzes for children and recorded the "Little Niles" project, our friendship and working relationship were growing, and I definitely wanted Melba to write the arrangements for *Uhuru Afrika*. When she consented I breathed a big sigh of relief, because I knew this project would be guaranteed successful.

## Enter: Langston Hughes

Over the years since we first met in the Berkshires, the great poet and writer Langston Hughes and I had become friends. Marshall Stearns brought Langston up there to speak at one of his programs, which is how we first became acquainted. Langston eventually wound up participating in our history-of-jazz presentations a few times as narrator, the same concept that first came from Marshall Stearns. These programs were structured so that we would play different pieces to illustrate the various evolutionary steps in jazz history and Langston would do the reading. We took the music on a trip from Africa to the Caribbean, then the black church, the 1920s and people like Ma Rainey and Bessie Smith, then on to the swing era. I particularly remember once when we performed it at City College with Booker Ervin on tenor sax and Langston.

Years later Langston eventually introduced me to two women who assisted us in the development of our black musicians' organization, which we called the African American Musicians Society. These women were Ramona Lowe and Adele Glasgow and they worked with Langston, though I think it would be unfair and would somewhat belittle them if I were to refer to them as his secretaries. These two sisters, who lived downtown at the time I met them, had a strong desire to move to Harlem, and eventually they opened a place in Harlem called the Marketplace Gallery on 135th

Street and 7th Avenue, near where the famous club Small's used to be. But before moving to Harlem they enabled me to lease their apartment in a building on 13th Street and Third Avenue, which was my first time living in Manhattan. This apartment was pretty impressive, with six huge rooms for only $76 a month rent. In this apartment they had one room loaded with nothing but books. These were two very literate women and through their many contacts they helped us organize the African American Musicians Society, and the Marketplace Gallery became our meeting place.

## Ray Bryant, pianist and composer

*Ray Bryant*: The African American Musicians Society came about because we started meeting informally to talk about the conditions we faced as musicians. The musicians' union was discriminatory in a number of ways, and we wanted to see if we could do anything about that. So we started kicking around some ideas and discussing what could be done about these conditions, including the music disappearing from the black neighborhoods.

The original members were Louis Brown, Nadi Qamar, Sadik Hakim, John Handy, Randy Weston, and I. Melba Liston came into the organization later and was elected vice-president. We decided to have a convention and invite musicians from across the Eastern Seaboard—from Maine to Florida—to inform everybody of what we were trying to do and invite certain black leaders to speak. A. Philip Randolph and John Henrik Clarke were two of our speakers.

One of our objectives was to insist that the musicians union include an anti-discrimination clause in all contracts, which we were successful in getting them to do; that clause still stands in all Local 802 contracts. All the union bigwigs were there at the conference and they consented to most of the things we wanted. The union had a trust fund, which consisted of surplus money in the treasury that was supposed to be evenly distributed among musicians for gig opportunities, but that wasn't happening, so we forced them to more evenly spread that trust fund money. We later organized to picket the building site of Lincoln Center because they were building that facility without any apparent awareness or plans for inclusion of black music; they just wanted to ignore black music completely.

This is what we sent out to announce the meeting and our intent:

*Notice: A Call To attend the Afro-American Musician's Conference Sponsored by Afro-American Musicians' Society*

Monday, August 28, 1961
St. Philip's Church
215 West 133rd Street
New York City

*Greetings: To all Afro-American Musicians and their supporters*

The Lincoln Center Project for the Performing Arts calls for the creation of a great cultural center. Plans provide for a Palace for Ballet, Symphony and Opera.

But a Palace for Jazz is missing. Why?

Jazz is an American Creation!

Jazz is from the heart and tears and hopes of America!

To omit a Palace of Jazz is to deny America's contribution to the music world.

It denies as well the soul of black men who took their African and American heritages to create jazz, from Dixieland to Modern.

To deny a Palace for Jazz is to deny democracy and to write off the Afro-American.

But this is not all—the whole project by-passes the Negro in equal job opportunities in every way.

There is not a serious voice among the City fathers raised in protest against this omission, nor is there a voice in the trade union movement rallying its members to change this abominable neglect.

However, it is not too late to correct this mistake!

Labor can help by supporting the demands put forth by the Afro-American Musicians' Eastern Seaboard Conference.

And above all, you and I can urge other Afro-American musicians to join us at the Conference.

Dear Friend,

We are calling your attention to: THE AFRO AMERICAN MUSICIAN'S EASTERN SEABOARD CONFERENCE.

12:00 noon, Monday, August 28, 1961
St. Philips Church
215 West 133rd St.
New York City

Enclosed herewith is an invitation from the conference committee to join us as a friend and patron at our initial organizing session.

Our speakers will include:

A. A. Philip Randolph
   President of the Negro American Labor Council
B. John Henrik Clarke
   Noted historian and scholar on Africa
C. Lofton Mitchell
   Author, Producer, and Guggenheim award winner

We need your support. Please return the enclosed pledge and contribution as early as possible so that we may register you, and guarantee you one of the few remaining seats we have set aside for our guests.

Thank you for your kind cooperation.
Fraternally yours,
Randy Weston
Chairman

At that time there was hardly any work for us. Discrimination and racism were as strong as they could be at this time in the early '60s; they didn't want blacks in symphony orchestras, they didn't want blacks in society orchestras. When you worked in a jazz club, if you were a leader, you might make $125 a week, with sidemen getting $90 a week . . . you *might* make that much. And I'm talking about the top clubs.

Ramona Low and Adele Glasgow introduced us to a man named John Walker, a labor organizer along with a guy named Bill Jones who is still involved in labor matters in Harlem; they in turn introduced us to A. Philip Randolph, who was a major figure in black history, particularly on the labor side of things. He was the man who organized the Pullman car porters. John Walker was a beautiful brother and he schooled us on labor matters, on how now that the former black musicians' union had been absorbed into the regular, white-led musicians' union, we must make certain demands. We didn't feel we had any union representation; they weren't giving black

musicians the union jobs and simply weren't recognizing black music properly for what it is. John urged us to work on a plan to present to the union;
plus he put us in touch with the big chief, A. Philip Randolph.

In 1962 a group of us got together at the Marketplace Gallery and worked
all night to process that mailing to musicians from Florida to Maine to attend our organizing conference. People were volunteering, typing letters,
and sending out invitations to this three-day conference. Reverend More-
land Weston, a Harlem minister who is not related to me, donated his St.
Philips Church to host our conference. A woman named Khadija organized
a group of sisters to cook food for three straight days for this conference.
Ramona and Adele arranged for the great intellectual John Henrik Clarke
to be one of our speakers, along with A. Philip Randolph.

Around that time I also became acquainted with a woman named Georgia Griggs, who became a lifelong friend and assisted me greatly on business matters. Georgia loved the music and she lived a block away from me
on 13th Street; she ended up being of incredible assistance to our AAMS
efforts. Sometimes people up in Harlem would harass this white woman
when she came uptown, but she didn't let that stop her. She was our editor and she was so fantastic I took her on tour with us to manage the band
when we toured Africa. Georgia also helped us take our whole concept program on the history of jazz into elementary schools in New York.

Our conference at St. Philips featured one agenda area for African culture—which John Henrik Clarke addressed; and the other agenda area was
for labor, with A. Philip Randolph spearheading that. It was kind of a black
musicians' think-tank conference. We wanted to talk with everybody who
attended, to get everybody's ideas of how we were going to form this organization. At this point we were only loosely organized as a kind of active
committee. But we had big plans and we were intent on trying to organize
as the African American Musicians Society.

After that I remember the AAMS giving a fundraising party downtown.
We approached the recording companies to get some support. We felt they
should donate because everything was going into their pockets and they
weren't giving anything back.

One time I remember a representative of the Teamsters Union boss Jimmy
Hoffa came to meet with us. Hoffa sent a brother down from Chicago, and
I'll never forget this guy because he was so sharp; he arrived wearing a hip
blue silk suit. He came offering to strengthen our organization and give us
some assistance. I think the reason for that was that Hoffa and the Teamsters wanted to form a union counter to the Musicians Union, and when

we started the AAMS they wanted us to be a part of the Teamsters. Unfortunately this Teamsters offer created major dissension in the organization, because some of us said no; we didn't want their help, while others said yes, they wanted the Teamsters' assistance.

Unfortunately we only lasted about a year as the AAMS, but we raised some hell, particularly with the musicians' union. The unfortunate part was we didn't have the critical support of the black bandleaders, and that was what we needed — support from the bandleaders. Ornette Coleman was the only bandleader who came to our conference. We missed Max Roach, we missed Charles Mingus, but at that time they had another musicians' organization called the Jazz Guild, an integrated musicians' organization which they were involved in. Eventually there were unfortunate efforts made by some of our brothers to break up the organization, which sadly did eventually happen. So some of us formed our own small splinter group and called it Ndugu Ngoma, which meant brothers of the drum in Swahili. Unfortunately that group didn't last very long either.

*Ray Bryant*: One of the things that really stand out in my mind is that conference [the AAMS] had at St. Philips Church. It was a great thing even though things didn't really happen after that the way perhaps they could have, it did show that people did want to get together. But unfortunately the enthusiasm waned after that conference. I really can't explain that, but I think that some very good points were made at that conference; it was a great day!

Langston Hughes was important to us in many ways, including in the formation of the AAMS. He used to attend some of our meetings as well and was very interested in our cause as musicians. But back to the development of *Uhuru Afrika*: I went to Langston and asked him to write a freedom poem for the introduction to the suite, which would have four parts. He was as excited as I was by the prospects for this suite, so he eagerly agreed to write the poem. The poem which we later had translated — a point I'll get to in a minute — became a sort of invocation for *Uhuru Afrika*. It was a key element in the "Uhuru Kwanza" movement of the suite. I also asked Langston to write lyrics for a section I wrote for African women called "African Lady," which became the eventual second movement of the suite. Langston's poem set an absolutely wonderful tone for that recording session. Remember, the whole point of *Uhuru Afrika* was to talk about the freedom of a continent; a continent that has been invaded and had its children taken away, the continent of the creation of humanity. And Langston felt that, he *knew* it deep down in his soul.

> Piano music is as old as the piano which as an instrument, in variations of its present form, dates back some 250 years. Millions of fingers have rippled the keys since then. But not until Randy Weston put the enormous hands of his 6′7″ frame to the piano did exactly what happens in his playing emerge from that ancient instrument. When Randy plays, a combination of strength and gentleness, virility and velvet emerges from the keys in an ebb and flow of sound seemingly as natural as the waves of the sea.
> —LANGSTON HUGHES
> (from the original liner notes for *Uhuru Afrika*)

After *Uhuru Afrika* Langston and I stayed close. In fact when he died in 1967 at a French hospital in New York, his secretary called and said, "Randy, in Langston's will he wants you to play his funeral with a trio." I thought, "Man, Langston is too much!" They had some kind of religious ceremony someplace else, which I was unable to attend. But the ceremony Langston really wanted and had specified in his will was at a funeral home in Harlem. It was a big funeral home that seated over two hundred people with chairs on one side of the place. In the other room was Langston's body, laid out in a coffin with his arms crossed. The band was Ed Blackwell, Bill Wood, and me. They had arranged for us to play in front of the area of the funeral home where the guests sat, surrounded by two big wreaths. Ed Blackwell got very New Orleans, very superstitious about the setting. He said, "Man, I'm not gonna touch those flowers. It's weird enough we're here in the first place." So we had some guys move the flowers so we could set up the band.

The people filed in and had a processional to view Langston's body. Lena Horne was there, so were Dr. Ralph Bunche, Arna Bontemps, and a whole lot of dignitaries. We set up the band and I went outside for a minute to get a breath of fresh air. Langston's secretary came out and said, "OK, Randy, its time to start." I said, "Where's the minister?" He said, "There's no minister, *you guys* start the service!" I stayed up all night the night Langston died and wrote a piece called "Blues for Langston" because I knew he loved the blues more than anything else in the world. He and Jimmy Rushing, those two guys really made an impact on me about the importance of the blues and what the blues really meant.

Before we played I stood up and said, "Well, folks, I wrote this blues for Langston Hughes since he loved the blues so much, so we're going to play the blues." We played one hour of all different kinds of blues and in between selections Arna Bontemps read some of Langston's poetry. The funniest thing I remember about it was that Lena Horne told me later, "Ya know, I didn't know what to do, I didn't know whether to pat my foot or not." But the story is that Langston put us all on. Two weeks later I got a phone call from his secretary, who said, "Randy, I forgot to tell you, Langston said to be sure the musicians are paid union scale."

As I was writing *Uhuru Afrika* I recalled so many images of the continent from my father's teachings. I called upon my cultural memory of the black church, of going to the calypso dances and folks dancing to people like the Duke of Iron; of going to the Palladium and hearing that great Latin music, and probably even going back to before I was born. I just collected my spirits, asked for prayers from the ancestors, and tried to create what came out of me. I had also spent time with a choreographer from Guinea named Asadata Defora up in the Berkshires. He introduced me to a lot of African music. So I started collecting African traditional music, because even with jazz music, even with spiritual music, learning it was a natural process of listening . . . but not necessarily listening with your ears; it's almost like listening with your *spirit*. I was constantly playing African traditional records in my house, absorbing this music as I cooked, ate, and went about my daily routine. I had this music going all the time and it wasn't as though I was just sitting there totally concentrating on that music, but just through having that musical spirit in the house I absorbed this rich spirit of Africa. When I wrote *Uhuru Afrika* all these elements just came out, like a sort of magical, supernatural process. Once again the spirits served me well.


## Uhuru Afrika: The Language

For the text I was very anxious to use an African language in *Uhuru Afrika*. I was still so upset by how African language was presented in the media. I could also vividly recall the ridiculous images of those awful Tarzan movies I had been so into as a boy, and how they depicted the Africans and their language. Tarzan had these blacks carrying stuff on their heads, saying,

"Bwana this, Bwana that, Bwana the other" . . . So I made up my mind that *Uhuru Afrika* had to use an authentic African language, not some gibberish or nonsense from television or the movies. I wanted to present this work of music where people would hear the beauty and depth of an African language, and at the same time show the power of the drum.

I spent time at the United Nations doing some research on African languages. It was a very exciting time because I had always wanted to have contact with Africa. Thanks to my friends at the UN, A. C. Thompson and Richard Jennings, who knew everybody, I was introduced to a lot of the African personnel at the UN. Whenever there was a party for Kenya, the Congo, or any of the other African countries, Richard would always make sure I got a ticket so I'd have a chance to meet these ambassadors.

I knew it would be difficult selecting one common language for the text; after all, it was my understanding at the time that Africa was a land of over nine hundred different languages and countless dialects. So I met with several African ambassadors and other Africans who worked at the UN. When I asked them which language would best represent the continent, they said Kiswahili. One of the people I met there was Tuntemeke Sanga from Tanganyika, which is now post-colonial Tanzania. This guy was a real revolutionary.

## Richard Jennings, retired UN official (1931–2010)

*Richard Jennings*: Sanga was there at the UN as a petitioner. During that time of decolonization, different groups and individuals would come in and speak to the UN trusteeship counsel on decolonization. Sanga was one of those petitioners, speaking to the decolonization committee as to why his country should be decolonized.

Sanga, who was a professor of Kiswahili, was something of a revolutionary even then, and he said that Africa would not be free until it had the atomic bomb. Melba Liston, me, and some of the musicians wound up studying Kiswahili with this guy. He translated Langston Hughes's freedom poem into Kiswahili, as you hear it on the record. Brock Peters, who sang the male part of the "African Lady" selection, was originally supposed to recite the freedom poem, but Sanga's voice was so incredible that we ended up using him on the recording.

## The Music

I saw *Uhuru Afrika* as the most important music I had ever written. The prelude was Langston's freedom poem. I wrote the suite in four movements: the first movement was "Uhuru Kwanza," the theme of which was that African people have a right to determine their own destiny. The second movement, the vocal piece that Brock Peters and Martha Flowers sang, was "African Lady," which was written as a tribute to all the great black women who had impacted my life, beginning with my mother; all those sisters toiling away to support their family, putting food on the table, doing menial jobs and putting up with all kinds of indignities. The third movement was called "Bantu," which signified all of us coming together in unity. The last movement was titled "Kucheza Blues," for the glorious moment when Africa would gain its full independence and black people all over the world would have a tremendous global party to celebrate.

## The Players

Since I wanted this to be a really important suite, I knew it had to be played by a thoroughly unique orchestra. Melba certainly had a lot more big-band experience than I did, she knew all the great big-band players. After all those years she spent playing in the Gerald Wilson, Count Basie, Dizzy Gillespie, and Quincy Jones bands—not to mention writing for Duke Ellington and numerous large ensemble recordings—I totally relied on her judgment when it came time to hire the musicians for *Uhuru*, and from that point forward whenever we had a big-band date. She always wanted several key players to be the backbone of the band, people she knew from her big-band days, people who were versatile and who would lend dexterity and distinctive voices to their particular section. So we started out with Budd Johnson on saxophones and Quentin "Butter" Jackson on trombone, they were very close friends of Melba. These were musicians who could read any music inside out, who could interpret anything; they were our foundation, the keys to develop this big-band sound I was hearing in my head.

We picked Charlie Persip to play the trap drums because Charlie was in Dizzy's band with Melba. Most of the other musicians I picked. She wanted to have a certain passage for double flutes, to capture the sound of the birds on "African Lady." So I got Les Spann to play the guitar and double on flute to go along with Jerome Richardson, another very versatile musician who could play all the reeds and flutes. I also wanted musicians that were in tune with our history; musicians who were aware, musicians who took pride in being black, pride in being African Americans. It was a combination of all those things and that's why we wound up with such a powerful lineup. We hired Gigi Gryce, Yusef Lateef, Cecil Payne, Sahib Shihab, Jerome Richardson, and Budd Johnson on reeds and flutes; Julius Watkins on French horn; Clark Terry, Benny Bailey, Richard "Notes" Williams, and Freddie Hubbard on trumpet and flugelhorn; Quentin "Butter" Jackson, Slide Hampton, and Jimmy Cleveland on trombone; and Kenny Burrell on guitar. That was one of the greatest orchestras you could put together, and we haven't even gotten to the rhythm section.

Africa is civilization's heartbeat, so the rhythm section had to be very special. We wanted to have a rhythm section that showed how all drums came from the original drum, the African drum. So we got Babatunde Olatunji from Nigeria to coordinate the rhythm section and play African drum and percussion. I got Candido and Armando Peraza from Cuba to express the African drum via Cuba. Max Roach played marimba, Charlie Persip played jazz drums—G. T. Hogan subbed for Persip on "African Lady" when he couldn't make the second day of recording—and we had two basses, George Duvivier and Ron Carter. To sing Langston Hughes's lyrics for "African Lady" I wanted two singers who knew jazz but were not necessarily known as jazz singers. So I got Martha Flowers, a soprano who was largely from the European classical tradition, and for baritone Brock Peters, who was primarily known for playing Broadway shows and singing folk music. Putting all these forces together was an amazing experience.


## Label Quest

Even though we had all these resources together, I still wasn't sure who would record *Uhuru Afrika*. At this particular time in my recording career I was signed to United Artists Records, where I had a three-year contract. This was the same company that had previously recorded my *Little Niles* record, in 1958. The reviews for that record were very favorable and I obviously wanted to record *Uhuru Afrika* for United Artists, due to the success of *Little Niles*. But they hesitated at recording such a big project. They said I wasn't that well-known at the time and perhaps I should do something more popular; the implication, I thought, was that after making this more "popular" record, *then* I could record *Uhuru*.

They suggested I make a record based on the music from a Broadway show. They said, "Look, Randy, if you do a recording based on a popular Broadway show, then we'll let you do *Uhuru Afrika* . . ." so I took the bait. I started checking around, reading the Broadway reviews and inquiring about the various Broadway shows playing at that time. For some reason, I'm still not sure why, I came up with a show called *Destry Rides Again*. *Destry* is all cowboy music by Harold Rome, but I chose it anyway. I asked Melba to write the arrangements and I chose to use just trombones and a rhythm section on the date. I got Benny Green, Slide Hampton, Melba, and Frank Rehak to play the trombones; Peck Morrison played bass and Willie Rodriguez played the conga drums. We did our best on that and I always laugh when I think about that date, because it was also the only time I recorded with Elvin Jones on drums.

I loved Elvin's playing; he used to come to the Five Spot and sit in with me. You know how powerful Elvin is, I could never hear myself when he played, but we loved each other and that *Destry* recording gave me the opportunity to have Elvin play the drums. Frankly we weren't that inspired recording *Destry*; I did it purely hoping for the opportunity to record *Uhuru Afrika* for United Artists. But finally we soon realized that United Artists just wasn't ready to record *Freedom Africa*.

The project finally found a record label, largely because of Sarah Vaughan's husband and manager at the time, a guy named C. B. Atkins. He was a heavy cat from Chicago and he later became one of Muhammad Ali's managers. I went to see him because I knew he liked my music, he had been to clubs to hear my trio. In those days we used to work a lot opposite Miles Davis, Dizzy Gillespie . . . the real heavyweights. So I met with Atkins and said, "Listen, I have this project I really want to record and it's gonna require a big band. It's in four movements and it's going to be called *Uhuru Afrika*, which is Kiswahili for 'Freedom Africa.'" I explained the various movements to Atkins and he was very interested. He said, "Okay, I'm going to talk to some people at Roulette Records and maybe you can record it for them." Atkins went to Roulette Records and he talked Morris Levy into it, which was no small feat.

## In Process

Working with Melba is always an adventure, and this project was no exception. She was very particular, very orderly, but she was also so creative that sometimes she would decide to make last-minute changes in the arrangements to get things just right. Sometimes she would write something and it seemed like the arrangement was all set; only to have her say, "No, I think I want to change this."

Needless to say, it was quite hectic and frantic up until the moment we started to record. Even with all of Melba's creative powers, Jerome Richardson and several of the guys were still copying parts the day of the first recording session. I was living in that apartment that those two sisters from Langston's office had leased to me on 13th Street, and up until time to go to the recording session guys were writing out parts. Melba had people copying parts on the ceiling, on the walls, on the floor; it was a comical scene. The poor copyist was on his feet so long that his legs were completely swollen by morning; he had worked so hard with no rest. What a scene: we had to actually carry this guy down the stairs in a chair to take him to the studio!

## The Session

We recorded *Uhuru Afrika* on two successive days at Bell Sound in midtown Manhattan. With all of those musicians, and all of those different personalities, what was ironic was that both recording dates were scheduled for 9:00 a.m. and everybody was on time. Nobody was late, two days in a row, which was incredible. When the session started it was actually the first time the musicians had heard the poem at the introduction. When the guys heard the Langston Hughes poem it was quite dramatic; you could see it on their faces and hear it in their expressions. They said, "Oh, man . . . ," because that was during the period when Africa was either a place to be ashamed of or a place that people had tremendous fear of; you were not supposed to identify with Africa.

Africa, where the great Congo flows!
Africa, where the whole jungle knows
A new dawning breaks, Africa!
A young nation awakes, Africa!

The freedom wind blows!
Out of yesterday's night Uhuru—Freedom! Uhuru! Freedom.
—LANGSTON HUGHES, *Uhuru Afrika* invocation

When the musicians heard Langston's freedom poem, the purpose of which is to bring us together, to say the freedom of Africa is a freedom for us, they instantly knew what feeling we were after; that poem really set the mood. The independence of some African countries is inspiration for us to search for our freedom and our identity. That recording session was an incredible experience, and the spirits of our ancestors were with us in that studio, everybody got into the spirit of Africa. At one point we needed a certain kind of percussion sound and some guys got the inspiration to use Coca-Cola bottles to make sounds. Everybody contributed their ideas, because when I record I like to get the ideas of some of the musicians. Sometimes they can hear things that I can't hear. I never like to completely finish a piece until I get to the studio, because we may be doing something and someone might say, "Hey, why don't you do it this way; let's try it this way." I always like to keep it open. This session was wonderful because there was the artistic control, there were the charts, there was the music, but at the same time there was a tremendous sense of freedom.

## The Players Remember

*Yusef Lateef, saxophone*: I think as a composer Randy's music represents a progressive refinement and development of African American music. What was going on in that studio was discovery and invention in the aesthetics of music, because there were decades of knowledge in that studio; Charlie Persip and all those drummers! It was an amalgamation of abilities that were exchanging ideas and formulating the outcome of that music. A kind of romance of experience happened at that session.

*Ron Carter, bass*: *Uhuru Afrika* was my first awareness that when you go to a record date you don't have any instructions; you should just be prepared for whatever is on the music stand. It was a stunning surprise to be in the midst of all those guys on the record . . . To walk in the studio and see Clark Terry, Richard Williams, Charlie Persip . . . and to have George Duvivier as a bass partner was quite an amazing environment to be in. When I got to the studio the first thing I noted was the pitch

of all those drums: you've got congas and bongos, African drums . . .
My first concern was whether I could find some notes to play that were
out of their range, even though I don't know when they're going to play
them necessarily, when they're going to hit those specific drums. I prepared my technique to be out of the range of those drum notes because
it takes a hell of a mixing job to get the bass notes out of that mud.

By the same token I was respecting and honoring George Duvivier's
presence, kinda hanging around to see what his approach is going to be
when those drummers start banging around. Is it going to be like mine?
Is it going to be different from mine in terms of where to play our parts,
and when the drums lay out how do we handle the ranges now that
we have the space? . . . So it was a real lesson in section bass playing,
not having played with another bass player in a jazz ensemble before.
George asked me what I thought and I said, "George, they ought to
record the drums the day after tomorrow! . . . In the meantime I guess
our best bet is to try to slide some notes in here where the drums aren't
playing so loud so that the bass notes, which are the roots of all those
chords, make the top part sound like it belongs there." George said,
"Well, we can do that." I said, "Well, let's give it a shot." I think he
was kind of pleased at my comfort at talking with him and that I had
some suggestions that clearly might work. I was basically a stranger to
George, I was just a new guy in town at the time . . . and George Duvivier is George Duvivier! But when he asked for my advice, I thought
that since Randy had hired me for this date, George knew Randy well
enough to trust that whoever he hired would be capable of getting the
job done; so I felt good about that.

*Clark Terry, trumpet*: Melba was always so laid back and relaxed, but
she was just a completely thorough musician. We had worked together
with Quincy Jones's band on *Free and Easy*.

*Martha Flowers, voice*: Opera was my field, but when Randy asked me to
do this recording I was delighted. The key "African Lady" was written
in, and how it lay as far as my voice was concerned . . . it was not written in a high key where my voice would sound very operatic. It was
written in a sort of medium key where I thought my voice had a kind
of mellow quality that would lend itself to any kind of jazz music, or
music that was not considered classical music. I just felt vocally right at
home because it seemed like it was just written for me. Randy told me

he had written this wonderful composition and he thought my voice would be very suitable to sing it. *Uhuru Afrika* had great significance for me. When I heard about this music and saw the score, and then going up to record it, I felt a great sense of dedication to this work, that this composition would really have a great impact on the music world. Politically it made a great musical statement, and this really fired me up. I was quite anxious to sing "African Lady" and was truly excited when I saw all the other musicians who were involved in it; clearly this was a top-quality engagement. I had great respect for Langston Hughes's lyrics, they were just perfect for what Randy had written. The experience was just electrifying.

*Charlie Persip, drums*: I don't remember getting any kind of preparation for the date. I remember Randy talking about what he was going to do, but I basically had no idea until we got to the studio. I really made the majority of my money during that time doing just that; I was called to do record dates and I had no idea what was going to happen until I got to the date. I think that's why Randy asked me to do the date, because he knew that I was very proficient in that type of situation, plus he liked the way I played with large orchestra. I had the score, so I was reading the music accompanying the orchestra; but as far as blending with the other drummers, I listened to the other drummers and I played with them. I didn't take over, I just listened to the drummers and tried to blend with them and at the same time play my part, which was accompanying the ensemble.

This was like the who's who of African and Caribbean drummers on this date, so I was trying to blend with these people. I was glad to be a part of it. When I heard the whole thing and I heard the narration, I began to get kind of inwardly emotional about it, because we were just starting to become aware of our African heritage and starting to really get our pride together as black people. Once I did the album, when I heard the music it kind of got to me, it really helped to get me more involved emotionally with my African heritage. Doing that music really helped me to get deeper into my pride as a black man with African ancestry.

# Postscript

*DownBeat* magazine gave *Uhuru Afrika* a three-and-a-half-star review. Some people questioned my Africanness, they were afraid to deal with Africa. Some people said we were Black Nationalist because we created a music based upon the African civilization. It was kind of a piece that shook up some people, because collectively we have so little education about Africa. When we go to public schools, when we go to the movies . . . we always get indoctrinated with the history of Europe, so all of our heroes tend to be European. *Uhuru Afrika* was a complete turnabout; we were saying, "Wait a minute, you know Africa is the original civilization!" The critical response was a combination of those things, but Melba Liston and I were tremendously proud of this creation.

The freedom message of *Uhuru Afrika* was so powerful that in 1964 the government-controlled Board of Censors of the Union of South Africa officially banned the record. This was during apartheid, when the South African government persistently denied black South Africans access to anything which spoke to black freedom. Copies of the album were seized in Cape Town and Johannesburg.

LENA'S "NOW" RIGHTS LP BANNED IN S. AFRICA
Copies of Lena Horne's hit LP of last year, *Now*, a vocal effort aiding the fight for civil rights in the United States, were seized in Capetown and Johannesburg as the Union of South Africa officially banned the album along with pianist-composer Randy Weston's *Uhuru Africa* suite . . . Weston's is a four-movement suite—"An American Salute to an Emerging Continent"—which grew out of the composer's interest in African music and culture.
—*Jet* magazine, November 12, 1964

SOUTH AFRICA BANS LENA HORNE DISC
In a recent action by the government-controlled Board of Censors, the Union of South Africa officially banned two albums by U.S. artists: pianist-composer Randy Weston's *Uhuru Afrika* and singer Lena Horne's "Here's Lena NOW!"
—*Amsterdam News*, October 3, 1964

The first time we played the *Uhuru Afrika* music in concert was on February 4, 1972, at Philharmonic Hall, which is now Avery Fisher Hall, at Lincoln Center. We performed it with the Symphony of the New World, which was conducted by Leonard de Paur, with many of the original musicians. We played it as part of two concerts that were devoted to black history, on a program that also featured music by William L. Dawson, Roger Dickerson, and Howard Swanson, all black composers. I think the audience loved it because with *Uhuru Afrika* we go through so many different expressions.

We also played Uhuru in 1998 at the Brooklyn Academy of Music's Majestic Theater, for 651 Arts. But musically it wasn't quite the same, because Melba was ill and we tried to pull it together in too short a time. We couldn't find some of the parts; Melba had stored the music but there were some parts missing. So we went through the usual with Melba . . . it's always an adventure! Sometimes in her travels and dealing with her illnesses, some parts of her work turn up missing. But despite that it was a powerful night and the spirits were high in that theater. Melba was in the hospital at the time, but we were able to pick her up so she could come to the concert that night. I insisted on wheeling her out in her wheelchair so the audience could see this woman whose contributions were so essential to my music. The crowd gave her a really warm standing ovation, and while she sat there beaming, all the musicians got up and serenaded her with their horns. It was wonderful to see her onstage with Billy Harper, Benny Powell, Talib Kibwe, and all the cats surrounding her, playing music for her; it was very special.

## 8

The Gnaoua musicians of northern Africa carry an exalted musical tradition. In the public squares of Marrakesh and Tangier,
they perform for ecstatic, all-night ceremonies. They accompany dancers and acrobats; they summon spirits; sometimes they
work what Westerners would regard as miracles—walking on
hot coals, or making wounds disappear. . . . The jazz tradition is
intimately tied to African music, but Mr. Weston has made more
direct connections with Africa than most American musicians.
—*New York Times*

## MAKING THE PILGRIMAGE

I had been dreaming of traveling to and even living in Africa for as long as
I could remember. My golden opportunity to travel there finally came in
1961. An organization called the American Society of African Culture (AM-
SAC), which was involved in U.S.-Africa exchange programs, and which
some of us later figured was one of many seemingly benevolent CIA fronts
of that period, chose twenty-nine of us to travel to Nigeria. Our task was
to spend ten days there exploring the relationships in art, music, philosophy, and linguistics between West Africa—particularly Nigeria—and African America.

Not long before this time I was going out with a German-American
woman named Jean Krentz. We had broken up by the time of this trip, but
we were still very close. She worked for this organization AMSAC, which
had an office in Manhattan in the East 40s, near the UN. They were doing
things like bringing a painter from East Africa to present an exhibition of
his work in the U.S.; cultural exchange between the U.S. and Africa was
their mission. The head of AMSAC was a man named John Davis, a graduate of one of the black southern colleges. For this particular trip they were
sending an entire delegation of U.S. artists to Africa, and actually the original jazz pianist they had selected for the trip was Phineas Newborn. There

was absolutely no question that Phineas Newborn was a master musician, but I was more deeply involved with Africa, and Jean Krentz knew that.

So one day she called me and said, "Randy, I'm coming by in a taxi. Gather up one copy of all of your LPs and I'm coming to pick them up." She came over, scooped up a bunch of my LPs, went to John Davis's office, locked the door, and wouldn't let him out until he agreed to send me on this trip to Nigeria. Muslims talk about making the pilgrimage to Mecca, but for me the entire continent of Africa is Mecca; and at last I was going back home.

They took twenty-nine of us on the trip: I brought along my tenor saxophonist Booker Ervin and the drummer-dancer Scoby Stroman. Lionel Hampton brought eight members of his band and the plan was for me and my two guys to play with Hamp's band. Others on the trip included the painter Hale Woodruff, the singer-actor Brock Peters (who sang on "Uhuru Afrika"), the dancer-choreographer Geoffrey Holder, Langston Hughes, the Nigerian drummer living in the U.S. Babatunde Olatunji, the wonderful classical pianist Natalie Hinderas, Martha Flowers, the great soprano who sang "African Lady" on *Uhuru Afrika*, Nina Simone, Ahmed Abdul-Malik, the Savoy Ballroom dancers Al Minns and Leon James, and Bayo Martin, a drummer who had long been involved in the Nigerian independence movement. We were to spend ten days in Lagos, the capital of Nigeria.

I was beyond ready. I can't stress enough how thoroughly conditioned I had been toward Africa by my father from the time I was a child. I'm sure it's a dream of every black person, every African American, every African Caribbean person to go to the continent, back to our place of origin. That was already deeply ingrained in my life. That's why I get so upset when people either overlook or avoid going there, or go there and don't grasp the spiritual significance of Africa—not what Africa is today, but what it was, and what our ancestors created . . . We came from that greatness, so I was very excited about this trip.

The night before we left they had a big gala send-off for our delegation, with Count Basie's Orchestra playing; that was where I met the great Paul Robeson for the first time. When we departed for Nigeria it was a typical cold January day in New York. We boarded an Alitalia flight to Rome and changed planes there for the trip to Lagos. The closer we got to the Motherland the more excited I became. Finally, when the plane came into Nigerian airspace the pilot said, "Now we're over Africa." I was so over the top in my excitement, I could swear I felt the rhythms of the plane engine change, which later inspired me to write a piece called "Lagos." I recorded that piece twice, once with trio on the *Berkshire Blues* album and later with septet on *Saga*, so there must have been something powerful about my impressions of that plane engine. I know it was my imagination, but that's where some of the greatest ideas come from.

The plane touched down at about 11:00 at night. When the door to the plane opened I'll never forget it because there were Geoffrey Holder, Brock Peters—who were both tall men too—and myself coming off the plane first. I can't describe it in words but there's a certain smell in West Africa, a certain fragrance, and it was really potent that night as we stepped into the night air. Africa at last! About fifty drummers were there to greet us, and a few in our delegation got down on their knees and kissed the good earth. Then all of a sudden amidst this whole scene, a guy comes running over to me and he says, "Well, you finally decided to come back home, you been gone four hundred years, what took you so long!" Man, the tears were streaming down my face I was so overjoyed. Lagos was incredible; it was incredible because here we are in Africa—we're in Africa, all of us for the first time.

On our first full night in Lagos Nnamdi Azikiwe, the first post-colonial president of Nigeria, had a big dinner for all twenty-nine of us at his house. He didn't speak formally, but he made us feel very comfortable, very much at home. There were many ambassadors there from all over Africa and each one of us was seated next to an African ambassador. There we met a very beautiful African American lady named Barbara Wilson, who kind of resembled a black Sophia Loren. She was director of the AMSAC office in Lagos and was our liaison while we were in the country. Fela Kuti, the renowned Nigerian music star, was invited and he brought his trumpet. There was a piano there, so Fela and I played together for the first time and were friends from that moment on.

A typical day on this trip included meetings and conferences in the morning, which might consist of things like readings from the distinguished Nigerian writer Chinua Achebe speaking about his work and by contrast Langston Hughes speaking about his, trying to make the connections between African and African American literature. Some of the other Nigerian participants included Steve Rhodes, Wole Bucknor, the television personality Art Idiye, and Ulli Behr, a German man who lived there and was a scholar on Nigeria; plus the musicians Bobby Benson and Bayo Martin, and Bobby's brother T. O. Benson, who was the Nigerian minister of tourism.

In the evening they would have concert performances such as traditional African dance on one side of the stage, and the two dancers from the Savoy Ballroom, Al Minns and Leon James, on the other side of the stage to illustrate the contrast and connections between African traditional dance and African American dance.

Other sessions included politics, philosophy, music . . . Every day there was something scheduled. The night of the biggest performance, which also featured Nina Simone, we were scheduled to play with Lionel Hampton. For Booker Ervin, Scoby Stroman, and my first rehearsal with Hamp and his eight musicians he pulled out a ton of music and we rehearsed about three hours . . . hard; when we played the concert he didn't call nothin' we'd rehearsed. He just went into his familiar routine, his "Hey Bab-a-Reebop," "Flying Home," and all of his hits. The stage we played on was really high, and that's when I realized what a juju man Lionel Hampton really was. He did one of his numbers and leaped off the stage, landing on his feet as if nothing happened. We were blown away, as was the audience.

The critics were not amused, and the next day they blasted Hamp's antics in the Nigerian newspapers. They said they wanted to hear the music, that just because Hamp was in Africa he shouldn't be coming there clowning. They were tough on him but the audience loved him. The critics blasted Olatunji too, because they said he was misusing their sacred rhythms. The audience had a ball, but this was what the papers were saying.

One day Olatunji took me to his village. On our way there, as we were coming down the road we could see a guy down the way a distance. When we got to where he was standing this guy kept checking us out with great curiosity. All of a sudden he came running up to us talking in Yoruba with Olatunji, and I couldn't understand a word they were saying. Olatunji turned to me and said this guy wanted to bet him that his friend is taller than me. We laughed and I said something like "OK, bring him on." This was like a scene out of *Gunsmoke* or something, because this other tall guy came walking down the road toward me as though we were about to have one of those wild, wild west gunfights. When he got closer we could see I was just a bit taller than he; we came together and embraced like long-lost brothers, and we all had a good laugh.

In the evening when the panel discussions, dinners, and concerts were over I was determined to hang out with the Nigerian musicians, also because I had designs on living in Africa even then. So I made up my mind that after all the evening's activities I was going to go into town and hang out at Bobby Benson's club. He was a drummer and guitarist who had a huge club in Lagos called Caban Bamboo. It was a typical African club, open air with tables surrounding a big circular dance floor that could accommodate several hundred dancers. I wrote a song named after that club called "Caban Bamboo Highlife" that I recorded on *The Music of New African Nations*, which followed *Uhuru Afrika*. Later Bobby's tune "Niger Mambo" became part of our band book. All of the young West African musicians used to hang out at Bobby's club, including Fela. That was back in the day when I used to drink. Bobby and I became friends, so he would always have a bottle waiting for me at the bar. Whatever I drank one night he would just make a line on the bottle, and when I came back the next night he would make sure I got the same bottle.

On weekends Bobby would feature traditional Nigerian music at the club. One Saturday night I was there they had a group playing traditional music from the countryside. The group had an enormous balaphon and the whole family was playing that balaphon: grandfather, father, son, mother . . . all playing this huge instrument. For the percussion several women were playing on bolts of cloth; they were holding these bolts and playing them like drums, something I hadn't even imagined. This music was so beautiful, and I'm sitting there at one of the tables surrounding the dance floor. With the plants and stuff the club was surprisingly intimate for such a big place.

The music was so inspiring that at one point I jumped up and got the spirit, I just had to go sit with these people. So I sat down with the group, just like I belonged with these people. The music started getting more and more intense and the next thing I knew I could feel myself leaving the earth. This music was so powerful I was literally levitating, or so I felt. I actually began to feel that if I didn't get away from these people I might still be going up and up in the universe somewhere! That was my first experience with the power of traditional African music. I panicked and jumped down off the stage, with everybody busting out laughing. I slinked back to my table, but fast. That music was too deep for me. After those ten glorious days I was determined to return to Africa as soon as I could.

Randy with unidentified Nigerians on 1963 tour.

## Back to Africa

The first time I went to Africa in '61 I made it my business to meet as many people as I could and I guess it paid off, because in 1963 I got an invitation to go back and do some playing and lecturing. This time it was just me and Elton Fax, the great African American illustrator who wrote the book *Black Artists of the New Generation*.

We returned to Nigeria, again sponsored by AMSAC, and this time our assignment was to visit universities and give lectures. I also did more play-ing that trip than I had in '61, including playing with five African drummers in a concert at Bobby Benson's place—just piano and traditional Yoruba drummers. At the University of Lagos I got a chance to hang out again with my man Fela, one of the originators of what has come to be known as the "Afro beat" sound. At that time Fela was still playing trumpet and hadn't started playing the saxophone. We wound up playing together. I met a lot of young West African musicians on that trip.


## Fela Ransome Kuti

Fela is the bravest, most courageous musician I've ever met in my life. He lived in a country which was controlled at that time by the military government, and military rule is always hard-core. As I mentioned, I'd actually met Fela on that first 1961 trip and was happy to see him this time; but by this time he was becoming an increasingly larger figure in Nigerian life. Remember, 1961 was right after many of these African nations had just gained their independence from colonial rule, and we had met President Azikiwe that first trip. He was a hero of the Nigerian liberation from the British. He was a beautiful man, very cultured, very educated. When we had that dinner at his house on that '61 trip they served a ton of food. At one point Azikwe said to me, "Mr. Weston, I don't think you've had this kind of food before." I said, "I'm sorry sir, but I grew up with this kind of food." And I told him about my father being from Jamaica, Panama, and about the okra, yam, peas, and rice and all that stuff I had grown up on, which is straight out of Africa. After Azikiwe came the military government, and they had all those coups and killings and Nigeria just went crazy.

Fela was also an educated man who was forever in opposition to these military governments, so he became a thorn in their sides because the people really loved his music; and as a result he became a global superstar. I don't know how Fela got such power, but I do know his mother was a very famous politician, a real revolutionary. By the time I returned to Nigeria in 1977 Fela had developed his own village right in the city of Lagos. Also by this time Fela was making recordings and he had formed his own organization called Afro Beat. That band Afro Beat was the most popular group in all of Africa except for the Congo, because in Congo they have the strongest rhythms on the continent.

Fela was growing ever more powerful among the people, saying stuff like he wanted to be president of Nigeria. He was constantly insulting the military government: calling them fascists, murderers, assassins, writing songs about them . . . They put him in jail a number of times. When I visited him and went through his village there were brothers all around with stands full of reefer smoke. When Fela walked through there he was the chief.

Randy Weston and the legendary Nigerian Afrobeat king Fela Aniku-lapo Kuti, whose life story became a Broadway musical, reunite at a concert by the African Street Festival group in Brooklyn, New York, 1995. *Photograph by Goddy Wichendu.*

Fela's mother was also quite an impressive woman. An illustration of that was an incident I heard about where she organized some opposition to one of the Nigerian chiefs. Somehow this cat wasn't doing the right thing; I don't remember all the details. But whatever the case, what he was doing wasn't correct with the women.

This trip also had its share of different kinds of unusual experiences. Elton Fax and I met a Russian woman journalist named Petra who knew her way around a bit and hung out with us while we were there. She took me to the juju market and apparently she was deep into the traditional stuff, which I didn't know, so that was a heavy trip. The juju market is in a town called Ibadan, and it's a huge market covered with tent material on poles. Even though we went there in broad daylight, when we went down the first three or four stairs into this market it was very dark and very weird there, like we'd entered another world.

Turns out the juju market is where you go to get stuff to put some kind of charm or spell on someone, supernatural stuff that I wasn't really into. They had everything for sale, from bird beaks to chicken legs, all kinds of weird stuff. The women who controlled this market had eyes that were like yellow in color, real spooky-like. I'm hanging out with this Russian woman because she was apparently quite familiar with this scene. We just hung out, we had no relationship; but I didn't know she was into this juju tradition. Almost as soon as I walked down into this market and checked the place out I wanted to get outta there. Petra got kinda mad and recognized that I was a bit spooked by this scene. She said, "What's wrong with you?" There was nothing wrong with me that just getting out of there wouldn't cure.

Another time we went looking to hear some Nigerian juju music, this time with Elton Fax and that beautiful woman Barbara from the AMSAC office. I've always been interested in the spiritual world, psychic phenomena and that kind of stuff, since I was a kid, but I guess not to the extent of that juju market. Nevertheless, I used to read books about psychic phenomena all the time, so I really wanted to hear this juju music. There was a club down on the dock in Lagos, so Petra offered to take us down there to hear this music. That was during my shirt-and-tie days, because that's what you wore in those situations. So Elton and I were clean and we were determined to go to this club.

When we got down to the dock Petra pointed out this club where they have the real juju music, and we started getting out of the car to go down there. This area was really in the "hood." Just as we're arriving at the club we spot this guy standing outside the place holding a big stick. We're still sitting in the car, watching this scene. I'll never forget that car, because it was a Volkswagen and my knees were pressing up against the dashboard. Elton Fax is sitting behind me and Barbara is sitting behind the Russian woman. We're checking out the scene and we spot this Nigerian brother and his woman, dressed sharp in traditional garments walking to the club. They walk to the door and all of a sudden this guy with the stick hits this brother right in the stomach, bam!

We're all wondering, "Do we really want to go into this club?" Next thing I know Petra starts blessing me out, calling me scared—probably remembering my hasty escape from the juju market earlier. By this time we had gotten out of the car, but when we saw that guy get hit with that stick we hesitated. Next thing we know the guy with the stick starts coming toward us. Everybody quickly got back in the car and we split; I never got to hear that juju music. I told Petra, "I'm not ashamed, my sister used to fight my battles." She kept insisting, "He's just protecting his god in the club." Me and Elton Fax said, "No way," and we split.

Another great trip to Africa came after I had my first opportunity to tour the continent with my band, but that's another story entirely. In 1977 I traveled there on my own to join a delegation of artists and great thinkers at the FESTAC event. FESTAC '77 was actually the second Black and African Festival of Arts and Culture. The organizer's idea was to bring over black representatives of the global arts and culture community from across Africa and the diaspora, including places as far away as Australia, which sent some Aborigine artists.

Once again I traveled to Lagos, which by that time was a bit different place than it was when I was there in the 1960s. For one thing cars had literally taken over the place, and the traffic was horrendous around the clock. The ancient country of Ethiopia, which I still haven't visited, is much older than Nigeria and except for an incursion by the Italians Ethiopia basically remained free of colonialism. Ethiopia was the host of FESTAC '77, even though Nigeria was the site. The Nigerian government reportedly put up huge amounts of oil money to stage this event. The whole idea is that we are one African people, that was the goal of FESTAC. No matter if we're in Mississippi or Havana, or Australia, or wherever; that was the whole point of the event.

They invited about twenty thousand artists from across the globe. I never counted them but that was the official number. I only wound up playing once, at least officially, though I did jam with Fela; but we'll get to that in a minute. Sun Ra was there and he played once. There was so much great artistry at this conference that you didn't need to play more than once. Representatives from the entire black world organized this thing. They hosted colloquiums throughout FESTAC on everything from education to health to music, all things involved with African people. It was designed to develop a sense of global unity. FESTAC lasted one month, throughout January. Each country sent groups and usually the groups would stay one or two weeks, then other groups would come. I stayed most of the month because I had come individually on my own; I didn't come with the American delegation because I was living in France at the time.

One of the artists there was a dancer named Percy Boyd from Trinidad, the husband of the great dancer Pearl Primus. He was a fantastic artist himself and a very brilliant guy. The scene was kind of chaotic in a way, with a lot of confusion over transportation. But Percy was hooked up; he had a bus and a chauffeur. Once he did his two weeks with his dance company and was ready to split, he said, "Randy, do you want this bus. I'll give you this bus and this is your chauffer, he'll do whatever you want him to do." So I had this big bus and a chauffeur like some kind of big shot—and meanwhile some of these visiting ministers couldn't even find any transportation.

They had houses for the artists, not hotels. Each country had its own housing: Ethiopia is here, Mali is here, Brazil is over there, Cuba is there, Libya is there, Tunisia, Morocco . . . it was an amazing scene. Plus you can imagine all the music; it was so powerful it was one of the most amazing experiences of my life.

The array of folks there was also incredible. For example I'd have breakfast and my tablemates might be Louis Farrakhan, Stevie Wonder, Queen Mother Moore, and a heavy Sufi master named Mahi Ismail. Imagine me hanging out with those cats. Stevie and I actually managed to stay in a hotel. When he arrived Stevie came into the hotel with his guitar, walked in the lobby, sat down, and started singing and playing his guitar; that's the first thing he did when he got there.

The Nigerians had built a special theater for this event, but the two brand-new Steinway pianos and one Bösendorfer they had purchased were waiting at the airport, hung up in customs apparently. Long story short: the pianos didn't arrive until the day of the concert. I was supposed to play first opposite some Ethiopian musicians. But they were late getting the piano there and I wound up playing second, on a new piano that had never been touched before.

Fela was one of the main people I wanted to see while there, and like some African musicians he had his own club called the Shrine, just opposite his village in Lagos. Fela's club was really big, it must have held about a thousand people, and the night I went there it was packed. When I got to Fela's village he was sitting in a corner, holding court and eating away. I'm stepping through all kinds of women, all surrounding this dude. It was quite a scene. He saw me and said, "Randy, come on and have some food." We talked awhile, then it was time for him to perform, so he put on his stage costume and we were stepping around all these women to get outside. As we were walking through his village it was obvious Fela was like a king to these people.

We entered the Shrine and this place, along with Bobby Benson's joint, really became my inspiration for wanting to open up my own club. Fela got his band together for the performance and he calls me over and says, "Randy, you sit there." He had an English film crew capturing his every move. He started by playing this little rhythm on the piano, then the band came in and he grabbed his saxophone. The rhythm was totally infectious, but you have to hear it live, you have to be where people are dancing to this band to fully appreciate this groove. At one point in his performance Fela grabbed the mike and said, "Ladies and gentlemen, I want you to meet my brother from America," and they brought me onstage. So we jammed a bit. Next thing I know he's talking on the mike again and he's got me by the hand and he's cursing out the military—and there were military guys in the club. I wanted to get the hell off that stage with a quickness, 'cause those cats don't play. Man, Fela was fearless, but I was sweatin' . . . what this guy *didn't* call the government . . . and he wouldn't let go of my hand. The people were cheering him on.

One week later, after we had all left, the soldiers raided Fela's village and destroyed the place. They threw his mother out of a window, beat him up and took him to prison, and raped all his girls. But when he came out of jail Fela was the same, still defiant. He said, "I'm the president of Africa"; he was against all that stuff that was in opposition to the true Africa, he was incredible.

As for FESTAC, which was over by the time all that madness happened to Fela, the final night was Stevie Wonder, Miriam Makeba, and Osibissa in a stadium with fifty thousand people in the stands. As I always say, we're all a part of this, all our music is different, and all our music is the same. But this FESTAC thing was too powerful; it was too big. The white press gave it absolutely no coverage, no more than they had given to our 1961 trip—which was nothing. But this was the most fantastic event I ever participated in up to that point.

## 9

[Randy Weston] is a dedicated student of African music, which he has been integrating directly into his piano music . . . and a tireless traveler. —*New York Times*

## TOURING THE MOTHERLAND

In 1966 my working band of Ray Copeland on trumpet, Booker Ervin on tenor saxophone, Big Black on hand drums, Lenny McBrowne on trap drums, and Bill Wood on bass broke up. It was a shame, because we had really gotten tight, both on the bandstand and as brothers. We were all totally into Africa and were very much in tune with each other and the music, but we simply couldn't get enough gigs to sustain the band. The sixties were a hard time for all jazz bands. Our last concert together was in September 1966 at the Monterey Jazz Festival, a performance which much later was released on CD by Verve Records.

While we were out in California for the Monterey Jazz Festival I got a call from the State Department in Washington saying they would like me to take a group on a tour of West Africa and North Africa, with side trips to Beirut, Lebanon, and Damascus, Syria, starting in January 1967. I had mixed feelings about making the tour, because this was a time of great turmoil in the U.S., with the civil rights movement, it was a time of riots in the cities and all that stuff, and I was just disgusted about the continued status quo of black people in America. So I questioned whether I wanted to represent the U.S. government in this way. I did a lot of soul searching, talked to some people I trusted, and they all said, "You must go on this tour because this is the first opportunity to take your own music to Africa, and all the compositions you've written about Africa." They all felt this would be a real good test, seeing how my music was received on the continent, since they all knew how important Africa was to my life. So I agreed to make the tour.

I talked with Booker Ervin about making it, but he had made some records as a leader and wanted to go out on his own; he decided to stay in California. Big Black absolutely did not want to make the tour and Lenny McBrowne's wife lived in California and he wanted to stay out there. I came back east and put together a group with Bill Wood on bass, Ed Blackwell on drums, Chief Bey on African drum, Clifford Jordan on tenor sax, and Ray Copeland on trumpet. Ray did a lot of the arranging for this sextet. Having Chief Bey on the tour was one of the keys to our success. I knew that in many places we were likely to encounter audiences that weren't real familiar with western instruments, but I knew Chief's drum would connect with the people. My whole concept of having African drum in my band—which is still the case today—goes back to hearing Chano Pozo with Dizzy Gillespie's orchestra, and hearing people like Sabu Martinez with Art Blakey. When I heard Chano with Dizzy it was like a revelation, nobody had played music like that before. From that point on having the African or Cuban drum in my band was very important to me. Having Chief Bey on this tour was purely a matter of connecting with our African audiences. That drum is their instrument. They may not be so sure about the origins of the other instruments, but when they see that hand on that drum they know that's theirs. I would never have gone to Africa any other way.

We met to discuss the tour and the conditions the State Department had laid on us. The only condition we weren't happy with was the edict that we had to wear suits and ties when we performed, though we had the freedom to wear African clothes when we weren't performing. My great friend, the indispensable Georgia Griggs, traveled with us as our road manager and wrote a piece for *DownBeat* magazine on the tour.

## Arranger's note
*(Given rates of inflation in the years since the 1967 tour—not to mention how performance fees and travel challenges have changed the touring game—we thought it might be interesting to revisit the original budget for the tour)*

*Randy Weston African Tour Fiscal Year 1967 Budget*
Pre-Tour
   Passports, visas, inoculations 7 @ $40.00 = $280.00
   Insurance Common Carrier 7 @ $18 = $126.00
   Uniforms 6 @ $150 = $900.00

Bass case 1 @ $145.00 = $145.00

Scoring and arrangements of music specifically for tour = $250.00

Presentations (expendable materials) = $200.00

Airport taxes 15 countries @ $7.00 = $105.00

Tour

Salaries: $33,000.00

a. Randy Weston 12 wks @ $750.00 = $9,000.00

b. Five sidemen 12 wks @ $350 = $21,000.00

c. Georgia Griggs mgr-secretary 12 wks @ $250 = $3,000.00

Contingency Fund: $500.00

We gathered at Kennedy Airport to leave on a bitter cold day in January. Our itinerary was to include performances in Senegal, Cameroon, Gabon, Ghana, Sierra Leone, Liberia, Mali, Niger, Egypt, Algeria, Tunisia, Morocco, Beirut, and Damascus. But Damascus didn't happen, because there were some heavy political problems in Syria at the time and they canceled that date. I had also decided to take my son Niles—who later changed his name to Azzedin—with me. He was fifteen and he had a medical problem with his leg, and the doctor told me that if I left him in New York without super-vision he'd be running around too much and might damage his leg perma-nently, so I needed to keep an eye on him.

When we arrived at our first stop, Dakar, Senegal, my son wanted to take a nap. But I was full of energy—back in the Motherland again!—and along with the State Department officer and Ray Copeland we went to take a look at the theater we were scheduled to play, because our first concert was the same night we arrived. When we got to the theater we saw a guy onstage with five drums. It was Dou Dou Ndaye Rose, who was a big Senegalese star that I was hearing for the first time. I got really excited, because my son was studying the drums. So I ran back to the hotel, woke him up, and told him, "Man, you gotta get up and hear this drummer!" We ran back to the theater and experienced Dou Dou Ndaye Rose playing these five drums. When we heard these five drums we heard everything; we heard echoes of Max Roach, Kenny "Klook" Clarke . . . everybody.

Our concert that evening was a big success. Those Senegalese brothers and sisters in the audience might not have understood some of the stuff we played, but they could certainly identify with Chief Bey and his traditional drums, and Ed Blackwell with that New Orleans beat; those New Orleans drummers have that beat for dance. We always ended our concerts with my tune "African Cookbook," and that night the people exploded when we played it.

The American ambassador, a young guy, was at the concert, and after the concert they had a reception for us at his residence. The ambassador called me aside to congratulate me on the concert and said, "Mr. Weston, I really love your music and I'd like to ask you a couple of questions." The first question he asked me was how come he didn't recognize any of the songs that he heard. I told him that's because I'm a composer of my own original music, which is about African American culture. Then he asked me why I didn't have any white musicians in the band, though he asked it very nicely and not in a negative way, more just his basic curiosity. I told him the reason was we are an African American people and I was chosen to do this State Department tour, I believe, because of my compositions and my interest in Africa.

It was an intriguing question, because most of the State Department–sponsored tours kind of specified that there had to be a white musician somewhere in most of the bands. The ambassador told me, "This concert was a big success and I want to tell you something: this is the first time I've been able to get these African diplomats to my house since I've been here; and that was the impact of your concert." So that was the first concert of our three-month tour.

The next country was Upper Volta, which is now known as Burkina Faso. We played in a beautiful park in the city of Bobo-Dioulasso for about six thousand Africans who had never experienced a live concert before, at least not of western music. It was very interesting, because during intermission the audience stayed right in their seats, they didn't move; others simply stood in place. As always we played our original music, but we used African rhythms and Chief Bey had that African drum, so the people gave us a very warm response. After the concert they all packed up their chairs on their bicycles and went back into the bush.

We had a funny experience at the zoo in Bobo-Dioulasso. We were accompanied there by some African Americans who worked for the State Department. There was a chimpanzee there that was the delight of all the kids, and Bill Wood wound up getting a bit carried away with this chimp. Bill was into smoking a pipe, which he was using when we spotted this chimp. Bill passed the pipe to the chimp and the chimp smoked it after watching Bill. Then they started exchanging this pipe, and somehow Bill and this chimp started doing a little dance together, imitating each other by beating on their chests and making sounds. Next thing we knew Bill lost his balance and tumbled to the ground. When the chimp saw this he tried to pounce on Bill, and Bill wound up scrambling away, literally on his back on the ground, with this chimp in hot pursuit. All the kids and everybody fell out laughing at the sight of Bill scooting away on his back, being chased by this chimp.

The next day we took quite a ride from Bobo-Dioulasso to Ouagadougou. All the roads in Upper Volta at that time were covered with a type of red clay. I was riding in a station wagon and the others in our group were riding in a truck. Our driver was totally out of his mind, driving so fast that he was hitting dogs left and right; they'd go flying in the air and he wouldn't even stop. Finally we stopped to get something to drink and went into a store for some Coca-Cola or something. We created a real sensation in that store. All the townspeople came out to get a look at us, not just because we were strangers but because by this time our hair and faces were completely covered with red dust from that clay. These people had a good laugh on us, we looked like creatures from outer space.

When we arrived at Ouagadougou we checked into a fairly modern hotel and a funny thing happened. We went out to the swimming pool to relax, and Chief Bey was tightening the heads of his drums, with everybody sitting around him just messin' around, when we noticed a recurring phenomenon: at 5:00 every evening there would be hundreds and hundreds of bats flying over the swimming pool. Clifford Jordan always walked with a limp, I don't know if he had one leg shorter than the other or what. My son Azzedin didn't miss anything and he looked up and saw all these bats flying around; then they started zooming over us and the swimming pool. We were spooked and everybody took off running. Even though he had that limp, when we got to the hotel Clifford Jordan was standing there waiting for us. I never understood how he beat all of us there.

During our stay on Ouagadougou the American embassy had a reception for us and had some local musicians come to perform. They had these stringed instruments and drums and it was really beautiful music. Their chief came, along with his wives; they all danced, and this was one of the most beautiful receptions we had the entire trip.

The next country was Mali. When we arrived in the city of Bamako we were ushered to this huge, Russian-built stadium where we were to perform. As we were getting prepared to do our history-of-jazz program, the Malians were arranging for it to be translated into French, so we were working with

Randy Weston Quintet at the airport in Bamako, Mali, on their State Department tour of Africa in 1967. From left: Clifford Jordan, saxophonist; Ed Blackwell, drummer; Georgia Griggs, road manager; Ray Copeland, trumpeter; son Niles in suit jacket under the "B" in Bamako sign; Randy, standing tallest in shades; Chief Bey, percussionist, kneeling with package under arm; Bill Wood, bassist (next to Chief Bey).

the translator. Suddenly we were surrounded by Malian youth who were very much into jazz; some played saxophone, trumpet, and whatnot, and we developed a beautiful rapport with them. My memories of Bamako also include the Grand Hotel where we stayed. This place was like something out of a spy novel, with Vietnamese on one floor, Chinese on another, and East Germans on another; it seemed to be a hotel of tremendous intrigue. It was a beautiful hotel but full of mosquitoes. So many that my son and I had to walk the streets at night, covered with mosquito bites; we simply could not sleep.

Next we went to Niger. When we landed at the Niamey airport I looked up and saw a young black man with a beard, and as he got closer I was delighted to see it was an old friend of mine named Ted Joans from my Five Spot days in the Village. Ted, who passed away in 2003, was a poet, a painter, a writer, and a great speaker. At that time he was traveling all over Africa, with a simple pack on his back, hitchhiking across the continent.

After we got settled at the hotel Ted took us out. He took us to places where we could get fantastic African food for something like 25 cents a bowl. I remember him taking us out to the desert to see the Tuareg people. They had me sit on a camel, but the saddle broke and I'm struggling, sliding down this camel with all the Tuaregs laughing at the sight of me dealing with this camel.

In Niamey we played at an extraordinary museum, one of the most beautiful I've ever seen in my life. There was local music playing constantly all day in this museum; there were animals, games, Hausa clothing, and lots of kids around. This was a combination museum and zoo and they even had a petrified forest. I vividly remember feeding a giraffe, with the guys taking many pictures of me feeding him; with my height next to this giraffe I guess it was a real sight gag for them. We actually had a full-scale replica of an African village as our dressing room.

When we got to Ghana we played at a Ghanaian trade fare in the capital city of Accra. Ghana has always had the finest school of African music, and they have a library of African music and world black culture. One of the things Kwame Nkrumah did as president was to emphasize Ghanaian culture as a key way of life. The University of Ghana in Lagon, just outside of Accra, invited us for a visit. We met a Professor Opoku, who was a master teacher of African dance. He gave us all beautiful African flutes. We stayed in Ghana ten days, which gave us an opportunity to meet many Ghanaian artists and hang with the people. I met the great Ghanaian musician Kofi Ghanaba, who was known as Guy Warren at the time. His composition "Love, the Mystery of" is something I close all my concerts with even today.

We heard about a sorceress located in a village not too far from Accra and we became very anxious to go up there and hear some of the music, which was supposed to be fantastic. On our way there we experienced some of the greatest music of our trip, from Ghanaian drummers, singers, and dancers who were celebrating a renowned chief.

Eventually we arrived at the home of the sorceress. When she started speaking with us Chief Bey suddenly burst into tears, because he said this woman looked exactly like his grandmother. It was kinda humorous and serious at the same time, because we didn't quite know how powerful this woman was. Unfortunately the musicians who were usually there were off somewhere else when we arrived. She did a libation ceremony for us, wished us well on our journey, and asked that the brothers and sisters in America come back to Africa. Ghana was one of the real highlights of the tour, because we had more actual contact with the local musicians than we had in some of the other countries.

The next country was Cameroon, which was the first country where we performed with a folkloric group, the Batous. The audience danced to my music, they danced to "African Cookbook." We played for a school somewhere out in the woods for the young people, we gave an indoor concert, and the rapport with the Cameroonian youth was just fabulous.

In Gabon I was really impressed with the American ambassador. He arranged for us to go into the interior and had us play in such towns as Bitam, Mouila, Franceville, and Libreville, the capital. The first stop was Bitam. When we arrived we went to a village and heard the people playing balaphons, the instrument that is mother to the xylophone and vibraphone. We were so fascinated with their music that we wanted to use the balafon in one of our concerts, so we got together with them and had a rehearsal. Our host was the mayor and he looked exactly like my father. That night after the concert my son disappeared and nobody knew where he was. It was pitch dark out and we were in the bush, so naturally I got very concerned. We called the police, the army, the Peace Corps, and had everyone looking for him. Hours later he came back, accompanied by two Bitam women, but he's never told me to this day what happened or where he went that night!

When we arrived in Libreville the night after, we witnessed a fantastic ceremony in the country just outside of town. It was some kind of Catholic-African religious ceremony where the people painted their faces white, the drummers played with long, thin sticks on another stick, two on each side, and they burned this incredible incense. It was just eerie, and I'll never forget that night because I recorded the music on the small Nagra tape recorder I had brought on the trip. That night I also went out into the jungle and recorded the sounds of the insects, which was the most natural of all orchestras.

Mouila was a real scene. Radio reception there was poor, and somehow they didn't get the message that we were coming. When we landed we had to get ready to perform almost immediately, and it was screaming hot. We had to set up in the middle of town, right in front of some municipal building. By this time my poor electric piano, which I was forced to play for much of the trip because they simply didn't have pianos at many of our stops, had just about fallen apart from overuse. We struggled through and got set up for this performance. The officials had to call out to the people to gather for the concert, since the people hadn't realized we were coming. Meanwhile we met this old man playing a stringed instrument that resembled a sitar. We loved his music so much that we invited him to play with us. He played throughout the set, the blues and everything else we played. He was just beautiful, and yet another reminder of the power of music to make connections between people.

In Liberia we had some really humorous experiences. The thing I most remember is President Tubman and his executive mansion. We were to play a concert for him and he had a theater in his mansion that could only hold fifty or sixty people. That evening it was a very stiff scene. The entire audience appeared to be people over sixty. Everybody was sitting around waiting for Tubman to arrive, dressed in these nineteenth-century colonial clothes, men in top hats, the whole bit. Remember, many of the Liberians were ex-slaves who migrated there from America. Somehow they hadn't rid themselves of that colonial mentality. Liberia really appeared to be an American colony; they used dollars there and the Firestone company seemed to control everything.

We were onstage waiting, and the stage was like a movie theater stage, very narrow, so we had to stand in a single line across the stage in order to perform. All of a sudden we looked around and saw this little man approaching the theater with this big cigar in his mouth. Suddenly everybody jumped up out of their seats and came to attention. We didn't know who this guy was. Finally he made his way through with his entourage and somebody announced, "Ladies and gentlemen, His Excellency President Tubman." He walked in with his big cigar and said, "All right, ya'll can sit down now." We were all snickering at all this pomp and circumstance, especially Ed Blackwell.

After the concert they had a little reception for us, which really wasn't much considering all that formality, because all they had were drinks and peanuts. At one point Tubman walked up to me and slipped me some money as a tip for my performance, all the while telling his ministers how much he had enjoyed our performance. On such State Department tours the musicians are paid by the State Department, which didn't want any of the locals to give us money. The American ambassador later told me he knew Tubman had given me this cash; he sorta winked and allowed me to keep the loot.

Excerpts from a Liberian newspaper account of this performance (*Liberian Age*, March 10, 1967):

Audiences in Liberia found that the six-piece Weston group has a strong sense of musical colour, building a blues waltz, a powerful ballad, or more often, a catchy riff with bright splatches, exotic shadings, and a texture which can almost be felt . . .

A performance at Cuttingham College on March 3, the only one outside the capital city, drew a capacity audience of extremely enthusiastic students and faculty who showed their appreciation by giving the Sextet the longest and loudest applause of the entire series . . . Mr. Weston collected much Liberian music on tape and noted prior to his departure that his African tour will probably influence his future compositions and performances in many ways.

We arrived in Cairo, Egypt, in April, and it was one of my most memorable experiences. The concert we played there was just explosive, perhaps the most powerful performance of the whole tour. We played "African Cookbook" to end the concert, as we always did. The vibes from the Egyptian people were so strong in that theater that at a certain point when Chief Bey took his drum solo on "African Cookbook" the audience got into it and simply took the rhythm away from us with their vigorous handclaps. They were actually throwing our rhythms back at us, as if to tell us, "We know that rhythm, that's *our* rhythm," which it was, of course. Chief Bey was tired, but he simply could not stop playing the drums; they wouldn't let him stop.

The next night we played a concert in Alexandria, then we went back to Cairo to play another concert. This time an Egyptian guy came backstage to see me and said, "Mr. Weston, the American ambassador told me to ask you not to play 'African Cookbook' for the people tonight, please play some rhythm-and-blues instead!" They thought our playing "African Cookbook" was inciting the Egyptians. I told this guy, "Sorry, we don't change our music." So we played, but the vibe wasn't as strong as it had been for the first concert in Cairo. Perhaps there was just something in the air in Cairo at that time because three months later war broke out with Israel.

The ancient Sufi masters say that music precedes everything. I once met an incredible Somali poet, a Sufi named Moussa. He told me, "Music is the voice of God, music is the source of information, of creation." In other words, creation couldn't happen without music, because music is the way the universe functions. He said, "The first thing that changes is the music, when the music changes then everything else changes." And I thought about that a lot when this war broke out soon after we left Egypt. In the theater that night of our first concert in Cairo I didn't know they were getting ready to go to war, perhaps even *they* didn't know they were getting ready to go to war. But it was in the air, because the spirited way that Egyptian audience reacted when we played "African Cookbook" was like a revelation; I'd never experienced that before. We just went *out* with the rhythm, it was an incredible experience. No place else did that kind of thing happen.

We visited the Cairo museum that trip, which was really something to see, with a six-foot statue of King Tut, displaying what accurate history teaches us was his true complexion, completely black. We saw fantastic Egyptian jewelry, and saw how the Egyptians embalmed their animals and their mummies for so many thousands of years. Later we went walking around the city and went to the pyramids. But it was dark when we arrived at 10:00, which was after tourist hours. Ray Copeland paid a taxi driver to have someone turn the lights on, and when the lights came on the size of the pyramids and the Sphinx was just overwhelming.

Algeria was interesting, because at that time in 1967 some of the Black Panthers were living there; Eldridge Cleaver was there at that particular time. Algeria was very much of the East and was of great concern to our government. On these State Department tours we're considered goodwill ambassadors of the highest level because they know the musicians can hang with both the very rich and the very poor. God has given us that language of music that we can reach whole civilizations of all levels of people. That's why Louis Armstrong, Duke Ellington, Dizzy Gillespie, and all those people were so important to the State Department tours they did; they were real ambassadors.

Our arrival in Algiers was prominently featured in the newspapers.

> For the first time since independence we can hear jazz, true jazz for, in spite of what some of my friends have said, we cannot call Woody Herman's music jazz. Tuesday evening, then, at the Ibn Khaldoun Hall, the Randy Weston Sextet will give us our first jazz concert, an event not to be missed by any jazz fan. —*El Moudjahid* (Algiers), April 4, 1967

The head of the USIS at that time, Robert Behrens, welcomed us to Algiers. He showed me that article in the Algerian paper which said, "At last, the Americans are bringing some real jazz, some real African music to Algeria." He was very happy. He also told us there was an area of Algiers, known as the blue area, where Americans were not allowed. But he told us that when we came they'd open up that area to us, which they did, though I don't re-

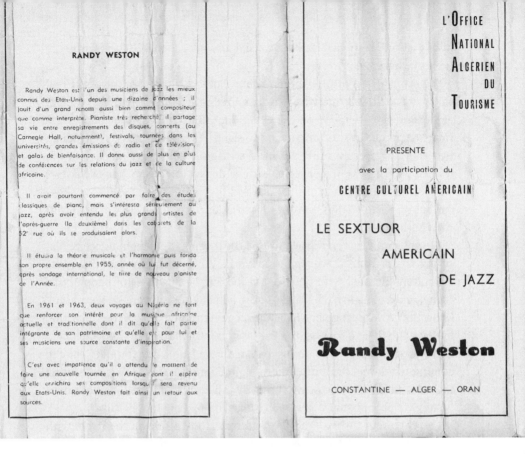

Typical tour program from State Department tour of Africa in 1967, Algiers.

member much about it; but it was a very wonderful thing to me, it showed the power of music.

Beirut, Lebanon, was simply extraordinary. First of all it's a fantastic city. They gave a big party for us, and while I'm standing there greeting people this kinda conspicuous blonde woman came over to me and said, "Mr. Weston, we're so happy to have you in Beirut and we really love your music." She said, "My name is Sabah, I'm a singer." Later on I asked somebody who she was and they said she's one of the great Arab singers. So when we got ready to leave the party I walked up to her and said I would really like to hear her sing sometime. She said, "Well, this Saturday we're having a benefit concert featuring all the great Arab artists; they're coming to Beirut to play a benefit for orphaned children." Again, another example of our natural responsibilities as musicians; you see this in Africa, you see it everywhere.

Sabah arranged to pick me up at my hotel at 8:00. I got dressed real sharp and told Azzedin, who was napping in the bed at the time, "C'mon, get up and go with me so we can experience this night of Arab culture." He said, "No, pop, I'm tired and I want to sleep." I went downstairs and Sabah was standing there waiting, wearing a magnificent caftan, decked out in jewels. We went out to her big chauffeur-driven limousine, her two sisters were sitting in the back of the limo and they were decked out too. These caftans they had on must have cost thousands of dollars. I'd never seen stuff like this before.

We got in the car and drove to this theater for the benefit concert, featuring artists from all over the Arab world. When we arrived the place was absolutely jammed with people. I'm looking at this mass of people, this scene, and asking myself, "What in the hell am I doing here?" Next thing I know the crowd recognized Sabah and came running over to our limousine and actually began rocking the car, pressing their faces to the windshield and the side windows. Coming out of my culture, I'm thinking they're coming to get me. I'm sitting there in panic mode. This mob is screaming in Arabic and I don't know what they're talking about. I said, "What's happening?" Sabah casually said, "Oh, those are just my fans."

The chauffeur turned the car around and took off down the street with people bouncing all over the place. He raced off and drove around to the back of the theater in the dark somewhere, parked the car, and told her, "I'll be right back I'm going to find out what's the best way to get you in this theater." So we're sitting in the dark talking and I'm thinking to myself, "Man, what kinda scene am I in now?" Next thing we know we see two or three guys walking in the shadows, they see our car, recognize Sabah, and here come these cats again. The door was slightly open and we were struggling trying to close it, it was like a scene out of a Charlie Chaplin movie. I was tripping out. Finally the chauffeur ran back to the car and we took off down the street.

When we eventually got into the theater the Lebanese army was holding the people back on both sides of a red carpet. What kinda scene is this!? We got outta the car and I'm walking with these three women, one a major star. This scene was like science fiction to me. We got inside the theater and she took me backstage to introduce me to all these great Arab singers, dancers, and so forth. When it came time for Sabah to go on I noticed her pacing back and forth. I asked, "Are you all right?" She said, "I always get nervous before I perform." That struck me, because sometimes you don't even know you're getting nervous, but you've gotta go out there like everything is cool.

She sang beautifully, and you know how those Arab singers are; they hit a note and it takes a half-hour to get to the bottom. She was wonderful. After the concert we all got back in the limo and drove to this nightclub that must have held about five hundred people. I walked in with these three ladies and all of a sudden everybody in the nightclub got up and began applauding. The next day I went to her house and hung out with her. This place was opulent, with emeralds in the ashtray and rugs so thick and plush that when you stepped on them it was like you were sinking down into a hole. We had a good laugh when she told me they all wanted to know who this black guy was that she'd been with the night before.

Our band played at the American university in Beirut twice.

From a State Department memo from the American embassy in Beirut, dated April 14, 1967:

> Both concerts were smash successes. On March 20, the sextet presented their "History of Jazz" concert to an audience of approximately 700 persons, most of them students. Numbers were frequently interrupted by applause and Escort Officer Harry Hirsch stated after the performance that the group had received its best reception of the tour. The next morning the French daily *Le Jour* carried a picture of the concert of its first page and the following comment by its music critic, one of the two or three most respected in Lebanon: "Finally, some jazz! Pure, true presented brilliantly, raucously, modulatedly . . . making every note afire . . . Randy Weston and his Sextet presented last night at A.U.B. a perfect lesson on true jazz, its African ancestry and its development today, tracing through spirituals, blues, swing, bop and 'free jazz' all the particulars which make this Negro American music the 'chant profound' of the whole world. Randy Weston and his musicians explode with the joy of living and playing. Go hear them Wednesday: it's not every day that we are able to hear other than the pale byproducts of jazz."

I met some Palestinian people and they took me to a Palestinian refugee camp. I saw the suffering of these people, which touched me very deeply. I also met some of the young Palestinian poets and writers and met some composers, including one who had invented a piano on which you could add more notes between the keys to play Arabic music.

The last stop on our tour was Morocco, where we played a concert in Rabat. Ed Blackwell took a tremendous drum solo during the concert and the audience went nuts. Blackwell being from New Orleans, everything he played was danceable, no matter how complicated the rhythms were.

From a memo from the U.S. Information Service office in Rabat:

In a country where American jazz rouses endless enthusiasm, but where it is usually purveyed by other nationalities (even Yugoslavs), the Weston group clearly established American superiority in the jazz field . . . It also received triple exposure over Moroccan radio. The radio, which played the VOA promotion tape prior to the group's arrival, originally planned only one broadcast of the concert tape, but gave in to a barrage of letters and phone calls (even threats) for a second airing of "the greatest moment in Moroccan jazz history."

One of our stops in Morocco was in Marrakech. They took us to the central square, Jemmaa-al-Fna, where you see the snake charmers, storytellers, soothsayers, and all kinds of interesting sights. We came upon a guy with this big bag on his shoulder, and in this bag he had all kinds of different snakes. When he saw us coming he took some of the snakes and put them in his shirt. There's one particular snake they used for tourists, I guess this snake was friendly. In Morocco they are very persuasive people.

This guy told us, "Our tradition here is you've gotta put this snake around your neck so we can take a photograph." We all looked at each other because none of us wanted to be a punk about this, we're all bad dudes and it's a question of our manhood involved here. This cat insisted that we do this. I didn't go first but I took my turn. Finally the last one was Clifford Jordan, and we could tell Clifford didn't want any part of this snake stuff. But Clifford was this bad Chicago dude and he knew he couldn't have the rest of the guys thinking he was punkin' out. Finally Clifford asked, "Is this part of the program?" In unison we all said, "Yeah." So Clifford very reluctantly put this snake around his neck, just like the rest of us, and allowed them to take a photograph. But just the thought of that sucker hanging around your neck was enough to shake anyone.

When our Morocco trip concluded it was the end of the tour, the band returned to the States, and I stayed behind for a few days to complete my State Department final report. This tour had really gotten my juices flowing; I was now totally dedicated to living in Africa. My first thought was Nigeria, but because the Biafra war was going on at that point Nigeria didn't look too promising.

The following is excerpted from an article that appeared in the July 13, 1966, issue of *DownBeat* magazine and is excerpted courtesy of *DownBeat*:

*With Randy Weston in Africa By Georgia Griggs*

This was one of those State Department overseas "cultural presentation" tours that jazz groups get sent on occasionally. This one was by the Randy Weston Sextet. For three months, from mid-January to mid-April they visited 10 countries in West Africa (Senegal, Mali, Upper Volta, Niger, Ghana, Cameroon, Gabon, Liberia, Sierra Leone, Ivory Coast) one in the Middle East (Lebanon), and three in North Africa (United Arab Republic, Algeria, Morocco).

They were accompanied by a State Department escort, whose duty it was to get us, our instruments, our baggage, and the tour equipment in and out of places; to act as liaison between us and the local U.S. personnel; and to keep an eye on our behavior and appearance at concerts and receptions and dinners given in honor of the group's visit.

The main thing wrong was the attitude of our escort and of some of the local U.S. personnel (though I hasten to add this applies only to a few, not by any means the majority) to Weston's music and toward our audiences. We were warned that African audiences would respond only to Dixieland numbers or to loud drum solos and had no comprehension of or affinity for any other manifestation of American jazz, especially modern jazz, and that we shouldn't expect too much from them, or play anything too difficult or sophisticated.

"Remember, they're not as sophisticated as U.S. audiences," we were told repeatedly, especially by our escort officer, a great jazz authority who wouldn't have been able to tell Coltrane from Beiderbecke, and undoubtedly had never seen a jazz audience in the U.S.

This puzzled us, because we assumed that one of the reasons Weston's group had been chosen to go to Africa was his interest in (and incorporation of) African rhythms and themes, which all the State Department and USIS people knew about. They had received advance detailed information about the music as well as Weston's latest record, and many of them had seen a recent 10-minute film that had been distributed throughout West Africa. In December, those in charge of the program in Washington had seen the group in concert, playing just what they'd be playing on the tour. If they knew what they wanted and knew what they were getting, why did they try to make us feel the sextet should have been a Dixieland band or a drum troupe?

The audiences did love "The Saints Go Marching In," which was played as part of the History of Jazz concert the band did as one of the two standard concerts presented on the tour, the other being a program of Weston's compositions, and they certainly liked the drum solos by Blackwell and Bey; but don't U.S. audiences respond the same way?

The Africans also responded very warmly to the blues in any form, to many relatively complex Weston compositions, to Basie and Ellington swing-era numbers, and to Wood's bass solos, Copeland's trumpet solos, Jordan's tenor solos, and even Weston's piano solos (though, I must admit, not as often).

The number they liked best—everywhere we went—was a Weston composition entitled "African Cookbook," which combines African rhythms, Middle Eastern melodic concepts, and just plain jazz—and which is long (usually running a half hour or so) and is considered "far out" by some non-African listeners.

That same patronizing attitude was also reflected in an inability on the part of some Americans to understand why the band members were so eager to hear African tribal music and to meet local African musicians and people interested in African culture. After all, if you believe that Africans are culturally deprived—and anyone who hasn't been sufficiently exposed to U.S. culture, whether he's in Harlem or Upper Volta, is automatically deprived as far as these people are concerned—what could they possibly do or achieve that could be of interest to Americans?

The men in the band were perfectly capable of making their own contacts to hear local music and meet local people, even if there wasn't official cooperation in any given city, so these attitudes didn't substantially interfere with what was really happening on the tour.

The other main problem was the tiny electric piano that Weston had to use whenever there was no regular piano available. This instrument (in this case a euphemism for "toy") was totally unsuitable for a pianist-leader, or for any pianist who plays with strength or who wants to express ideas. At times, it sounded like a grossly overamplified guitar, at others like the cheapest electric organ, and it could never be gotten into proper balance with the other instruments. Not only did it sound dreadful, but it looked absurd when Weston—all 6 feet 7 inches of him—sat down at it.

But what really counted was the music the band played, the music and dances of the Africans, the African people themselves, the beautiful interaction between band and audiences, the experience of just being there.

A million scenes crowd in—voices, faces, music, rhythms, food, beauty—and of course, some pettiness, misunderstanding, and inconvenience too. But best remembered are the vibrancy and the beauty, which the band absorbed and—even if in a small way—enhanced by its presence. The State Department can't be all bad if it was responsible for an experience like that!

The following review, excerpted with permission, appeared in the June 29, 1967, edition of *DownBeat* magazine, in a section titled "Caught in the Act":

*Randy Weston, Freetown University, Freetown, Sierra Leone*

It was one of those warm, sultry evenings typical of a tropical night. There had been a lot of publicity on radio and television and in the papers and the audience was a reasonably large one. The occasion was a concert by the Randy Weston Sextet, sponsored by the U.S. Embassy in conjunction with the U.S. Information Agency.

Amid the hubbub of expectancy, the concert started about 25 minutes late because of last-minute efforts to get Weston a piano on which he could be "heard." He had been lugging a knocked-about "mini" piano over half the continent. However efforts failed, and Weston had to be content with his portable.

The concert demonstrated that Weston's music has adequately welded the tonal and modal expressions of African rhythms and music with those of jazz. The group exuded such rapport and cohesiveness with the leader, along with individual expertise, that none could doubt their belief in their work. The audience was stirred to its roots by the echoes of the indigenous environment and established complete rapport with the musicians.

At the conclusion of the concert, the audience gave the sextet a standing ovation. The scene was pandemonium.

The music itself was sometimes ethereal, sometimes ephemeral, alternately mystic or full of hot, throbbing sensations evoking ancient rituals. It was sometimes down-to-earth, sometimes plain funky and mean, and sometimes arch, with dynamic and strident Ellingtonian overtones. The musicians are as fine a group of gentlemen as ever came out of the United States. They were fitting ambassadors.—Dr. E. Otis Pratt

## Randy Weston's Official Post-tour Report to the State Department (excerpted)

*1. Estimate of the Tour's Success*
. . . Our tour was a very successful one. As we saw it, our purpose was to perform our music for African audiences and to establish contact with Afri-

cans not only through our music but through our interest in their music and culture . . .

A. *The type of music my group plays*
. . . Although most of our audiences were not educated or sophisticated in regard to American jazz, they have a basic feeling for the music because of its relationship to their own music. And since we emphasize this relationship not only in our History of Jazz program but in the African-inspired pieces we play in our regular program, I think there was, truly, a real rapport established with our audiences, even by the supposedly unsophisticated ones.

B. *The attitude of the musicians*
Each man in the group is so genuinely interested in all aspects of American life, culture and people that he could establish rapport with the people off the stand as well as on. This isn't necessarily a matter of color, but of sincerity and genuineness of interest, for we believe that Africans generally respond warmly to anyone — of whatever color, nationality or background — who is honestly interested in them and respects their own culture and way of life. Many times we arranged trips on our own to hear local music (in Accra and Freetown, for example) and were very enthusiastic whenever the posts went to the trouble to make such arrangements for us. Thus the desire of the members of my band and myself to learn from as well as share with the African people we met can be considered a real factor in the tour's success in addition to the goodwill created by the concerts themselves. This is attested to by the fact that we were often told that African government officials were unusually willing to attend both our concerts and the receptions held in our honor . . .

C. *Help and understanding on the part of U.S. Government*
*personnel at most of the posts visited*
Wherever the aims of the tour were understood and supported by the local posts our job was made much easier and our presence more effective. The highlight of the tour, in this respect, was Gabon, where Ambassador Bane and his staff were fully in accord with what we considered to be the real, underlying aims of the tour . . . Also to be mentioned in particular are the late Ambassador Rivkin, in Senegal, whose encouragement at the very beginning of the tour helped reinforce our own determination; Marshall Berg and Owen Roberts in Ouagadougou, who had a group of local tribal musicians play for us

at a party held in our honor there, which was a scene of great warmth and sharing . . .

D. *Encouragement and response from Africans*

We were also heartened because so many of the Africans (and Europeans who had made Africa their home) we met and talked to told us that they were really pleased that we were interested in their music, were incorporating it into our own and were so willing to meet, talk to and perform with local tribal musicians . . .

[Here we skip past the sections dealing with day-to-day tour logistics to Randy's sense of the tour's assigned State Department escort, with whom Weston had several differences.]

6. *Other advance information*

C. *State Department escort*

We would have liked to know just what the functions of the escort were and how much authority he had over which areas of the tour. We assumed that he was to act as liaison between us and the local U.S. personnel, at least until we got to know them ourselves; take care of travel arrangements and getting the tour equipment, luggage and us in and out of places; set up and operate the sound equipment; help us with any problems that might arise concerned with traveling; share with us his more extensive knowledge of traveling and the countries being visited; and keep an eye out regarding our appearance and behavior at concerts and other official appearances and be aware of any major real or potential problems among the group and deal with them in an effective way if they arose. In some areas our escort was admirable, but in others he was a distinct stumbling block and occasionally antagonized not only us but local U.S. personnel. He often offered disparaging opinions regarding the music and wearing apparel during off-duty hours, complained about things that had nothing to do with the tour, and was generally inflexible when it came to dealing with members of the group, collectively and individually, thus creating unnecessary resentments where none would have existed otherwise. Sometimes, in areas where he was right and his observations and suggestions entirely valid, his attitude and manner of dealing with us were so inconsiderate and inappropriate that his opinions weren't respected. And, worst of all, he seemed to have a general disdain for what we considered to be the main purpose of the tour—that is, to establish rapport with the African people in order to share our cultures and to encourage understanding between the peoples of their countries and ours. Group morale is very important on a tour such as this, and the men in the band worked hard, both on the bandstand and off (even though they enjoyed their work), and it was demoralizing to be subjected to unnecessary criticism and tension as it tended to distract us from our main purpose and caused us all to waste time and energy on matters that could have been handled easily and tactfully . . . It is a shame that the United States ever sends people with what we (and many Africans) consider to be "colonial" mentalities any place overseas, for they make a very bad impression on nearly everyone who meets them.

### 111. Further Thoughts

. . . The idea of the Cultural Presentation tours is a fine one, but it could be deepened and expanded along the line I've mentioned and be much more effective. U.S. artists actually living among the people and working with them could have an impact no group passing through for a few days could ever hope to have. After talking to many Africans in every country we visited about this I feel that such a program would be enthusiastically accepted everywhere, even in those countries supposedly unfriendly toward the United States. There are, really, unlimited possibilities in such a program. It might seem far-fetched now, but I'm sure at one point the Peace Corps seemed far fetched too, although it has come a long way and done a great deal of good in very concrete ways.

## 10

Son, never forget what you are. You're an African. Though you were born here in the United States of America, you are an African. An African born in America, do you understand? Your motherland, the home of your ancestors, is Africa. Wherever you travel all over this planet, you must always come back to her. Africa is the past, the present and the future. Africa is the four cardinal points: the North, the South, where the sun rises and where it sets.—FRANK EDWARD WESTON, as conveyed to his son Randy Weston from childhood

## MAKING A HOME IN AFRICA

During the mid-late 1960s, when I began to seriously contemplate making a life in Africa, considering my two earlier trips there, Nigeria was naturally my first choice. It was an English-speaking country, so I figured there wouldn't be a communication barrier; most of the educated people in Nigeria spoke English, and I had gotten to know many people, from the governor general to various Nigerians in television and radio, sculptors, painters, and assorted other artists. Nigeria just seemed the most obvious African country for me to migrate to.

There were other possibilities on the continent as well. At that time, largely because of the successful independence movement there in '59 and the charisma of Kwame Nkrumah, Ghana was then the most celebrated African nation in New York. I had many Ghanaian friends at the time. But Nigeria still presented the most obvious migration possibilities to me since I had such positive experiences there, including friendships with Nigerian musicians like Fela Kuti and Bobby Benson. I had recorded Bobby's tune "Niger Mambo," so there were many reasons why Nigeria was the most obvious place in my mind. The Nigerians had really impressed me with the pride they had in their culture, and I was so impressed with the art there. It really is a fantastic country; the climate is great as well. But the Biafra war raging at that time was a real deterrent, so that took care of that, and I never really came close to moving to Nigeria.

Besides my lifelong fascination with Africa, stemming first from my father's teachings, there were some negative factors related to the music scene in the U.S. at the time that I found personally distasteful or troubling which increased my desire to move to the continent. When the Beatles came on the Ed Sullivan show and I saw the hysterical reaction to their music, I saw everybody flipping out about that music, I said to myself: "Oh, man, black music in America is in trouble now." At the same time, the jazz scene in the mid-late '60s—at least as far as the press and the critics were concerned—was being heavily infiltrated with a growing fascination for what they referred to as free or avant-garde jazz, not that the musicians who were labeled that way would have agreed with those labels.

What exactly is free jazz? For me the freest jazz I ever heard was Louis Armstrong. I never heard anybody play freer than him. The very concept of free can be intricate things, different kinds of things, which I have no problem with. But when it comes to free, with jazz, we must never lose touch with our ancestors, because every note, all that music we had been playing up to that point was really for freedom because we were under serious oppression between the slavery and the very powerful, mental and physical racism. Jazz is freedom music at its root. So I had to ask myself, "What are they talking about 'free' jazz?" It was like when they came up with what they called *cool* jazz, when Miles Davis came out with Gerry Mulligan and *The Birth of the Cool*, playing those relaxed tempos, and all of a sudden everybody was saying, "Be cool when you play, don't sweat when you play . . . ," be like the Europeans in essence. But with us we sweat . . . so that notion didn't really work for black musicians in general, at least not as I saw it amongst my peers. So these labels, like free or avant-garde, or cool jazz, which have largely been convenient for the press, haven't held much meaning for me.

Despite all this critical euphoria over what they were calling free or avant-garde jazz, when I heard what they were referring to it didn't excite me in the least and seemed so opposite black music. Coupled with other disturbing things I was witnessing, I really got turned off to the music scene in the U.S. and began turning my thoughts more and more toward Africa and an African existence. I really began to feel as though I needed to remove myself from all that. One night I saw Max Roach's band opposite Dave Brubeck's quartet at a club in New York, I was appalled at how the audience seemed to completely overlook Max's mastery and went wild for Brubeck's so-called cool sound. It struck me that the collective audience was losing its taste for black culture, for what makes our music unique, what makes the music that black people produce different than other kinds of music; and I truly wanted to stay in that tradition. But in the U.S. we seemed to be drifting away from that in so many ways.

Nobody wrote more great music than Ellington, and I don't care what Duke played or wrote—you always heard the blues underneath. He wrote for the queen of England, he wrote for the emperor of China, but you'd always hear the blues underneath. For me, the blues feeling is *us*, it's what makes our music unique; and to be modern you don't have to play *free* or play a lot of notes. Our masters proved that: look at Count Basie or Thelonious Monk. The music I was hearing at this time, which really was captivating the press and in many respects the audience itself, seemed to be getting away from our basic traditions. When we play for people it's supposed to be a spiritual, healing process. It can be done with Coleman Hawkins playing "Body and Soul"; it could be Clifford Brown playing "I Remember April."

There's a certain romance, a certain love in our music, a certain emotion despite all the adversity we've faced. When you hear Coltrane with Duke and they play "My Little Brown Book," there's a certain romance, and *that's* what I wasn't hearing in the music anymore. We were taught that to play jazz you gotta be able to play the blues, you gotta be able to play for a woman, to romance her. I felt that the music of that time in the 1960s was getting more and more like machines with the electronics that were also entering the scene, and those other things. If you don't have a pretty sound it just doesn't reach the people. The music was getting more and more western, for me it was getting away from the so-called black tradition, that *feeling*. So those were some of the music scene factors that sealed my desire to migrate to Africa, at the same time and for many of the same reasons that some of my peers were pulling up stakes and moving to Europe. Ironically my migration point was not to Europe or what for me might seem to be the more obvious West Africa, but North Africa.

One month after returning from Morocco after our 1964 tour stop there, I got a letter from the USIS in Morocco saying the Moroccan people are completely crazy about your music and they want you to come back. Our final concert on that 1964 tour, after three months on the road in Africa, was in Morocco. During our performance Ed Blackwell took one of those classic drum solos that just drove the Moroccan people crazy. When I came back

Performance in Tangier.
From left: Randy, Bill Woods, Ed Blackwell, Azzedin Weston.

to New York after the tour I found that the Moroccan people had been writing letters that were forwarded to me from the USIS office in Rabat, saying they were still talking about our concert and they wanted me to come back. So I later figured out Morocco chose me, I didn't choose Morocco. This letter I got after our appearance there pretty much sums up the Moroccan response.

> The Foreign Service of the United States of America
> May 11, 1967
> Rabat, Morocco
>
> Dear Randy,
> It's been nearly a month since you left Morocco, and the fans are still roaring . . . As you know, Radio Maroc broadcast the Agdal Theater performance . . . once. The fans are outraged! The DJ has received about 100 phone calls and letters asking for a second airing of the tape, including one letter from Marrakech in which a young listener literally threatened the DJ if he did not play again "this greatest moment in Moroccan jazz history."

The radio has decided to run the tape again. But more than this, our office has been besieged with demands that you come back to Morocco June 22 for the USIS-sponsored "1967 Festival du Jazz" at the American Embassy gardens in Rabat.

When you were here, you mentioned the possibility of going to Beirut this summer for a private engagement. You also suggested you might be able to stop over in Morocco on your way.

Do you think you could arrange to be here June 22 for the Jazz Festival? You'd really make the show, and placate 2,500 wildly enthusiastic fans.

Again, the Weston sound at the Embassy gardens would be a real sensation. We'd love to see you back, and await your soonest reply.

Best regards,
Charles L. Bell
American Embassy

One thing led to another, and by 1967 I was finally ready to make the move. At the time I was living in the apartment on 13th Street in Manhattan that I had gotten from Ramona Low and Adele Glasgow, Langston Hughes's friends. In preparation for leaving I was able to transfer the lease on that apartment to Booker Ervin and his family. So everything in that apartment, my piano and all the furniture, I left with Booker Ervin and his family. The only things I took with me to Morocco besides my clothes were my papers, books, and music. And because I wanted them to experience life in Africa firsthand I took my children, Pamela and Niles, to live with me there. And this was despite the fact that I didn't really know anything about Moroccan culture. The vibrations and the spirits were just right. Morocco was calling.

When I arrived in Morocco in '67 I found there was such a great appreciation there for the music that I became involved with their culture almost immediately. They have such a diversity of music, from the Atlas Mountains to the Sahara Desert, so I was always looking for their traditions. There's a tendency on the part of some folks to feel that Western culture, or the Americanization of things, is supreme. That might mean that a McDonald's becomes more important than the traditional cuisine, like the traditional Moroccan tagine (or stew) for example. Because the West has dominated the world they've also created a kind of musical colonialism in a way; you'll find American pop music almost everywhere you go. The Moroccans were very protective of their musical traditions, and that really appealed to me, drew me deeper into their culture.

When we first got to Morocco, after landing in Casablanca, we went straight to Rabat, because that had been where the concert that was our last tour stop in '67 had taken place and it was also where those many letters had come from the USIS office, so it seemed like a natural first stop. Besides, it's the capital city of Morocco. We wound up staying in Rabat for one year, and if it weren't for one very important factor involving my kids I might still be there, but I'm getting ahead of myself.

The American ambassador at that time, based in Rabat, was a Greek-American named Henry Tasca, and he was very much in tune with my music. There was also a brother stationed there who was one of the deputies at the U.S, embassy, a man named Bill Powell. Bill was interested in helping me find my way there, and in helping me to create a base for African music in Morocco; to eventually have bases, or cultural centers, in different parts of the African world where people could come and study the culture, learn about it, take pride in it, and encourage the young people to continue the culture. That was my major goal in coming there. So we stayed in Rabat because there were people there who were willing to help me with my projects. I didn't know anybody in Casablanca, I had just met some people there, but Rabat was like the center. It's not as large as Casablanca but it's a very beautiful city.

Embassy of the United States of America
July 18, 1968
Mr. Randy Weston
Villa no. 3
Route des Zaers, km 3.800
Rabat

Dear Randy:
Since your first performance in Morocco in 1967, I have followed your career with great interest and much admiration. I feel that you are making an important original contribution both in your research on African folk music and in your original compositions inspired by African themes and adapted from African rhythms. I have been particularly pleased with the enthusiastic reception which your compositions based upon Moroccan themes, such as the "Marrakech Blues," have had in Morocco.

I am sure that the benefits which will be derived from your research work on African folk music will be of major significance. As you so very well understand, Africans must be helped to rediscover their own music.

They must learn to value their folk music, as you value it, realizing that the music of no other civilization can rival African music in the complexity and subtlety of its rhythms. At the same time, your research will help Americans to understand more fully the great debt that American jazz, blues, and spirituals owe to African music. Inevitably, the result of your work can only draw the African and American continents closer together. I feel that you are uniquely qualified to carry out this important work. Your great talent as a composer and as a jazz pianist, combined with the warmth of your own personality, have won you friends wherever you have gone. You have been of great assistance to the American mission in Rabat, and I hope you will be able to continue work in Morocco for many years to come.

With warmest best wishes,
Sincerely,
Henry J. Tasca
American Ambassador to Morocco

I met a man named Lahcen who owned a restaurant in Rabat called Jour Nuit (Day-Night), and he also owned a hotel right on the beach. When I came to Morocco after they had persistently asked me to come back, I went back with a trio, with Ed Blackwell on drums and Bill Wood on bass. We played at the Hotel Rex and this guy Lahcen was very interested in the idea of opening up a nightclub with me.

One thing I had observed from my travels in Africa was that many of the prominent musicians there, guys like Fela and Bobby Benson in Nigeria, owned their own clubs. This gave them a base of operations and the opportunity to present music and musicians they favored. I was really into the idea of owning my own club; little did I know then what a headache that can be. But back then I thought it would be a great idea because I wanted to have a place where I could present *our* culture, the way *we* approach music, the way we approach life. That's why I stayed in Rabat that year. Lahcen and I spent about a year negotiating this club deal, but ultimately it never happened, for one reason or another.

We stayed in the Hotel Rex for three months, and then I had to get a house because I was able to arrange for my children Pam and Niles to come over and join me after getting my divorce and gaining custody. Plus Ed Blackwell and his wife and three children were with us and we needed the space. I met a chauffeur for one of the Moroccan government ministers and he arranged for us to rent a house just outside Rabat. We all shared this house, Pamela, Niles, Bill Wood, Ed Blackwell, and his wife and three little children, all in one house. It was a two-family Moroccan house and everybody had a bed.

Besides making plans to open up this club we had also arranged through a Moroccan organization called DIAFA and the minister of culture to do a tour with the sextet. Ultimately they couldn't afford to bring the sextet so we went a few places as a trio. We performed in Rabat, Casablanca, Zagora, Erfoud in the Sahara, and Marrakech, on about a three-week tour of Morocco. The Americans wanted to solicit the other places we had performed in Africa for return engagements because we were a big success on that 1967 tour. America always needs that good image through art and culture, so we were ideal; we were African American, nobody was a drunk, and we were always on time. We did a little playing here and a little there, but the main gigs didn't happen so the tour idea fizzled out. As usual with musicians there were many plans for the next gig, but those next gigs were few and far between. And since I wanted to put my children in school and had learned that the best American school in the country was in Tangier, we moved there after that first year in Rabat. If it weren't for that school I would have stayed in Rabat.

In retrospect it's difficult to see how we sustained ourselves in Rabat that first year. But the rents were very cheap at that time and our basic needs, like food and things, were very inexpensive. And like I said, I arrived in Morocco with a few dollars because I was determined to live in Africa, so I had a little backup.

Tangier is right across the Mediterranean Sea from Spain and it isn't very far from Portugal, so it's a real international city. I met a lot of so-called American expatriates hanging out in Tangier, people like the writers Allen Ginsberg, Paul Bowles, and others, who all appeared to be looking for something, I don't know what. But they all lived in Tangier at the time, which made it even more of an international city. Besides that these artists and writers seemed genuinely interested in having someone like me, a so-called jazz musician, coming from the States to live there.

When we first arrived in Tangier I arranged to move into an apartment that had about four rooms, so both the kids and I had our own rooms. In Rabat I had a Moroccan woman named Khadija who did all the cooking and cleaning in our house, and I was able to bring her with us to Tangier for a short time. Eventually we were able to rent a big house right on the beach through an American guy who must have been about eighty years old and had been living in Morocco a long time. It was a nice place with three terraces facing the Mediterranean. I hired a Jillalah chieftess named Haemo to be the cook of the house and take care of us. The Jillalah are like the Gnawa, another Moroccan spiritual sect which I interacted with later. Haemo was a very strong woman and a superb cook. Each morning she'd go to the market and buy that day's fresh food. We lived in that house for over two years, with no telephone.

At the time I was going with a French woman named Genevieve McMillan who had some money from investments and was totally into African art. She and I talked with this old guy and rented this great house. These days Genevieve has a major collection of African art. She lends things out to museums all over the world. We got along well, but in the end she didn't get along with my children so she had to go. She gave me an ultimatum, "It's either me or them," that kind of thing, so I said "Bye." We split and left the house to her. The kids and I wound up moving to a small apartment, then to another very nice apartment on Boulevard de Paris. It was in a pretty modern apartment house, with four rooms, very spacious, lots of sunshine.

The American school was my major motivation for moving to Tangier, it wasn't like I had been promised any gigs there. We did manage to play a couple of concerts, played a gig for the Hot Club of France in the city of Meknes, played at a couple of hotels and that kind of thing. Many people I met in Tangier were deeply into the arts and culture and there was a lot of talk about opening a jazz club in town, but for me it was just a challenge finding a useful piano, much less the commitment to act on such plans. The first year there I didn't make any real money.

I felt like I was on a scouting trip because I wasn't able to do very much playing. In '67 I had become friendly with a guy from the USIS office in Tangier, a very nice guy who was a writer. Once again we tried in vain to hook up a tour of Africa through the USIS that fell apart at the last minute.

Wherever I go in the world I'm always interested in connecting with, or at least hearing, traditional music and musicians, and Morocco was no exception. The first of the Moroccan spiritual brotherhoods I connected with was the Jillalah, who I met through my friend Abdeslaam, who was a government police official at the time and who loved the music. I met him in a bar through a woman named Trudy from Vienna, Austria. She had her own club where they would play Viennese waltzes and sing. He immediately said, "Man, I've got your record *Uhuru Afrika*." I was shocked! Abdeslaam soon invited me to his house, and I met his gorgeous wife Khadijah, who was a great cook; I had my first home-cooked dinner in Tangier at their house.

From that point on Abdeslaam and I were partners, we became one with his family. He's the one responsible for introducing me to the Jillalah, he and a Moroccan named Muhammad Zane. This was about the time I was just getting that house, and they introduced me to Haemo, the Jillalah woman I hired to take care of the house. She was a strong Riff Mountain Berber woman; there was nothing glamorous about her. So because of her there would often be Jillalah musicians at the house. Jillalah is a Sufi sect; they see their instrument as a direct communication with Allah. They play these end-blown flutes called a qsbah or gisbah, and drums called bendir; that's their way of communicating with the Creator.

There actually were three spiritual Moroccan musical traditions I connected with. Another was the Joujouka, who Ornette Coleman later connected with and made a record with. The Swiss writer Brion Gysin was part of that European and American writers' circle in Tangier, along with Paul Bowles and those guys. Brion was very much into the music. Through him I heard about this village in the Riff Mountains called Joujouka. By this time in '67 everybody I was in contact with knew of my interests in connecting with the traditional musicians. Mel O'Connell, from the U.S. consulate, would arrange for government cars to take us to particular villages to hear the traditional music, so we all went up to Joujouka together.

For the trip to Joujouka you drive to a certain point where the mountain starts to rise and cars can't go any further, so you either go by donkey or you walk. Joujouka is a village that has no electricity; it's really soul Morocco, with a beautiful view of the surrounding mountains. The Joujouka musicians are healers; they play a double-reed instrument called the ghaita, kind of like an oboe, and they play those frame drums called bendir. They worship the god Pan, the god of flute. They have certain ceremonies where they prepare for three days or more. One of their mystics dresses in goatskin; they create huge bonfires and play their own Joujouka rhythms. People go into a trance and jump through the fire, and they also have a special room where they treat people for various illnesses by using that cold mountain water accompanied by certain tones they get out of their instruments. I've never had that experience so I can't tell you what happens, but the Joujouka are reputed to be great healers. We spent three wonderful days with the Joujouka, enjoying the ceremony, the music, the dance, we ate fresh eggs, completely fresh food, the cooking was wonderful, and I thoroughly enjoyed being with the Joujouka. But ultimately the Moroccan spiritual people I connected with most deeply were the Gnawa.

Randy Weston at twelve in Brooklyn,
wearing his "first pair of long pants."

Randy's Berkshires Trio: Sam Gill, bass, Willie Jones, drums,
Frank Heppenstall, saxophone, circa 1950s.

Randy at the piano rehearsing with
Babatunde Olatunji (talking drum) during the AMSAC trip, 1961;
Bobby Benson is standing at far left (with cap).
*Courtesy of Moorland-Spingarn Library, Howard University.*

Randy with President Azikwe and delegation from the historic AMSAC tour to Nigeria, 1961. *Courtesy of Moorland-Spingarn Library, Howard University.*

Randy (top step) and delegation arrive at the state dinner with President Azikwe (in white). *Courtesy of Moorland-Spingarn Library, Howard University.*

Randy (middle) with members of the AMSAC delegation to Nigeria, 1961, including the soprano Martha Flowers (to his right) and the dancer and choreographer Geoffrey Holder. *Courtesy of Moorland-Spingarn Library, Howard University.*

Part of the AMSAC delegation about to embark on its historic journey to Nigeria, 1961, including Randy (third from left) and (from his immediate left) Nina Simone, Martha Flowers, and Ahmed Abdul Malik. *Courtesy of Moorland-Spingarn Library, Howard University.*

Randy Weston, piano, and Booker Ervin, his tenor saxophonist (sax in lap), performing with Lionel Hampton's band in Nigeria during the AMSAC tour of Nigeria. *Courtesy of Moorland-Spingarn Library, Howard University.*

On tour of Africa in Gabon, 1967.

Randy with
Professor Opaku,
University of Legon,
Ghana.

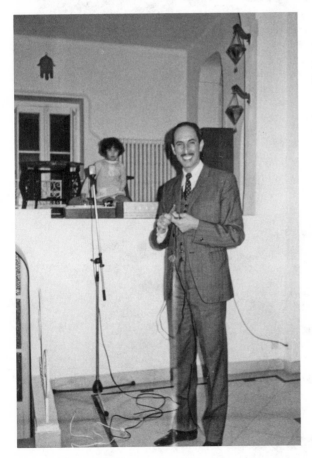

Randy's partner
in the African
Rhythms Club
(Tangier),
Abdeslaam
Akaaboune.

Gnawa musicians and Randy
at Randy's home in Tangier,
circa 1967.

Randy with Gnawa musicians at Randy's home in Tangier, circa 1967.

Randy's oldest Gnawa friend and collaborator, Abdullah El Gourde, with his guimbre, circa 1969.

Randy in concert with Mohamed Zain (flute),
Abdullah El Gourde (guimbre), and Yeiki
(dancer), Tangier, circa June 1970.

(*opposite*)
The night Fatou first heard Randy in concert.
From left: the bluesman Johnny Copeland;
TK Blue, saxophonist; Ahmed Ben Outman,
Gnawa musician.

Randy's African Queen: Fatoumata Mbengue.

From left: unidentified man, Aunt Carey (in fur coat), unidentified man, Dad (in coat and tie), Randy, Mom (wearing white scarf), Randy's sister Gladys (holding cup), family friend Scott Gibson.

At recording session for The Splendid Master Gnawa Musician for Verve
Records, Mamounia Hotel, Marrakech, circa 1994.

Randy and Melba Liston onstage at the Montreal Jazz Festival, July 1995. *Courtesy of Diane Moon.*

Randy with his old friend Richard Jennings, his key United Nations contact as he laid the groundwork for the Uhuru Afrika recording session.

(*facing pages*) Some of Randy's closest spiritual
mentors and advisors

Randy and Fatou with Aime Cesaire

Randy and Mahi Ishmail.

Dr. Ben

Wayne Chandler and Randy backstage
at the Ancient Future concert, Lincoln
Center, circa 2006

Dr. John Henrik Clarke and Sybil Williams Clarke, circa 1997

Randy (*center*) with members of his Marrakech Gnawa family, including Ahmed Ben Outhman (*fifth from left*), M'Barek Ben Outhman (next to Randy), and the photographer Ariane Smolderen (holding child), Marrakech. *Courtesy of Ariane Smolderen.*

Randy with boyhood Brooklyn friend
and fellow jazz master, drummer Max Roach, 1997.
*Courtesy of Ariane Smolderen.*

Concert performance of the African Rhythms Quintet with the Gnawa
Master Musicians of Morocco, Fes Festival of World Sacred Music,
Fes, Morocco, circa June 1998. *Courtesy of Ariane Smolderen.*

From left: (*standing*) Chief Bey, Brian Baccus, Tom Terrell, Alex Blake, unidentified man, Min Xao-Fen, Benny Powell, Neil Clarke, (*seated*) Melba Liston, Randy Weston, at the recording session for Khepera for Verve/Gitanes, 1998. *Courtesy of Cheung Ching Ming.*

Randy's commemorative sidewalk paving stone, Brooklyn Botanical Gardens, circa 2003.

Randy with his first record producer, Orrin Keepnews, Riverside Records, circa 2006. *Courtesy of Willard Jenkins.*

Randy receiving an honorary doctorate, Brooklyn College commencement, June 2006.

Randy performing with son Azzedin Weston (congas).

Randy and daughter Pam Weston sharing the fruits at
the Garden of Sultan's Palace in Tangier.

(*above*)
Randy's daughter
Cheryl Weston.

Randy's daughter
Kim Weston-Moran.

Four generations of Weston men—left to right: son Azzedin Weston, grandson Niles, Randy, father Frank Edward Weston.

Africa is not the geographical area that it occupies, nor is it the people living in Africa, nor is it anything we physically feel or see. For me, for people like Randy Weston and a few brothers, Africa is the spirits of our ancestors according to the African religions. You can't buy them with libations; you can't buy them with celebrations or dances for the spirits of the ancestors. They are choosey; they pick the people who they come to. And when the spirits of our ancestors pick on you, then you fall in love absolutely, and without qualifications, you fall in love with Africa. You fall in love with what is Africa. You feel the pulse of Africa within your own constitution and within your own heartbeat.
—MAHI ISMAEL (Sudan)

## CONNECTING WITH THE GNAWA

The Gnawa people and their music represent one of the strongest spiritual connections I've ever experienced. A lot of the songs they sing are about Bambara, which was one of the great city-states of the Mali Empire between the fourteenth and seventeenth centuries. The Mali Empire had a great influence on humankind with their writing, their culture, their civilization, and their music. The Gnawa in Morocco sing these ancient songs about Bambara. One of the Gnawa elders who I met in Marrakech, a man named Laayashi, told me, "We come from ancient Egypt." I have no doubt about that, because when the Egyptian Empire was invaded a lot of the people left and they went in different directions, creating new empires, traditions, and ways of life. In Egypt they have instruments that you see, inside the pyramids, inside some of the Egyptian museums that look and play a lot like the Gnawa stringed instrument known as the guimbre.

The Gnawa actually have a close kinship with African Americans, they're our brothers and sisters. Their ancestors came from the same region of Africa as the great majority of African American ancestors. While our ancestors were brought to the Americas and the Caribbean aboard Atlantic slave ships on the Middle Passage, Gnawa ancestors were crossing the Sahara to North Africa in bondage. Some of the same faces you see on the Gnawa in Morocco you see in the U.S. and you would never know the difference until they opened their mouths. My Gnawa friend M'Barek Ben Outhman from Marrakech, who has made tours and records with me in more recent times, could be a brother from Brooklyn, could be from Cleveland . . . until he starts to speak. The physical characteristics of African Americans and the Gnawa are very close.

I once met a Congolese filmmaker named Balufu Bakupo Kanyinda who insisted that the Gnawa story is the most important story in Africa to have been revealed to the rest of the world in the twentieth century. I asked him, "What do you know about Gnawa, you're from the Congo?" He said, "Man, let me tell you, the story of the Gnawa migration to Morocco proves that black institutions, black civilizations were so powerful that even if we were taken away from our homeland, taken away as slaves, we created new civilizations." That was also quite an interesting observation to me because when I first came to Morocco the Gnawa were viewed as street beggars, undesirables. Some Moroccans initially tried to discourage me from having anything to do with Gnawa. They'd ask me, "What do you see in these people?" Everywhere you go the black folks are always on the bottom. But now the Moroccans are all touched by Gnawa; all the young, educated Moroccans are all influenced by Gnawa culture—black culture. They've now seen the importance of Gnawa traditions to overall Moroccan culture.

The way I met the Gnawa is in retrospect one of the many mysteries of life I've encountered along the way. In 1968 my trio, with Ed Blackwell and Bill Wood, played a small performance at the American school where my children Pam and Niles attended. I met one of the teachers there, a man whose name I forgot almost as quickly as I learned it, and that's where the mystery comes in. I never even saw this man again after this initial encounter, yet he was very important as far as my introduction to Gnawa culture. That day after our performance at the school this teacher came up to me, introduced himself, and said, "Mr. Weston, I've heard you're interested in traditional music. You haven't heard African music until you've heard the Gnawa." Needless to say he certainly got my attention with that comment.

I told him yes, I was certainly interested in knowing more about these Gnawa people. We arranged a time when he could come to my apartment and when he arrived he brought one of the Gnawa with him, Abdullah el-Gourde, who played the guimbre. Abdullah and I have been connected ever since; he was the one who really introduced me to Gnawa culture and customs. As for that mysterious teacher, neither Abdullah nor I ever saw this man again, and neither of us can remember his name.

At the time Abdullah worked for Voice of America radio in Tangier. I'm not quite sure what he did there, but he worked there for a long time and it was great because it gave him the opportunity to learn to speak English and learn something about the American people. He told me about the Gnawa and their lineage, their culture, and he would often mention their spiritual ceremonies which they call Lilas. I became particularly intrigued by what little he told me of these Lilas, and I really wanted to attend one purely to observe. But at that time it was strictly taboo for so-called outsiders to attend these spiritual ceremonies, it was that deep. But I was persistent and kept insisting that my only interest was as an observer, not as a participant. Finally they relented and enabled me to attend a Lila.

The Gnawa have a color chart and each of their songs has a corresponding color. They have different rhythms for every color and each color represents a certain saint, a certain spirit, and they consider some colors more dangerous than others.

COLORS OF THE GNAWI MUSIC

*White*: The color of opening of the ceremony; it signifies peace, love and goodness.

*Brown*: The color of the spirit called "Hammadi."

*Sea Blue*: This color has many pieces of music in which they sing the greatness and depth of the oceans as well as their danger; for the sea gives a lot to mankind.

*Red*: The color of a slave called "Bacha Hammou"; a butcher who was courageous, slaughtered sheep, etc . . . and saw blood. This spirit shows strength just as the color red.

*Green*: The color of the great Marrakechi saint "Moulay Brahim" who loved Gnawis and used to treat them very well. Gnawi loved him too and this color is recognition and in honor of this saint.

*Dark Blue*: In this color you find the sky spirit with all that the sky represents, that is greatness, beauty, ambiguity, etc.

*White with Black Dots*: The spirit of the "Hawsas" tribe of ancestors.

*Black*: This color represents the spirits of the woods, enigmatic, magic, and powerful.

*Yellow*: The color of the girls and ladies' spirits who are the daughters of "Bacha Hammou" of the color RED.

*Orange*: The spirit of "Sidi Samharouche," a great "fkih" and astrologist and who controlled "D'jins." He is buried on a mountain which bears his name. The mountain is in Moulay Brahim. The spirit of Sidi Samharouch is venerated by Gnawi.

*Multicolors*: Le "Bouhali" used all the color, thus unifying all the spirits. Multicolors is the end of the ceremony. The last piece means "God is unique and replies when one makes appeal to Him."

I remember very vividly an incident a friend told me about later regarding these colors. My partner in Morocco, Abdeslaam, told a story about an encounter his wife Khadija had with Gnawa.

He said that what happens in Morocco, three days before the Muslim holy period of Ramadan, people with large houses give their homes over to the Gnawa so they can have their ceremonies, where they do their spiritual thing. Abdeslaam said that a long time ago this Gnawa man was in a trance and he was dancing to the music and spinning around, and whatever the color was it was a very heavy color. So whatever this guy was dancing to, Abdeslaam's wife and little girl started laughing at this spectacle and the result was that his wife responds to the color yellow because of this incident.

On another occasion after this yellow incident, I was with Abdeslaam and his wife and the Gnawa were playing at my house. There was another Moroccan guy there, a would-be flute player who had pulled out his instrument itching to play with the Gnawa. This cat with the flute is one of those types of guys who have no talent, but he'd even go so far as to have the nerve to take out his flute and start playing if John Coltrane was onstage. I warned him, "Man, don't play that flute!" So Abdeslaam asks the Gnawa to play the color yellow for his wife Khadija, who was reclining on the couch nearby. When the Gnawa played the color yellow all of a sudden a strange voice started coming out of Khadija, who is a very dainty woman. This voice starts coming out of her and she says something to this wannabe flute player in Arabic. Next thing I knew this cat grabbed his flute and started dashing for the door. Whatever she said it was so powerful he had to split immediately.

Meanwhile my bassist, Bill Wood, had bought a motorcycle that he wanted to ship back to the States because he got such a good deal. He bought the motorcycle in Rabat and thought he had arranged to have it shipped to Tangier so that he could put it on a boat to be shipped back home. But when he got to Tangier there was no bike, and nobody knew what happened to this bike. So he called back to Rabat and they said, "Your bike is still here." Bill went back to Rabat and they told him his bike was in Tangier! Mind you this was a big bike but he didn't know what happened to it.

Back to that night and the Gnawa are playing the color yellow while Khadija relaxes on the couch. This was not a real ceremony, the music wasn't as strong as it can get at a Lila, they were just playing their spiritual music, what we might call just jamming. But whatever they were playing it really affected Khadija to speak in this strange voice. Suddenly she told Bill Wood to go to a certain restaurant where he would see seven people and inside the restaurant would be his motorcycle!

The next day Bill and my son Azzedin went down to the beach to this little soul Moroccan restaurant down there. They go in the restaurant and sure enough, there are seven people inside and there's the motorcycle. He never got that motorcycle out of Morocco. He finally had to give up because every time he'd send it away, the motorcycle would come back. That was just an example of the Gnawa folklore.

My first experience with a Gnawa spiritual ceremony, an actual Lila, came in 1969. As I said, at first they wouldn't let me experience a Lila. It was not permitted to attend one if you were not part of that society, because they always said people have gotten physically harmed if their spirit wasn't right when they were in the room during a Lila. But I was determined to go. The chief was steadfast in not wanting me to attend a Lila, but I told him I felt I had to go there; there was just something about it, perhaps it was the spirits directing me to do this. By that point I had been hanging out with the Gnawa, particularly Abdullah el Gourde, for two years, so I thought I was more than ready to attend a Lila.

The chief finally relented, but he insisted that I had to bring Abdeslaam with me because he spoke Arabic, so if something happened he could protect me. I wore a djellabah, or traditional Moroccan robe, and just quietly sat in a corner to observe this ceremony. In the midst of all this music and dance I began to experience the colors; I saw red, and I particularly saw blue, which turned out to be my color as determined by the Gnawa. So I had this spiritual experience with these people. I was supposed to return the next night, to experience the color black and whatnot, but I declined. I think my mind had been blown enough by that point.

The Gnawa Lila ceremony generally lasts all night and consists of music and dance that often induces trance in the participants. At one point they played the color blue, and I swear I went into a trance that lasted two weeks. I'm not suggesting I was incoherent or unconscious for two weeks; it wasn't as though I was sitting in one spot in a coma. I was physically moving and otherwise going through my normal life, but I was in another dimension because this music had been so powerful. If you can imagine hearing the black church, jazz, and the blues all at the same time, in their original form, with all these rhythms coming together, that's what it was like. And these people were all dressed in their colors. There were those dressed in the color blue that would start beating themselves with ropes and you'd see actual marks on their arms. I saw a guy in a trance hit his head on the ground, saw blood oozing out of his head, when all of a sudden a guy walked up and rubbed his hand across this head wound and the blood disappeared completely. I'm not an ethnomusicologist or a spiritualist, but when you're with these people long enough you don't laugh at this stuff.

The first tune I wrote in honor of the Gnawa was "Blue Moses," a translation of their reference to Sidi Musa that is based on one of their songs. But the chief Gnawa in Tangier forbade me to play it. He said, "Don't play that in public, that's sacred music." So for one year I wouldn't play that piece. Finally I went back to him to ask his permission. His name was Fatah, so I said, "Fatah, I think the world needs to hear this music and I'm not going to commercialize it or disrespect it in any way. I'm going to put all the proper spiritual power behind this music because I respect you and I respect the Gnawa people." Finally Fatah relented and said OK, that I could finally perform "Blue Moses." But you can bet that if he didn't give me the OK, there was no way I was gonna play that piece, because I've seen some strange things happen in Africa when there's even a hint of crossing the spirits. Ironically, though I've played "Blue Moses" countless times since then, the first time I recorded it was in 1972 on the *Blue Moses* album for CTI that was a real hit record for me.

When I'm with what I refer to as traditional people, like the Gnawa or the Joujouka for example, I feel as though I'm going to music school, because in the West we have the tendency to believe that we started music. We tend to look upon Europe as the foundation of music and we tend to ignore the music of ancient cultures—India, China, Africa, etc. The African concept of music is much deeper than the western concept and it's based upon very powerful, spiritual values and supernatural forces, and pure magic. I've had some amazing experiences with traditional music that I had never experienced with any other kind of music. The sheer power of music makes

Fatah, the Gnawa chief who permitted the public performance of Weston's composition "Blue Moses," Tangier.

you realize that it's not only the origins of music, but when music is based upon certain spiritual values.

When a Gnawa is playing his instrument he has to say certain prayers before he does something like cutting a tree down. We in the West go into a music store, and if an instrument sounds right we buy it. But in Africa they are directly in tune with Mother Nature. The Gnawa told me things like "God has given you this gift of playing the piano, he's given it to you and he's going to take it away, so make the most of it while you're on the planet." In later years, after these early Morocco experiences, when we would tour with Gnawa musicians, we would all watch and listen and we found that each note has a certain power. They made me realize the value of one note. That's why I was attracted to Monk, because I heard magic in Monk's music; I heard something that no one else could possibly capture. When I heard Gnawa music and hung out with these people, my spirit evolved, because I knew I was with my origins, I felt I was going back to the beginnings of music. They can do things with music that we cannot do. These people are very humble, very respectful, and very spiritual.

## Khadija Ouahamane
*[this Khadija is not Abdeslaam's wife]*

*Khadija Ouahamane*: I met Randy Weston long before he was aware that I even existed. During my adolescence in the late '6os I would hear about this "crazy" American who plays this mystical music with the Gnawa, up north. I was in Rabat and I wasn't very worldly, being a girl raised in Muslim society; you go to school and you come home. Randy played a concert for the USIS in an auditorium in Rabat, I think I was about sixteen then. It was a very small room filled with mostly diplomats. It's magical the way Randy plays. It was incredible music and he was playing solo piano. I heard *us*, I heard Morocco in his playing, and I identified with it. I didn't try to analyze it then, I don't try to analyze it now, it was home, and it was like a part of me he was playing.

As time evolved I was fortunate to spend eight years of my life working with the USIS in the '80s. My job was to promote an understanding of America through arts and culture, most specifically music, because people really respond to music in Morocco. I planned tours of U.S. artists. Once we set the budget and sent out invitations to the particular music groups we wanted to have perform in Morocco, Mr. Weston was number one on our list.

In 1985 we arranged a short tour of Morocco for Randy with three stops: Rabat, Casablanca, and Marrakech. I covered the northern parts, up to Casablanca, but for Marrakech our USIS branch there took over. While Randy was in Rabat I got a call from the royal palace and they said, "We understand Mr. Weston is here and we would love for him to come and share his music with us"—this was a request from the king's sister! So we arranged it and he was very gracious, even though he wasn't going to be paid for it. It was an intimate royal performance, at the golf club in Rabat; she invited a select group of friends, very high-level people, maybe an audience of thirty-five. That was in contrast with the concert he played in Rabat at the National Theatre, which is the largest in the country; there about three thousand people came to the concert.

One thing I must explain is that perhaps as are all Africans, Moroccans are really very suspicious of anything that is sponsored by western governments. They may go and attend something . . . maybe, maybe not, even if it's free, not with the idea of enjoying the music, but they figure it's propaganda so they can go to diss it, and maybe the next day they write negative letters and call in. But that was never the case with Randy, because we consider Randy one of ours, he's our son, he's our master. Randy has put our music on the map. Who would have ever heard of Gnawa music, how would they have the renown they have now if it hadn't been for Randy? And that was almost forty years ago when he first started with them. Randy Weston is absolutely revered in Morocco . . . period. We don't explain Randy; Randy is Randy . . . that's it.

The thing about Morocco is it's a Muslim country but it's also a Judaic country as well. We had a big Judaic population which was mainly Berber, and after the Inquisition started, when Queen Isabella shoved us back across the Straits of Gibraltar, the Jews were going to be burnt at the stake so they fled; it's only nine miles south of Spain. Morocco and Europe kiss, you just have this little partition. But we're not truly Muslim in the sense of Islam, like from the East, because we're essentially profoundly African.

In Morocco you have all the hues. When Islam came to Morocco a lot of the ancient beliefs, be they originally purely African or afterwards Judaic, and then Islamic, were incorporated into our Islam. Any Islamic purist who examines Morocco will say, "These people aren't Muslim." It's just something that we can't shed; a lot of it has to do with mysticism, and we have several musical brotherhoods that all adhere to colors. They're the ones that really propagate Moroccan music, including the Gnawa. The older generation of Moroccans at least used to have a different view of the Gnawa. For instance my mother hates the Gnawa, but I love the Gnawa. When I was a kid they would come around and play their music and she would shutter the windows and everything. Meanwhile I would be responding to their music inside the house and I would have to hold it inside. Their music scared the hell out of her, and it still does. I think that's because some Moroccans are not at that level of consciousness, that level of appreciation. I guess that's my color of music.

What Randy did for me personally, and I'm sure what he did for countless people back home, is to make us acquaint ourselves with our own culture, our own music, and our own roots. I remember when I went to Randy's concert in Marrakech, even though the USIS office there was in charge. After they finished the concert we went to the foot of the Atlas Mountains with the Gnawa to their homes. These were very modest homes, adobe homes, and these are master musicians with subsistence living. They performed a whole ceremony, and I was the only outside woman who was permitted to hang out. It was outdoors and it was a lovely spring day, there was still snow on the Atlas Mountains. They had this huge bonfire and the ceremony went on until 4 o'clock in the morning; the chanting and the playing, the women bringing more and more food . . . I nearly got scared because I had never had that kind of experience. This was more than a visit, this was a communion. Randy enabled me to stay, and discover my own roots, my own people. As a result I have a different eye for discovering my own people and music, and a different eye in how to perceive the gifts we have. It should come from the highest authorities to recognize the contributions Randy Weston has made to my nation and my people, and the world at large.

As I've said, in Morocco I went to school. But you must understand, it took me two years to adjust to living in Morocco because you can have this vision of being an American or African American and you're going to go to Africa and just because you love Africa everything will be cool. It doesn't happen like that, because it's another way of life and you sort of have to unlearn, and it took me two years to do that. But I was determined to stay, I gave myself five years when I left the U.S., because I knew if I came back before that folks would tease me and give me hell about failing to adapt.

At that time so many other musicians were talking about moving to Stockholm, London, Paris . . . Europe was the mecca to the musicians, everything was about Europe and Africa just wasn't in their consciousness. So for me it was so incredible to discover the spiritual power I found in Morocco. With every one of these sects or tribes, societies, brotherhoods, Allah is always the most important ingredient. I discovered with our people, wherever you find us, the Creator is of utmost importance, whether we're in Jamaica, Brooklyn, or wherever. When I started my life in Morocco the first thing we had to learn about was God, that's number one.

What happened to me in Morocco is something magical and very mysterious, the same as what happened with my relationship with Thelonious Monk. When I heard Monk I heard something special, and when you hear something like that you want to live with it, you want to be with it to try and understand. So I had to live with these Moroccan people, eating, drinking mint tea, watching them and their customs, listening, breathing, inhaling the culture, the food . . . the way of life, the children, the weather, their ceremonies, the whole bit; its kind of like a magical thing. Africa led me to truly understand the spirituality of all of our people, we're truly an African people, and I could adapt on that level. At that time I had no command of their language at all; no Arabic, no French, no Spanish, no Berber, no nothing . . . but love. So it's a very mysterious process. What you hear in my music now is the spirit of Mother Africa.

By being with all these traditional societies over the years, they get in your heart and it comes out in your music. Music describes and characterizes life and in modern life we're always rushing around. These traditional people bring you back to earth; they say, "Slow down, take your time." I discovered civilization in Africa. My young interpreter in Tangier was eleven years old and this guy spoke about seven languages, including dialects. After a while all the kids knew me because I'm so tall. Sometimes I'd walk in Tangier and all the kids would follow me and I'd think, "Man, these kids are geniuses, if they ever had an opportunity for advanced education . . ."

I really discovered the genius of our people in Africa. I learned all of these spiritual values and realized where we come from; and we've been able to survive because we maintain some of those values even though we've been cut off, not knowing where it came from.


## Khadija Akaaboune

*Khadija Akaaboune*: Randy Weston's experience in Morocco is wonderful in a very special way because his ancestors came here against their will and he went back home on his own, and he's free to go back and forth, he's built a bridge.


## TK Blue, saxophonist and music director, Randy Weston's African Rhythms

*TK Blue*: I believe it was the warmth of the Gnawa people that attracted Randy to them, and of course their music. That warmth and hospitality coupled with Randy experiencing their spiritual Lilas and seeing some of the things they do with music, greatly attracted Randy to the Gnawa.

The spirituality in Gnawa music really reached him. When the Gnawa play their music they're praising God, which runs throughout everything they do. If you talk with any of those Gnawa brothers about the spiritualism in their music they always point to the sky, to the Creator. That was deeply attractive to Randy; I know it certainly had a deep attraction to me when I first met the Gnawa and had an opportunity to play with them.

The Gnawa are very giving people. I remember meeting Abdullah el Gourde for the first time, going to his house and having food; that's a deep tradition in Africa and you find it in the south more than you find it in the north of the U.S., that tradition of inviting people into your home to have food, just real basic stuff. Here in the U.S. we call that southern tradition but I think it goes back to Africa.

For the Moroccan people the color blue is a very, very powerful color. I've always had a deep affinity for the color blue and I know Randy feels strongly about the color blue. When Randy's mother passed in the mid-1980s we were playing in Marrakech with the Gnawa, we went to a mosque with the Gnawa and had a very special remembrance ceremony with our Moroccan brothers. That really moved Randy, to see these brothers giving special tribute to his mom; there's definitely a spiritual connection between him and the Gnawa. We all have nothing but love, admiration, and respect for the Gnawa and their music, and they feel the same. Everybody that I've played with who have played with the Gnawa all say the same thing.

Gnawa music, their rhythms, is something you feel in your heart. A lot of it is their aura. I remember a funny story about touring with the Gnawa. Once we were somewhere in Europe and I woke up one morning extremely hungry. I went down to breakfast and was dismayed to find there was hardly any food left—no croissant, no fruit, nothing. The Gnawa brothers had just finished eating and they had wiped out all the food. I looked around and asked my Gnawa brother Mbarek, "Where's the food, where's the croissant?" He reached back in the hood of his djellabah and handed me a croissant!

## 12

Embassy of the United States of America Rabat, Morocco
Mr. Randy Weston
c/o Mr. Roberts
USIS                                                    October 18, 1967
Rabat, Morocco

Dear Randy:
Enclosed you will find $100 in dirhams as a contribution to the
wonderful work you are doing in combining modern jazz and Moroccan music. This modern treatment of traditional Berber music
is very interesting and I was particularly impressed with your
composition "Marrakech Blues" last evening.

   I know my guests enjoyed the evening very much.

Sincerely yours,
Henry J. Tasca
American Ambassador

# BUILDING A LIFE IN TANGIER

## The African Rhythms Club

The city of Tangier is the northern gateway to Africa, where people from all
over the continent—and from all over the world—mingle. A trip to Tangier
is the easiest way I know to make a standard European vacation something truly special, because even though there are European influences,
you know you're in a different culture when you're in Tangier. It's less than
twenty miles from Europe, accessible from Spain by ferryboat. Tangier is
a truly special city, built on hills with a beautiful beach and the incredible
Tangier Bay at its feet. Tangier is at the northernmost tip of Africa, where
the Atlantic and the Mediterranean meet in the Straits of Gibraltar, and the
bay is an ever-changing blue and green, always fascinating. You find your-

self forever running into that view when you're walking around the city; wow . . . suddenly . . . there it is.

Several of my buddies came to visit me during my time in Tangier, and a couple of those visits were truly memorable. Ahmad Jamal came over and spent one week with me in 1970. He didn't come to play, just to visit and hang out, seeing Tangier, experiencing Morocco. I introduced him to all the people I knew, the writers and so forth. That was when Ahmad first had an opportunity to hear my son Azzedin play. Jamal really appreciated Azzedin's conga playing and actually wanted to recruit him for his band, but he didn't tell me this directly at the time, out of respect for the fact that Azzedin is my son and was playing in my band at the time. So he told our mutual friend and bassist Jamil Nasser. Jamil came back to me and said, "Hey, man, Ahmad sure likes your son, but he didn't want to ask you directly." I got excited for Azzedin and said, "Tell Ahmad to take that dude . . . yesterday! Azzedin playing with the great Ahmad Jamal, are you kidding me!" It was a golden opportunity for Azzedin's growth as a musician, and that's how he came to play with Ahmad Jamal for those years.

My old Brooklyn buddy Max Roach came over to hang out in Tangier for a week. He came with his wife at the time when she was pregnant with their twins. One thing I vividly remember about Max's visit is that the trumpeter Bill Coleman played a concert at the local theatre that week, so Max and his lady Janice and I went to the concert. At one point the announcer said, "Ladies and gentlemen, we have Mr. Max Roach in the audience." The audience was cheering for Max, and the guy said, "Come on up and play some, Max." Bill Coleman was from a generation of musicians before us and he played some New Orleans kind of number and Max played that stuff perfectly, just like he was Baby Dodds or some traditional drummer like that, it was incredible and just showed how deeply Max is in the tradition.

## The African Rhythms Club

It had long been my intention to establish some form of cultural center, or base of African culture, on the continent. When I came back to Morocco to live in the summer of 1967, that idea simply intensified, particularly when I found the culture there so rich, what with all those spirit music brotherhoods like the Gnawa, the Jillalah, the Joujouka, the Hmadcha, and others. I had experienced so much great culture in other parts of Africa as well that

I wanted to develop some form of cultural center that would bring many African cultures under one roof.

At the same time I had always been impressed by some of the prominent African musicians I met along the way and how so many of them had their own cultural bases in their country, primarily in the form of nightclubs. One of the things that really impressed me about going to clubs like the Shrine, which was owned by the great musician Fela Kuti, and Caban Bamboo, owned by the guitarist Bobby Benson, both operating out of Lagos, was that their clubs enabled them to have a base where they could always play their music, as well as a place they could present artists they were musically and spiritually in tune with. So in addition to investigating my cultural center idea I also had in my mind to operate my own club. Morocco seemed particularly ripe for both ideas when I first got there. So many of the people I met were receptive to my plans.

When they asked us to come back to Morocco after our first tour stop there, I returned with the trio, with Bill Wood on bass and Ed Blackwell on drums, and we got a short gig at that restaurant in Rabat called Jour Nuit (Day Night). When I met the proprietor Lahcen at the Hotel Rex where we stayed, we talked and it seemed we both had eyes to operate a music club, so we decided to see if we could partner to open one. Even though that idea eventually fell by the wayside, a year later when we moved to Tangier I was still focused on that notion. Meeting several literary types in Tangier, those expatriates who were kind of living there in self-exile, like Paul Bowles and Brion Gysin, just increased my desire to open my own club. They were encouraging and it appeared that they were some of the people who would be quick to support such a venture, not with money or anything like that but with their patronage.

I met and became friends with other important people in Tangier who also supported such a venture. Jacques Muyal, someone I'm still in touch with today, was one such person. When I landed in Tangier in 1967 Jacques and his brother Massaoud, who we always called Marcel, were totally into the music with a real passion. When Jacques was fifteen years old he was a jazz disc jockey in Morocco. Jacques was also great friends with Dizzy Gillespie; he stayed at Dizzy's home for two weeks documenting Dizzy, and was at his hospital bedside when Dizzy passed. Jacques and his brother were examples of people I knew I could count on if I was going to realize this dream of opening a club in Morocco; and besides that they seemed to know their way around the "official" channels.

I remember when we first arrived in Tangier during the State Department tour; the moment our car pulled up to the hotel Marcel was the first guy there to meet us. He and his brother are of Spanish-Jewish descent, both wore glasses, and Marcel was always quick to laugh, he had a great sense of humor. He was one of those cats who if you just looked at him you'd laugh. When we pulled up to the hotel that day he said, "Randy Weston, how you doin', man? Booker Ervin, that's my man!" I had never met this guy and he immediately starts talking about Booker. Marcel was our first contact in Tangier and I soon met his father and mother. His mother was a great cook who would make dinner for us sometimes. Jacques at that time was an engineer for the Nagra Company in Switzerland, and he was also an inventor.

This desire to open a club actually dated back to my upbringing with my dad. Don't forget, even as a kid I was in the restaurant business with my dad, so the entrepreneurial spirit was deeply ingrained in me. I just thought it would be a great idea to open a club or cultural center, because I wanted to have a place where I could present black culture, the way black people, African people, approach music and just the way we approach life. That seed the Moroccan businessman Lahcen planted was enough for me to stay in Rabat exploring that dead end for a year before we moved to Tangier, where I started scouting around for a place in earnest. That first year in Rabat I didn't really work much, a couple of concerts here, playing a couple of hotels there, playing a concert for the Hot Club of France chapter in the city of Meknes—that kind of thing. I didn't really even have access to a piano much of the time; so from that standpoint it was a somewhat artistically frustrating year in Rabat.

So when I got to Tangier and met people like Marcel and Jacques Muyal, Abdeslaam Akaaboune and his wife Khadija, those expatriate writers like Paul Bowles and Brion Gysin, and others I felt artistically stimulated and started gathering my resources and exploring the possibilities. Abdeslaam eventually became my business partner; he was the only real investor in the club. And it was through his contacts that we found the space that became the African Rhythms Club, which was a story in itself—typical Morocco.

I came to Morocco to live as a kind of "star"—a star in the sense of advance billing, having played that State Department tour there, playing big concerts in Rabat and Casablanca; so we had all this great press, they knew about me there. I enrolled Pamela and Niles in the American school in Tangier and I played a concert at the school. This combination of things meant I knew a lot of people in Tangier—plus with my physical size if I didn't know them they knew who I was. Tangier, Morocco's northernmost port, was really like a small international city.

The center of Tangier is small but then it spreads out into the hills; it's definitely smaller than the other major Moroccan cities like Casablanca, Rabat, Fes, and Marrakech. Tangier was at one time a major port for smuggling of all kinds. Before I got there they had two hundred banks in this little town, which was unbelievable, and which gives you some idea of the kind of money floating into and through that town. Jacques Muyal used to tell me that when he was a kid growing up his father had a cart in the medina (or old city) in Tangier openly trading dollars. Tangier seemed to have a different police force every week. It was somewhat apart from Morocco as an international city, so it might be Spanish police one week, maybe French the next week. It was an unbelievable place. I arrived there at the very end of the exciting times in Tangier. There certainly weren't two hundred banks there by the time I arrived. When Morocco gained its independence from France they began neglecting the northern part of the country. Tangier had been living this high life while the rest of Morocco was still occupied. But when Morocco gained independence they neglected Tangier, so it lost a lot of its character.

My friends helped me in my search for a suitable space for the club I envisioned, and since Tangier is such a relatively small place word got around quickly that I was looking. There was a yacht club on the beach in Tangier which was run by a guy named Kadaoui. He also had this vacant space in town, right in the central area of Tangier, upstairs above the Cinema Mauritania, which I'm still not sure if he actually owned; in Morocco you never know, but he ran the place. My partner Abdeslaam was a police lieutenant by day and he knew everybody. He and this guy Kadaoui got together and somehow arranged for us to rent this vacant space; it was a very complicated process. Securing the space took a relatively short time in retrospect, but at the time it seemed like a long time. There was a lot of bureaucracy and red tape that was foreign to me; you had the old French system plus the complex Moroccan mentality to deal with, and all this besides the fact that Tangier was strongly influenced by a variety of cultures, including nearby Spain. So three months might seem like six months. Time-wise the whole process happened very quickly by comparison, but it was exhausting—probably something like a bit longer than six months.

Tangier in those days was a bright place full of light. The interior of this space above the theater was the complete opposite because it was dark inside, all dark-wood paneling, and though we talked about lightening it up we never did. To get to the club, whose entrance was next to the theater, you had to climb up a long spiral staircase. When you got to the top of the staircase there were two wooden, Spanish-style doors with glass windows that opened out to the club. As you opened the door there were three additional stairs before you actually entered the space. It seemed to be a suitable place for what we wanted to do. The space might seat about 150 people with tables and chairs. Right in the middle of the room there was a fireplace, though it wasn't working.

Everything came together rather quickly once we settled on this space. The Europeans warned me that things moved so slowly in Africa that it would take at least a year to get a liquor license for the club; I got my liquor license in three months. We had to do a lot of other politicking to get the OK to open this place. We had to meet with the governor and various officials to assure them of our proper intentions, to let them know that we planned on making a positive contribution to the community. We got the OK from the head of the tax department in Tangier, and all the various officials whose approval was required.

There was an American brother living in Tangier at the time, an artist from Florida named Wijo. He did some free-form painting on the walls leading up the staircase. When you walked in the club the bar was to the right and around the curved bar were high chairs. In the back the place had stained-glass windows, and we hung some of Wijo's paintings there. He also painted the ceiling with different images of Africa. We left the area around the fireplace open to create a dance space. As you entered, on the right side of the club is where we arranged the stage for performances. Unfortunately, because the place was so dark with all that wood, we never really got any good photographs of the interior.

We hung various African art paintings on the walls and tried to decorate the place to make it distinctly a place of African culture. We wanted to have a real distinguishing sign out in front of the club. Because the theater dominated the block, we needed something to let people know the African Rhythms Club was in business upstairs. Wijo went somewhere and found a forty-five-foot telephone pole that had fallen down. He got some Moroccan guys to saw this huge log down to about twelve to fifteen feet and he carved a symbol on the pole that resembled kinda like an African version of a swastika—not a real swastika but something shaped like that, which I guess you could say was an Africancentric variation, at least that's what it brought to mind when I first saw it. But this carving was so huge the city said no, they didn't want this pole on the street and made us move it immediately. My house had three terraces with a big backyard and I wound up putting the pole there, where it remained.

Next we needed a piano, the search for which became another minidrama. I heard through the grapevine that an Englishman named Peter who owned a bar right by the beach had two pianos and one was an upright that he supposedly wanted to sell. His mother had died and left him a Bechstein grand piano that she made him promise to keep the rest of his life, which he stored in a warehouse. I went to this guy's bar almost everyday to have a drink and try coercing him to sell me that Bechstein. After one month he finally relented and I got this wonderful piano for a thousand dollars.

Another hurdle was liquor, which though it wasn't what I was into you've apparently gotta sell if you're going to have a successful club. Technically it is difficult to serve liquor in an Islamic country, and liquor is generally only available in the international hotels and such, but we were able to obtain a liquor license through official channels despite that, which had a lot to do with the fact that Tangier was such a diverse city. As it turned out some of our Muslim patrons could really put away some scotch!

Those were some of the kinds of struggles we had in opening this place, but we made it. Primarily because of the nature of the club and our liquor permit we decided to sell memberships. Many of the so-called aristocrats came to Tangier—sons and cousins of people like the queen of England, rich bankers from Switzerland, Italian princes, and whatnot. The cost of living was low and they could buy all the property they wanted inexpensively. There was an Englishman named Rex Nankingwell who had a big house up in the mountains full of very fine paintings. I hadn't been in Tangier long when this guy had a big party at his home to bring all the artists together. He invited painters, sculptors, musicians, writers, and the like. Azzedin and I were invited to play; they had the Gnawa play and others. Through people like this guy Rex I met a Swiss woman named Louise duMeuron who was some kind of countess; I also met Princess Respoli from Italy, all of the aristocrats of Tangier. So we started our club membership with these folks.

The very first members of the African Rhythms Club were Evelyn Waugh, the British author of *Brideshead Revisited*, and his brother the writer Alec Waugh. Membership was only $20 a year, which these folks could certainly

Advertising flier from the African Rhythms Club, Tangier.

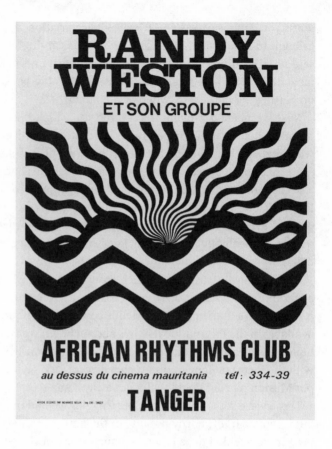

RANDY WESTON

ET SON GROUPE

AFRICAN RHYTHMS CLUB

*au dessus du cinema mauritania*     *tél : 334-39*

TANGER

afford. There was a United Nations headquarters in Tangier, so many UN personnel bought memberships. It wasn't as though we didn't permit non-members into the place, but membership provided them a kind of cachet. Some of our members also provided us with their expertise, including one of the members who had a print shop and printed our fliers for a very reasonable price. Paul Bowles, author of the book *The Sheltering Sky*, who was also a composer, used to patronize the club frequently. He was very prestigious, and if people knew Paul Bowles was going to be at the club they would come. It was a collective effort at establishing a cultural club in Tangier, a place with a certain identity.

The concept of the club was mine and I was the main proprietor of the place. It was difficult to get local management types who understood such a business, so Azzedin and I did most of the work ourselves—bookkeeping, managing, and the like. It was my idea so I had to be the person in charge.

On the weekends we might have three waiters, on weeknights maybe one or two, all wearing African clothing. We served some light snacks but no meals. We wanted to serve food but we weren't able to get the space to have a proper kitchen. Being all wood and located over a movie theater, there were certain legal restrictions on serving food.

My drummer-son Azzedin and I were the musical foundation of the club; we played there most nights from April through September. We opened the club at 6:00 p.m. for the young people, and then the regular club opened up at 9:00. Since Tangier is so heavily influenced by Spanish culture, everything stays open late, just like in Spain. At 6:00 was when we had programs featuring the recordings of American artists like Ray Charles, James Brown, and Marvin Gaye. In Morocco they had limited exposure to African American music. So from 6:00 to 7:00 we let the young kids come in, and they would dance, and me and Azzedin, who spoke very good French, would talk about this music.

Otherwise these young people only got small doses of real black music through Voice of America broadcasts, but they were crazy about our music. James Brown was number one in all of Africa. But in Tangier and other parts of Morocco they only got weak imitations of our music through Europe, where cats would play an imitation of black music. Obviously we didn't just cater to the aristocrats. Local folks with money—businessmen, hoteliers, travel agents, military people, doctors—the professionals patronized the club. There was no cover charge but the common folks really wouldn't have come anyway.

Actually when Abdeslaam and I began planning this place my preference would have been to have a teahouse, to bring the culture there and establish a base in Africa where we could come and experience each other's music; that was my real spiritual reason for having this club. Abdeslaam loved the music and my ideas, but he wanted to go more in the direction of a bar; he liked to drink scotch and so did his buddies. For them once the club opened they could hang out and do what men do; it became like their clubhouse. Basically we compromised because the cultural elements of the space were my idea. There really was no other place like this in Africa as far as we knew.

We decided the African Rhythms Club would be open six nights a week, and to start out I played every evening. When we started I had my son [Niles] Azzedin on percussion, and there was a sister living there at the time, a dancer named Diedre from Washington, who worked with us. So the original trio was piano, percussion, and dance; that was it. The place had a capacity of 150 so it was a nice size as clubs go. Those who weren't interested in joining but just wanted to come and hang out simply bought their drinks and sat down.

The Moroccans loved the place. They're a very sophisticated people; they're really quite interested in other cultures, so this place was very much to their liking. I think it became a kind of hip place to see and be seen, but it wasn't superficial in that respect, they were really into what we were doing musically and culturally. I managed the club myself, and we hired Moroccan women to clean the place. For our audiences we depended a lot on tourist groups, with whom we made arrangements for group rate prices, and the local people were really excited to have a jazz club in Tangier.

We did bring some other artists into the club. We brought in a blues band from Chicago led by a guy named Doug Turner. We brought in some Congolese singers and we also brought in the pianist Sadik Hakim from the U.S., who played a couple of nights. There really was no such thing as an average night at this place. Sometimes visiting diplomats dropped by, UN people patronized the place, and sometimes very colorful tourist groups came by. I certainly can't say our audiences were ever what you would call average. Every night there might be a different group either playing or in the audience.

In Morocco and throughout North Africa there's a tendency to look to the North or to the Middle East, so the focus was either Spain, other parts of Europe, or countries like Saudi Arabia or Yemen; that was their world. They had a spiritual, physical relationship with West Africa, of course, but they sort of failed to recognize the importance of their culture and the broader culture of Africa. So from that perspective I thought the African Rhythms Club could make a tremendous contribution. We had singers from the Congo, we had the Gnawa perform at the club, we had Chicago blues, and we had all the latest black American records; we provided them with top-notch entertainment and culture.

The effects of owning and operating this club were many, most of them positive, but it was a tough business. At some points I thought I was totally crazy. After all, I'm in a so-called foreign country, owning a club, and I don't even speak the language. I had no really serious financial backing and was kind of living by the seat of my pants; some people promised money but they never really came through. People would be thinking—and sometimes even wondering aloud—about my motives, as in "Why Africa? You're supposed to take from Africa, you're not supposed to give!" By the same token, through this venture I met many wonderful people from all over the planet. We had a guestbook at the club entrance, and in this guestbook you might see signatures from a Saudi Arabian pilot who was in the club, an English writer, an Irishman . . . Because of that club I was able to meet all these incredible people in Tangier. That's why it was such a wonderfully crazy time in my life: trying to play the piano and keep an eye on the bartender at the same time. So it was destiny; but I would never do anything like that again because it required so much commitment and sacrifice. But I got so much in exchange; whatever I gave I got more than that in return.

In the 60s [Randy Weston] moved to North Africa, and in the next seven years he soaked up musical styles from diverse parts of the continent. He probably knows more about African music than any other American jazzman today. — *New York Post*

# FESTIVAL BLUES, THEN DIVINE INTERVENTION

## *Blue Moses*

Aside from establishing the African Rhythms Club, developing a unique Pan-African cultural center was still a burning ambition of mine. C. B. Atkins, the wheeler-dealer who helped us get our *Uhuru Afrika* recording project released on Roulette Records, in the late 1960s, early 1970s became Muhammad Ali's manager, and I really wanted to meet Ali so I could talk to him about my cultural center idea. Ali was such a conscious brother, and I figured he'd at least be interested and perhaps might even consider contributing toward the project. One time, while I was living in Morocco and visiting New York, C.B., who knew I wanted to meet Ali, called to say Muhammad was going to leave for the airport and would be at his hotel on 8th Avenue and I should run over and try to catch him there because he was flying out that day. Unfortunately the timing was off; I was on my way back to Morocco and didn't have much time to catch Ali.

I wanted to see Ali because at the time I was endlessly thinking about economics and how to finance this cultural center project, so I figured I needed to meet some of the brothers who had serious money to invest in this cultural center I wanted to establish in Morocco. Even though I was pressed for time and had to catch a flight myself, I rushed over to this Manhattan hotel and by the time I got there coincidentally Ali was coming out of the hotel door as I was coming in. C.B. grabbed my hand and introduced

Randy with Muhammad Ali in New York. *Photograph by Efton C. Masters.*

me to Ali. But obviously he didn't have any time to talk with me. Ironically, as it turned out Ali was going to Casablanca to fight an exhibition match with a boxer from Senegal; this was about 1971. I was thrilled, figuring I might actually have a chance to catch him in Morocco. When Ali came to Casablanca for this exhibition fight, I drove down from Tangier and went straight to his hotel, where I spotted him with his entourage. He saw me and said, "Come on, man, sit down." I sat down with Ali and his wife but couldn't say anything because everybody was talking at once, there were photographers snapping pictures, Moroccans happy to see the champ, the whole bit. Everybody wanted a piece of this guy.

At that time Muhammad Ali and James Brown were like the biggest African American superstars in Africa, so everywhere Ali went he was treated like a king and mobbed with people. Finally I said, "Ali man, listen, I'd like to talk to you, but I know you're busy now." He said, "Don't worry man; you just come by the hotel later." I waited around and later that night rang his hotel room, he answered the phone and said, "Come on up." Excellent! I was actually gonna get a one-on-one with this elusive guy. I went upstairs and Ali was in his room in just his pants, with his fantastic physique. Meanwhile his wife was in the other room asleep. We sat down about 11:00, and when 2:00 a.m. rolled around he was still talking. It wasn't as if *we* were talking, *he* was doing all the talking; it was fascinating but I couldn't get a word in edgewise, much less talk about my ideas. That brother is highly skilled; he's a master talker who can go on for days. He talked about Elijah Muhammad, about Islam, about this, about that . . . Finally I said, "You've got a fight tomorrow and you'd better get some rest, but I really want to talk to you about this project." He said, "All right, man, I'm going to be in training camp when I go back, so we'll talk then."

I knew Ali was interested in music because Big Black was there in his training camp with his drums, helping him train in Zaire when he was getting ready to fight George Foreman. So Ali was totally into music, just like Sugar Ray, Henry Armstrong, Archie Moore, all the heavy fighters who were into jazz music. Anyway, that night in Casablanca when I got up to leave, I opened the door, he let me out, and I rang for the elevator. Ali leaned out the door and said, "Hey, Randy, one thing . . . the only problem is I like all kind of babes," and that was all he said. I laughed all the way back to Tangier. Later on I tried to get to his training camp since Black was there, but the timing never worked out. That was my Muhammad Ali encounter.

The African Rhythms Club was located about a ten-minute walk from the center of Tangier. Just to illustrate what an international city Tangier was, there was a hotel on the corner and right across the street from the club was a bar owned by an ex–lion tamer named Lilly, a German woman. Next to her place a few doors down was that bar featuring the Austrian woman who played piano and specialized in Austrian waltzes. The Moroccans were very open and interested in checking out everything. Each of these places had its own unique character, and everybody would spread the word about each other's places; there really wasn't a feeling of competition between us. Even though Tangier was a relatively small city we had a nice camaraderie between our clubs.

We put posters and fliers up around the city announcing the African Rhythms Club, but for the most part we operated largely on word of mouth. Since the city wouldn't allow us to place Wijo's massive telephone pole sculpture outside the club, that word of mouth was essential, because if you drove down our street it was dominated by the Cinema Mauritania, and you just might miss the African Rhythms Club if you weren't looking closely. We were just a rather inconspicuous black door next to the cinema . . . though we did have the letters A.R. posted on the door.

One never knows what the spirits might have in store. I remember in 1969 when we opened, the hot news in the region was that some of the Black Panthers, including Eldridge Cleaver, were living in exile in nearby Algeria. We had made plans to visit Algeria because I wanted to go and see Cleaver, but every time I tried to leave Tangier for Algeria something weird would happen. In Morocco all of the cities have their own mythologies; the mythical story of Tangier is that once you get inside of Tangier it's very difficult to leave. Some people who came to Tangier ended up dying there, never returning to their origins; that's the mythology of Tangier.

An example of that mythology was our weird efforts at traveling to Algeria to meet with Cleaver. The first time I tried to make the trip I got on an airplane, the plane took off, and as it was ascending, a flock of birds hit the windshield and the pilot was forced to return to the airport. Another time I tried to go to Algeria by car and something strange happened to the car's engine. Then another time I planned an Algeria trip, suddenly my liquor license for the club appeared out of nowhere so I couldn't leave if I had wanted to. It seems the Creator said, "No, you're not going to Algeria, you've gotta stay here and open this club."

We had our share of successes with the club, coupled with the usual trials and tribulations of running such a place. By late 1970 or so I started plotting to realize what had become of another related dream of mine, to present a festival of African and African diaspora music in Morocco. That goes back to my childhood dreams; I would forever be asking myself what I could do to unify my people, that's always been on my mind. My main desire was to establish cultural centers of our music in every country in Africa and bring the best of our minds from America to Africa and teach Africans our knowledge of music in the West. At the same time I wanted to help document their traditional music; learn about the music of Ethiopia, Cameroon, Gabon . . . that was my aspiration.

The whole idea was to get to Africa and establish these cultural centers. I envisioned having access to radio, television, tapes, and archival resources, and we would help to document and protect our music because inevitably everything is taken from Africa. In this case we would be contributing to the Motherland. So that was the foundation of my thinking. Part of that aspiration meant having a festival once a year where we could bring African American musicians to Morocco, along with African musicians, and we would have them perform together.

There were a number of people who were eager to help me realize this festival. One was an Englishwoman living in Tangier named Marie Miller; God bless her, she was such a fierce fighter. She was a classic Aries, and Aries women are very honest, very assertive. She helped pull together important people to support the festival, like the head of Spanish radio. She approached the governor of Tangier, and he thought it was a great idea that would bring culture to the city, attract tourism, and put Tangier back on the map. Remember, after Morocco achieved its independence from France somehow Tangier began to dissipate in importance as a Moroccan center. Bottom line in my thinking is that our music is not just about sitting in the club and listening: our music is the force for bringing us together as African people, for healing.

Yin and yang, the festival wound up being culturally successful and a financial disaster. The Moroccan tourism office promised financial support, as did the American government . . . at the last minute they both abandoned us and withdrew their promises. But I understand why, because from an American perspective it was an African thing; if it had been an integrated plan it would have been a different story. We talked to Iberia Airlines, to the head of Moroccan radio, talked to numerous local people in Tangier . . . In the end it was a total Tangier effort; we got absolutely no help from anybody else in Morocco.

We went to the ministry of tourism and I said, "Hey, this is gonna be great for Morocco; give us so and so support." The American government approached me; I didn't go to them, which was logical since we were bringing over a large American delegation of artists. The guy who was in charge of the USIS in Rabat ironically was the same decent guy from our tour who had previously been in charge of the USIS in Algeria. In 1967, when we made our State Department tour stop in Algeria, I'll never forget meeting this same guy Robert Behrens when we landed in Algiers. At that time the Algerians hated Americans and the feeling was mutual.

Embassy people rotate assignments, so by the early '70s this same guy Behrens was now stationed in Rabat, Morocco, and when I met with him he offered me money to support the festival, but something went down and we never got the money. It was never fully explained to me because I left the country soon after the festival. You never know what happens with governments, but politically I understood all too well because I don't think they ever really wanted African people to come together in this way. Despite these unfulfilled promises of financial support for the festival idea, we made it happen because we got all sectors of Tangier involved: the Spanish, the Portuguese, the English, the French, the Germans . . . in terms of people volunteering to help and spreading the word . . . but no one brought the big money.

Embassy of the United States of America
Rabat, Morocco
October 4, 1971

To Whom It May Concern:
I have known Randy Weston some four years personally, and have known of his excellent professional reputation for a much longer time.

Randy is engaged in producing a music festival in his adopted city of Tangier, a project which I find most exciting in its potential.

Speaking for the cultural part of the United States Embassy in Rabat I can say that we heartily endorse this project. We not only endorse it in my words but we are prepared to give it support in other ways (publicity and financial) as well.

The Weston idea of such a festival as he outlined it to us sounds positive and feasible—that is why we are happy to associate ourselves with it.

Robert H. Behrens
Counselor Embassy
for Public Affairs

Royaume du Maroc
Ministère de l'Information
18 October 1971

To Whom It May Concern:

I first came to know Mr. Randy Weston in connection with my work in broadcasting and television in Morocco. He has an excellent reputation as a musician, and more specifically, as a composer writing modern music based on the rhythms and melodies of traditional Moroccan folk-lore. I have much admiration for his work as a musician, and it has been my pleasure, more recently, to make his acquaintance on a personal level here in Tangier.

Mr. Weston has performed in Rabat and Casablanca for the national radio and television network on a number of occasions since he came to live in Morocco in 1968. Radio Tangier has recently put into service a new transmitter with a capacity of 200 KW, enabling Morocco to broadcast as far as both New York and Cairo, and we are looking forward to collaborating with Mr. Weston on his return from America, in putting out programmes of modern creative music for our increasing audiences.

Radio Tangier is also extremely happy to participate in the proposed "Jazz Festival 1972," to be held in Tangier next June. This project has recently received official sanction from H.E. the governor of the Province of Tangier, and it is hoped that the event will be repeated annually within the overall framework of Tangier's summer festivities.

Minister of Information

We had gathered a local festival organizing committee in Tangier, and I had also arranged for Max Roach and my good friend Mary Jo Johnson to be our U.S.-based liaisons. In order to get things done in Morocco you have to jump through a lot of hoops, go through a lot of red tape, and meet with a lot of people. At long last the festival was finally scheduled for September 1–3, 1972, with three days of nighttime concert performances. The first two nights were in a huge bullring, probably too huge in retrospect, but that was the most suitable venue we could arrange. The third night was also scheduled for the bullring, but there was a sandstorm coming in from the Sahara, and if you've ever been in a sandstorm . . . so at the last minute we had to open up the Teatro Cervantes for the concert.

This Teatro Cervantes hadn't been used in a while, so we had to get a group of people to furiously clean up this place in a short period of time to try and have it ready for the third night's performances, and we succeeded. The sandstorm made it impossible to present the third night in the bullring. This wasn't designed as a moneymaking venture, this was a cultural pursuit. Tickets were priced very cheaply at $2–$3 so the people from the medina could come.

It was a superhuman effort pulling this festival together, mainly because such a thing had never happened before in the history of Morocco. We had to deal with Iberia Airlines to arrange flights; some of the people assisting me extended their credit cards to cover our expenses, all kinds of crazy stuff. Then when it came time for the festival, unbelievably the plane carrying all of the artists from the U.S. didn't arrive in Tangier until about 6:00 p.m. of the opening night . . . and the festival was set to begin at 8:00.

On that plane were the group Mandrill, Pucho and the Latin Soul Brothers, the great singer Odetta, Max Roach's group—sans Max because for some odd reason that still hasn't been explained to me, my boyhood friend Max didn't make the flight, despite the fact that he had worked on the U.S. side to organize the whole thing. My dear friend and bassist Ahmed Abdul-Malik came, as did the flutist Hubert Laws and a few others. On the African side we had scheduled the Gnawa and some of the other Moroccan spirit music brotherhoods to perform.

Since they arrived so late and so close to the scheduled start time of the first night and there was no such thing as a sound check, much less a rehearsal, we got together and had a big debate about who was going to open the evening. We dropped the weight on Pucho to start first, so he gathered all his cats together and they opened the festival. The whole idea behind the festival was to show the connections between African people, the diaspora, and the continent itself, with an emphasis on North Africa. So as a sort of invocation for the festivities, lined up on one side of the stage we had three Berber flute players and Hubert Laws playing western flute on the other side. They started playing and improvising in their respective traditions, and slowly walking toward each other to join in the center of the stage. The purpose was to show the connections between our people.

Pucho and the Latin Soul Brothers performed right after that flute invocation. The tone was beautifully set. Then Max Roach's group sans Max played, including Cecil Bridgewater on trumpet, Billy Harper on tenor sax, and Juney Booth on bass. As I said, Max and Mary Jo Johnson headed up the festival committee in New York. They coordinated all the details on that side, including making sure all the musicians got on the plane on time. Odetta performed, Mandrill, Ahmed Abdul-Malik on the oud performed solo, and we also had two masters, the pianist Kenny Drew and the saxophonist Dexter Gordon, who came in from Europe. The trumpeter Richard Williams, who had been part of my *Uhuru Afrika* recording orchestra, showed up from out of nowhere; he had been in Spain performing, so he came down on his own.

We had about forty performers altogether. I played with Abdul Aziz, a percussionist from Tangier, and my son Azzedin on percussion. The remaining festival musicians were Jillalah, Gnawa, and other traditional Moroccan musicians. In the true communal spirit there were a number of impromptu performances as musicians got comfortable; Billy Harper even played the drums for a minute, subbing for the master with Max's musicians. The combinations would vary from night to night, but each of the three nights all of these musicians performed in different sets. And then afterwards everybody would come over to the African Rhythms Club after the concert to jam. This was historic and all of us knew we were involved in something we had never experienced before. The musicians were very happy despite the admittedly somewhat haphazard arrangements; there was a real lack of coordination, a lot of last-minute stuff got in the way, but they all loved Morocco. Their lodging wasn't a problem since they all stayed at the five-star Hotel Continental. The problems were more related to logistics, transportation, and stuff like that.

The newspapers absolutely loved the event, they ate it up. The fact that we were bringing all these top musicians to Tangier, just that in itself was very important and they felt much honored. Here's just one example of how crazy this scene was: we had a guy on our local committee who was the head of the tax bureau for Tangier named Ouazzani. He was a beautiful guy who really loved the music. The main venue, the Plaza de Toro bullring, was kind of a far distance outside of town. Once you got there the place had many different entry gates and ticket windows all the way around. So we had different people collecting the ticket money at the stations all the way around this huge place. Some of the tax department personnel took it upon themselves—unbeknownst to their boss Ouazzani—to collect ticket buyers' taxes right there on the spot. Ouazzani then had to run all the way around this huge venue to all the ticket windows to tell these guys to stop collecting these taxes. That was just one example of the disorganization; this kind of event had never taken place before, so a lot of this confusion was understandable. But the audiences loved it. With the United Nations presence in Tangier there were a number of other Africans and internationals in the audience as well.

The fact that all these musicians made it to Morocco in the first place was incredible. Years later in 2001, when I was strolling through the medina in the seaside town of Essaouira during the Gnawa Festival, to have so many Moroccan people come up to me and greet me with such warmth says it all about the efforts we made with the African Rhythms Club and the festival; they all remembered those times. If I made a million dollars tomorrow nothing could replace that feeling. It was something so incredible, and you KNOW the Creator was in charge.

How else could you explain how I was able to eventually pay off all of the enormous debt that came with the festival? That was some kinda miracle, it was spiritual intervention. Since the promised sponsorship money largely didn't come as expected we really fell short of the necessary dollars. We were only able to pay some of the musicians, some we didn't pay, and others said they would gladly donate their services. But these were my fellow musicians, and I really wanted to pay all of them as we had promised. I wound up completely strapped for cash after this festival. I had to borrow a plane ticket just to take my kids back to New York. I was forced to close my club; I had no money and all these musicians to pay. I also knew that some of these musicians were disappointed because they came there expecting some kind of African paradise, with no struggle . . . But the reality was a real struggle. They apparently thought they were coming to Utopia. Despite all that I know I made a contribution to my people, and to me that is the highest honor any black man can have.

But back to that divine intervention from the Creator: my dear friend Mary Jo Johnson had worked particularly hard to make this festival possible from the stateside perspective. At that time she was serving in a kind of managerial capacity for me, and besides her festival duties she was trying to arrange a record date for me. This resulted in the *Blue Moses* album. She said she went to fifteen record companies and nobody wanted to record me. Finally she met with Creed Taylor, whose very successful record company in the '70s was CTI. He recorded people like Freddie Hubbard, Hubert Laws, George Benson, Grover Washington Jr., Stanley Turrentine, Milt Jackson, Bob James, and others. He made all his records at Rudy Van Gelder's famous studio, using a stable of studio musicians which also included the leaders he was recording.

My idea was to record a program of music focusing on Morocco, and

I wrote four pieces for the date. "Ifrane," named for a small town in the mountains near Fes, was about my first trip through the northern part of Morocco. We had arranged to do some concerts at some hotels in Morocco and I had this little automobile. I drove this car through the Atlas Mountains with my son Azzedin and Ed Blackwell. When we passed through this town called Ifran there was actual snow. Ifran is a skiing village, and I didn't know they had snow in Morocco. I was so moved that I wrote a piece about it.

"Blue Moses" was simply the translation of Sidi Musa. Musa was Moses for the Gnawa people; for them the color representing Moses is the color of the sea, the blue of the sky. When I attended a Gnawa ceremony in 1969 in Tangier it was my first of several Lilas with the powerful Gnawa elders. As I said earlier, I was in a trance for a couple of weeks after this ceremony, it was so powerful, and this one particular melody stayed with me. So instead of Sidi Musa I called it "Blue Moses," based on traditional Gnawa music that I adapted and rearranged. When I first wrote this piece the Gnawa elders forbade me to play it in public; but after about a year they finally relented after I pleaded with them that people needed to hear this melody.

"Night in Medina" was about an experience I had when I was living in Rabat, the capital of Morocco. I stayed at the Hotel Rex, right in front of the old city; the medina is the old city, where the traditional marketplace sells all kinds of spices, kaftans, and other Moroccan goods. During the day there are hundreds of people on the streets of the medina, but at night it gets real quiet. One particular night I couldn't sleep and something urged me to go into the medina, so I went there at 3:00 in the morning. The streets were deserted and it was very mysterious, sorta spooky. I walked around these deserted streets and this melody came to me. Fortunately nothing happened to me, but it was a very powerful experience of having frequented the medina during the day when it's crawling with people, then at night when there's nothing but shadows. I also wrote "Marrakech Blues" in honor of the city of Marrakech, a city that is really magical. The buildings have a wonderful reddish hue. So that rounded out my program for this proposed *Blue Moses* date.

Creed Taylor insisted that the only way he would agree to do the date was if I played it on Fender Rhodes electric piano, which was popular back then. I can't stand the electric piano, but I really wanted to make this record. Creed also insisted on using his regular musicians, which was OK with me because they included Ron Carter and Freddie Hubbard, who had played with me on the *Uhuru Afrika* date; Hubert Laws, who ironically played the festival in Tangier; plus Grover Washington Jr., Billy Cobham, and the Brazilian percussionist Airto. I brought my regular bass player Bill Wood and Azzedin on congas to make the date as well. We recorded *Blue Moses* in March 1972. Despite my lack of control over some of these important elements, incredibly *Blue Moses* became my biggest-selling record.

Besides his regular crew of excellent musicians, Creed Taylor was known for a certain sound on CTI, and his house arranger was Don Sebesky. We recorded the date using Melba's arrangements of my compositions. I wasn't happy with having to use that electric piano, but the recording session came out much to my satisfaction. So following the session I went back to Morocco and got busy with the African Rhythms club and festival planning. *Blue Moses* was released just before the festival, and I remember being in the club when one afternoon a dub of the record arrived in the mail. I immediately put it on the turntable and out burst all this added orchestration from Don Sebesky. I couldn't believe it. But the true success of *Blue Moses* happened after the festival.

It was truly Allah's way; He said, "Man, we gotta help this brother." As I said, it turned out to be my only hit record, even though I'm playing the electric piano with all this added orchestration over which I had no control. But with the royalties from that record, thankfully I was able to pay all the musicians from the festival and I paid the back taxes on the club. People tell me they really enjoy that record. If it wasn't for *Blue Moses* I never would have been able to pay all those musicians. It was truly a miracle.

## 14

> Randy Weston has the biggest sound of any jazz pianist since Ellington and Monk as well as the richest and most inventive beat. —STANLEY CROUCH, *Village Voice*

# POST-MOROCCO AND
# THE ELLINGTON CONNECTION

My connection to Duke Ellington was equal parts musical and spiritual, long before I met the man himself. Duke was everything, going way, way back. Duke was always such a classy gentleman and his music was so powerful. Duke and Basie were alike in that those two giants were totally a part of the black community; they never forgot their roots even though both achieved worldwide fame. I loved Duke's music—Ben Webster, Harry Carney, Sonny Greer, Jimmy Blanton, and all those masters he employed had a huge impact on me. When I first heard the Gnawa in Morocco and heard them play that guimbre I heard echoes of Jimmy Blanton's bass and where that sound came from ancestrally. If I had to pick one giant of our music over all others I'd pick Duke Ellington because he was so complete, and like Coleman Hawkins he stayed forever young; he recorded with artists ranging from Louis Armstrong to John Coltrane. He recorded with Max Roach and Charles Mingus, so people like him and Hawk covered the whole spectrum of our music, they stayed young and always advanced.

In the '60s we used to give rent parties at my apartment on 13th Street to benefit the Afro American Musicians Society. One particular night we featured my good friend the pianist Ray Bryant. Big Black and I cooked food all day long: ribs, stew, and all that stuff; we sold liquor and food at the party to raise money. On this occasion Reverend John Gensel, who started the jazz vespers at St. Peter's and was an all-around jazz clergyman, brought Ruth Ellington, Duke's sister, to the party. It was a really soulful party, people were all over the apartment; we jammed maybe 100–150 people in this apartment and everybody was having a ball. That's when I met Ruth Ellington. I always laugh when I think about that party: she swore Big Black had spiked the party food because that night she felt mighty high, even though she never messed with any drugs.

Eventually Ruth and I got to be very close. Duke had given Ruth and his son Mercer beautiful homes on Riverside Drive and 106th Street, but Ruth also had an apartment on 59th Street. I went there once and played some piano for her and she got excited and said I was the next Duke; she used to tell me that all the time. Even after I moved to Morocco, whenever I came back to New York I would visit Ruth; at one point she actually wanted to marry me, but I was afraid of marriage, I didn't want to get married . . . no way, no how. She only wanted me to play solo piano and she was very critical of my recordings because I wouldn't play much piano, I'd just feature the other musicians in my band. We even gave a big birthday party for my mother and father at Duke's house.

Ruth always called Duke "Edward," and one day while I was there she said "Edward's got to hear you," and she was intent on arranging that. Duke did a concert of his "Night Creature" with the New York Philharmonic, with his trio, and Ruth arranged for me to play the reception, myself and Peck Morrison on bass. After the concert they had the reception in a bar in Philharmonic Hall, and we were playing at one end of the bar when up walked His Majesty, the Duke. He checked us out and gave me a great look, an approving look, a look as if to say, "Everything is OK."

Later on Duke called Ruth one night while I was at the house and she said, "You must hear Randy Weston." So she played "Blue Moses" on the phone for Duke. At that time she was running Duke's publishing company, Tempo Music. When I finally met Duke, we talked and he told me he wanted to start another publishing company with just my compositions and his compositions. I was blown away! So I put twenty of my compositions in his publishing company, Tempo Music. Duke had started a small recording company called Piano Records and he wanted to record Bobby Short, Earl Hines, Abdullah Ibrahim, and myself. That wound up being the record date I did titled *Berkshire Blues*, which was later sold to Arista Records.

Sometime later I encouraged Ruth to set up a big concert at the Cathedral of St. John the Divine to raise money for the seven West African countries of the Sahel Region, because they were experiencing a terrible drought. The great dancer-choreographer Geoffrey Holder was the producer of the concert. We had the Symphony of the New World, we put together a big band with Melba Liston conducting, we had the Joffrey Ballet, and we

Randy with Duke Ellington at Ruth Ellington's apartment.

raised about $7,000, which was basically just symbolic, and presented it to the president of Mali. I must admit I had an ulterior motive in my relationship with Ruth, and that was to encourage her to establish a house of African American culture and music. She had a friend who had the ideal house for this purpose up on the Hudson. We were kinda playing games with one another; she wanted to get married first, I wanted to get the house first.

Duke treated Ruth like a queen, and she was only surrounded by certain kinds of people, for me very bourgeois kind of people. I'm still basically a street dude, and for a while it was OK being around these people, but I got bored with that stuff, all that pretense. Once I talked her into having a party for Josephine Baker, because recently the king of Morocco had given Josephine a large sum of money for a research project she was spearheading. At the same time I was still intent on establishing that dream cultural center in Morocco and I wanted to reach the king. I figured I might be able to do that through Josephine, thinking that perhaps this party might be a step toward that.

So we had this party at Ruth's house the night after Josephine's last appearance in New York, in the late 1970s. I hired Danny Mixon to play the piano so that I could co-host the party with Ruth and mingle freely among the guests, but my real motive was to connect with Josephine Baker. Unfortunately, even though I met her I could never get to talk to her that night because throughout the evening she was surrounded by these ex-chorus girl friends of hers. It was almost like they were protecting Josephine.

Ruth had a big heart and we really became like family; my daughters Cheryl and Pamela, my father, we'd be at her house all the time. But she lived such a sheltered life and it seemed there were few people she could trust. She was a wonderful, wonderful person; very kind, very generous. We might have possibly married but she never wanted to go anywhere by herself, you always had to go with her, she was really sheltered. Whenever she would go out she had to be decked out, had to have her jewelry, her rings, had to wear her furs; she was an Ellington lady after all. She'd always feel better having a strong man by her side; eventually she married McHenry Boatwright.

Through Ruth I got to know a lot of the guys in the Ellington band. Reverend Gensel started the original jazz vespers services back when his church was on Broadway at 93rd Street. I actually played the first jazz vespers and played Billy Strayhorn's piano, which Billy had given to Gensel for his church. It was as a result of that connection that I wound up playing at Strayhorn's funeral.

Ruth actually felt that I could be the next Ellington; she wanted me to take over the orchestra after the master passed in '74. But the orchestra was Mercer's, and Ruth handled Duke's compositions. There was always a kind of friction between her and Mercer because Duke had given Ruth everything. He was like a father to Ruth. You'd go to her house and in her bedroom there'd be maybe twenty-five different kinds of crosses, which Duke would send her from the road; silver crosses, gold crosses, wooden crosses, all kinds. She took care of business for Duke's publishing company, Tempo. Our relationship was romantic, but for me it was more about the culture than about Ruth as a woman. During that time we also gave a benefit for my club in Tangier where we had twenty-five pianists play at the Ellington devotee Brooks Kerr's mother's house, an East Side townhouse. Ruth and I were very close and the core was Duke himself.

## Life after Tangier

After the festival I was left in a bad way financially, so I went back to the States and stayed at my dad's house on Lafayette Avenue in Brooklyn for a minute. But I wasn't a kid anymore and that didn't work, he and I just got in each other's way, so I moved in with my friend Pablo Ferro, a Cuban-American filmmaker. Pablo lived right around the corner from where I used to live in Manhattan, on 13th Street and 2nd Avenue. He had an apartment strewn with nothing but circus posters on the walls, and Budweiser lights flashing off and on . . . he was out there. Pablo once made an animated film called "Be There," and his partner Norman Skinner had me write the music. But after being in Africa that many years, coming back to the States afterwards was too big a change, I just couldn't get back into that pace. I only wound up staying in the States about two years.

I never was real interested in Europe, even though for a lot of musicians Europe was the key . . . everything was focused on Europe as an escape from the U.S.—but not for me, I always preferred to go to Africa. I was blessed in being able to go to Africa many years before I ever went to Europe. I didn't get to Europe for the first time until 1974, when I performed at the Montreux Jazz Festival in Switzerland. We arranged to make a record of that festival performance for a questionable Englishman named Alan Bates, which was eventually called *Carnivals*. My group on that occasion included William Allen on bass, Billy Harper on tenor sax, Don Moye on drums, Steve Berrios on congas, and my buddy Ahmed Abdul-Malik on oud. Billy was at the festival playing with Gil Evans at that time, Don Moye was there with the Art Ensemble of Chicago, so it was arranged that they would record with me.

Duke Ellington had just passed away, so I did a seven-minute solo piano tribute to Duke, trying to paint colors, trying to capture his spirit. When I came off the bandstand people stopped me and said that I should definitely play more solo piano; so that was the beginning of my really playing solo piano in major venues. I've actually played the Montreux Jazz Festival five times now, more than any other festival.

I met a Swiss guy named Paul Meyer who had a fantastic record shop in Geneva with all the best jazz music. He came to my hotel in Montreux accompanied by a French lady named Colette. Paul wanted to start a small recording company and he wanted to name the company Hi Fly, after my composition. He wanted me to make a solo piano record for his new company. I'd never been to Europe before and I didn't know who these two people were, so I wasn't too interested in that idea. I asked about the money and they said, "Oh, we'll negotiate later," which also made me quite leery.

It turns out this woman Colette Giacomotti lived in Annecy, France, near the Swiss border. She had a nice house there, she was friends with the South African pianist Abdullah Ibrahim, and she loved piano. This guy Paul wanted me to go to her house and make this solo piano record on her piano. After much coaxing on their part I finally said OK, I would at least visit this woman's house and hear what they had to say. So they took me to Colette's house in Annecy, where we were met by other people I didn't know, including the French drummer Daniel Humair. When I walked into Colette's house the first thing I spotted on the wall was a big picture of Melba Liston, and that blew my mind because I had never seen Melba's picture in anyone's house.

I also quickly learned that Colette is a great cook when she dished up all kinds of delicious food. Meanwhile Paul and Humair are steadily trying to convince me to make this recording for a relative small sum of money. We argued almost all night while Colette kept bringing out various refreshments and being a wonderful host. Finally I said, "OK, I'm going to do this record strictly because of her," pointing at Colette, "not because of you guys." That night they set up all the recording equipment, I sat down to the piano at Colette's house, and just played straight for one hour; and that was the beginning of my relationship with Colette Giacomotti. The session eventually came out on Paul's small Hi Fly label. But as I later learned, he was a con man and a very cheap guy who was using Colette to get to me.

Annecy is a beautiful town in the French Alps, with a lovely lake and lots of swans, a very peaceful town. Colette's home is not far from the water. She's a warm, wonderful woman who loves the music and is very spiritual. She also has a great love of African culture. Her house became my base in France, and from there I did a lot of performing in Europe. I wasn't much interested in living in Paris; I wanted to be someplace where I could be away from the hustle, so Annecy was ideal. The natural resources there are very vivid and beautiful, but unfortunately I'm not crazy about snow and ironically Colette was the director of a ski lodge. So sometimes I'd have to go up into the mountains and all that ice wasn't happening for me. But you have to adjust in life and I adjusted for a while.

I've found that with European women they can love you to death, but they cannot experience what it means to be black. There are certain things about us that are different. While I was up there in Annecy—and I wound up staying there at Colette's off and on for nearly ten years, using it as my base—there were only two brothers I connected with the whole time; one from the Ivory Coast who had a beautiful African shop, and Andre Paccard and his wife Jacqueline who had a gorgeous home where I'd often go to use their piano. I really missed black people in Annecy. Colette couldn't quite understand that. But we had the same feeling about Africa, she loved the music, and she had a big collection of our music. She's a woman who is very happy to know about black people.

During this time George Wein and the other jazz promoters in Europe wouldn't book me. Colette, who is also very shrewd and business-minded, started booking me because nobody was interested in hiring me in Europe otherwise. Eventually she contacted the French Ministry of Culture to try and arrange some performing opportunities for me. Through her persistence, her clarity, her energy, she learned the business and she booked me in a very professional manner. All I had to do was put my ideas on paper, show up and play the music. Colette was fantastic. Because of her I was able to perform in places like Guadeloupe, Martinique, and Tahiti, all around the world through the connections she made with the French Ministry of Culture. She arranged for me to do history-of-jazz performances and solo concerts all over the world. One time I was able to bring a group over with Idrees Sulieman, Big Black, James Spaulding, and Benny Powell. I had found a woman who loved the music, loved the culture, and was willing to fight for me to work as an artist in a very top-professional way. Everything with her was first class, her letters on my behalf and everything.

I maintained my base at Colette's home for nearly ten years. I'd come back to the States on occasion but essentially I was based in France. I brought my mother and father there to Colette's house, my oldest daughter Cheryl visited there, as did Azzedin, Pamela, and my grandson Niles, because wherever I go I always try to take my family. Colette's efforts assured me some work through the Ministry of Culture; I actually played in Tahiti three times through that arrangement.

One memorable occasion was a gig she arranged for me in Algiers with my trio. She would generally accompany us on these trips as manager. Sometimes when you deal with Africa, especially in those days not too long after independence, things can get strange with the tickets, with boarding the plane, there's always some extra nonsense or red tape to deal with. This one time when we were traveling to Algiers we got to the airport in Lyon, France, got our tickets, and this woman from the airline says, "Listen, we're sorry but the plane is full." We insisted we had to travel that day, we were on our way to a festival gig, and we had to make this flight. She said, "I'm sorry, that won't be possible."

While we argued with these ticket agents the pilot and co-pilot walked past and this agent went over to explain our situation to them. The pilot said, "What! come with me." We went through customs and got on the plane. The pilot made three people get up and get off the plane. Remember, this was Air Algiers, the official airline of Algeria. We were kind of embarrassed when we saw those three people coming off the plane. They seated us and Colette sat in the cockpit of the plane.

About halfway over the Mediterranean Colette remembered that she had forgotten some important posters we were supposed to deliver to the festival in Algiers. So she told the pilot that we had left the posters in the car. He said, "Where's the car?" She told him it was in the airport parking lot; he says, "Give me the keys and when I go back to Lyon I'll bring back the posters on the next flight." He actually did bring back the posters, arriving right before our concert started. With Colette I was really protected, I was treated as an artist is supposed to be treated, meaning I didn't have to deal with any contracts or paperwork headaches, all I had to do was go over to the piano and play, she took care of everything.

Another funny incident happened when she and I traveled to Tahiti for a concert. I love honey, and in Tahiti they have the most incredible honey,

honey like you've never tasted before; you taste it and the flowers literally burst in your mouth. Tahiti is all volcanic earth, I remember the grapefruits there were the size of watermelons. I bought these wonderful cans of this special honey, we're talking about nine-quart cans of honey, and I've gotta carry this stuff by hand, I can't put it in my luggage.

On a trip like this the French government took care of the roundtrip from Paris to Tahiti. Normally we would return after the performance. But we found out that by paying just a few more francs we could go pretty much around the world on our way back to Paris. Colette had been contacting Yamaha in each city to see if they would sponsor a tour of the band, because all we had to start with was the solo piano gig in Tahiti. We ended up going to Bahrain, Singapore, Hong Kong, Egypt, and Rome for just a few more francs. In every country the police would make me open up each and every one of those cans of honey. They'd have to look at it, and this honey is dark, so who knows what I might have had in there, but actually there was nothing in those cans but pure honey.

Finally, just before we were to go to Bahrain, I got this brilliant idea in Singapore: I would just take the honey and get some of those plastic containers and that way when I went through customs they could see through the plastic that it's nothing but honey. Only a genius could think of a solution like that, or so I thought. So I put all the honey in these plastic containers. We're on our way to Bahrain, carrying this honey. We took our seats on the plane and meanwhile the honey is in these containers in a bag with a lot of papers because it was easier to carry it on that way. I jammed the bag under the seat. By the time we got to the hotel in Bahrain there was honey everywhere. It was all over the papers, all over the contracts . . . We had to put the bag in the bathtub to get the honey out. For the next year we would find honey stuck on something.

Life was great at Colette's house, but Annecy itself was so lacking in color that I became starved for seeing black people. Besides those folks I mentioned earlier, Colette introduced me to a very interesting African musician named Papa Oye McKenzie. He was a brother from Ghana who lived in Switzerland. Annecy is just over fifty kilometers from the border and he lived in nearby Geneva. He was a spiritualist as well as a musician who was involved with some mystics in Zurich. He used to drive all over Switzerland in this distinctive white van with the words "Rhythm is the Secret" spelled out on the side. He was also teaching African drumming at various schools in Switzerland.

Papa Oye played thirty-three instruments, and he would set up his drums just like our traditional trap drum set, but everything was African. He took a gourd and made a sock cymbal out of it, everything was made from African materials. This guy played trumpet, oboe, and all kinds of percussion instruments; he was like a one-man band and he knew many of the traditional African drumming techniques. He and I instantly hooked up because we had the same vision of a strong Africa, which was our mutual concern. Because we knew if Africa became strong all of us in the diaspora would become stronger. We would discuss things like that all the time.

He was a guy who was interested in spreading the message of the importance of African traditional music. I'd go to restaurants with him and he would always eat with his hands, and he always wore African clothing. He once told me something very interesting: he said that he grew up in a traditional village but was forced to go to a Christian school in Ghana. He was from the town of Kumasi and he grew up with these two different ways—the western man's concept he got from school, and the traditional Ghanaian concept. He would always stress that all music comes out of African traditional music, that Africa represents thousands of years of magic and greatness that we know nothing about. Only the griots and the Gnawa and people like that who keep these songs alive to give us a taste of what happened before truly recognized these truths.

Papa told me one day that he was at a funeral in his village and he heard some traditional music, and the songs they sang were very sad songs, but very beautiful. Then later on he started playing some of those traditional songs on the trumpet. At the same time the Christian school was where he learned western techniques of music. When he finally left Ghana he went to Dakar, Senegal, because Dakar and Lagos, Nigeria, were two big centers where a lot of West African musicians migrated and hung out. He said that one night he played a gig with other African musicians at a club and some of them said, "You sound like Miles." He had no idea who they were talking about Then he started listening to Miles Davis and he thought they were right, because when Miles Davis played it was very beautiful, but it's a very sad beauty, you could feel the sadness in his playing. Like Billie Holiday, you can hear a certain sadness in her music.

So Papa surmised that Miles's ancestry comes from the village of those same ancient funeral songs, which are very beautiful but at the same time very sad. He said that's the reason why they thought he played like Miles, because he was playing these ancient funeral songs. He said he was convinced that every style of music that we call jazz, from Art Tatum to Dizzy to Coltrane, can be traced directly back to a traditional village.

We played several concerts together; I'd play piano and he'd play all his instruments. Other musicians would run at just the sight of his drum set, thinking it strange and too complicated, but he had all these instruments working together. He really opened up my eyes about the styles of the music. He said that Dizzy Gillespie's ancestry was absolutely from North Africa; and I certainly heard Dizzy's style out of the North of Africa. Out of a traditional village there is music for every single activity. The rhythms go beyond shades and color, and I'm convinced that is true.

Papa and I started working on a book about these things but unfortunately he died quite mysteriously; they found him dead of unknown causes in Switzerland in the early '80s. The authorities didn't know how he died, but I do know he was involved with some occult people, which I didn't know anything about. But our book plan was to trace the so-called musical styles, how the music changes everything . . . The Sufi teaches us that the music is the first thing that changes. When you have ordinary times you get ordinary music, and everything follows the ordinary music. When you have a creative time, that's when you have the powerful, creative music, not just here but all over the world. But when the music changes, when you get the junk and things are copied, you get an ordinary society.


## Return to Maroc

I had been living in Annecy for the bulk of ten years, with this incredible French woman Colette Giacomotti and her family; they treated me like royalty. But it suddenly dawned on me that in the ten years I was there I didn't really have any friends. At the same time I found myself more and more closing inward. There was one room in Colette's house where everything was related to black folks—the photographs and everything. I found that I was really missing black people. Finally I had to leave, I couldn't take it anymore.

What really did it, what finally drove me to leave, was sheer racism. Every Sunday when I woke up I went out to get fresh bread, beautiful, just-baked bread. I left the house this one Sunday and I saw signs around town about this fascist French politician, Jean-Marie Le Pen. This French politician, who is still there, had big signs up in town about his ideas of driving all immigrants out of France. His posters were up all over, and it really turned me off to see that. So I said to myself, "OK, if I've gotta deal with racism I'd prefer to be on my own turf, not somewhere like this." Nothing overt ever happened to me, but that really turned me off.

There was also an architect in town who wanted to hit on Colette's very beautiful daughter. I needed some work done on a new brochure and this guy knew some people who could design it, so me and this guy had lunch together. He was really interested in Colette's daughter so he was on his best behavior, he was dressed sharp, speaking politely, a real pretty boy in his manner. I thought we could do some business. That same Monday, Colette and I were looking at television at a report on the French elections. The Socialists had their support and this far-right racist Le Pen had his support as well. They showed a picture of a meeting with this Le Pen, and that's how we came to find out that this same architect was the president of Le Pen's party in Annecy. This was 1985, the year I left.

Colette is a great lady, and what she did for me I cannot describe, but this poisonous Le Pen atmosphere was just too much for me. I hated to leave Colette, but I couldn't take it anymore. I packed up all my stuff in my car—I had a Citroën back then—and left. It took me three days to drive from Geneva, through France, Spain, and directly to Tangier by ferryboat. When I arrived back in Morocco people were truly happy to see me. It was just incredible to realize how Moroccan people had missed me, even though it had been thirteen years since I'd left; it was a wonderful feeling.

Not long after I arrived my old friend and partner Abdeslaam in Tangier arranged a tour for me through a friend of his who was a major in the army and the head of the Crescent Rouge, which is the Islamic world's equivalent to the Red Cross. One interesting thing about Morocco is that the military and police are very much into culture. The police actually built the conservatory of music in Rabat. So these guys got together and arranged for us to do a tour of Morocco, the purpose of which was to raise money for the Crescent Rouge children's services.

The USIS was involved with the tour, and the person there who was responsible for the tour was my friend Khadija Ouahmane, who now lives in Brooklyn. The tour was set up to last a couple of weeks, with performances in Marrakech, Casablanca, Tangier, Rabat, and Fes. We played in hotels, sometimes special clubs like the officers' clubs, sometime at one of the princesses' houses or places of recreation, so it varied. We weren't necessarily spending any time with the traditional people, but it was great to be back in Maroc nonetheless.

## 15

# COMPOSITIONS AND SESSIONS

A great piece of music never grows old, that's the first thing you have to keep in mind. Someone may tell you it's old, but there's no such thing as an old song, not a real classic composition, it's never old. "Body and Soul" will never be old. I used to wonder why Duke Ellington would constantly play tunes like "Take the A Train" and "Sophisticated Lady"; I'd wonder why he wouldn't do something new—after all, this is a man who was always writing new stuff, but he would always play those standards of his. By contrast, I talked with Monk about that and he would say, "They haven't learned to play what I've already written," at least not his way.

It goes back to African traditional music, which has become my major influence. There's no such thing as an old song in African tradition; the music is timeless. That means you can play "Caravan" a thousand years from now, the key thing is what you *do* with "Caravan." It's a classic piece, what you would call a standard, and it's hard to create another "Caravan." I could never create another "Hi Fly," but there's no limit to what you can do with "Hi Fly." Sometimes I play it as a ballad, sometimes I switch up and do it as a waltz, sometimes 4/4, but if you look at the music itself any tune is a challenge, and when you improvise I don't care what song it is, you've gotta do something fresh, even if it is the same song you did before.

In our tradition you have to always be able to compose what's known as improvisation on top of an existing composition, so it's always a challenge. Each piece is a message; it's like speaking, you can speak and people can get bored to death with what you're saying, but when you speak if you put certain accents on certain words your speech can be more interesting. I learned from Duke that you have to constantly tell the story of that song; you're not just playing changes, you're not just playing solos, it's not so much about the technical aspects that reach most people . . . As Lester Young said, you have to compose on top of a composition, and that's your constant challenge as a musician, to improvise something fresh over an existing composition.

In the western concept we talk about things as being old, as passé . . .
In so doing we tend to forget what Duke Ellington, Eubie Blake, and all
those cats were doing as far back as the 1920s. For example, I've got a Duke
Ellington record where Duke is playing stride piano in 1928. I listened to
this music and I said: Wait a minute . . . that whole concept of flatted fifths
that people talk about being peculiar to bebop beginning in the 1940s, man,
Ellington and those cats were doing flatted fifths a long time ago. We tend
to be brainwashed by people saying, "This is the latest," as if what happened before is out of date, but it's just the reverse, what happened before
is the strongest, just like with African traditional music.

Whenever you hear the Gnawa play you always hear the same songs.
But those songs are so powerful that there's no such thing as "that song is
old." Their song "Chalabati" will never be old, it is timeless. I approach my
music the same way, through the influence of Duke and Monk. You have to
keep it fresh, because if you play the same solo every night you're finished.
When I play a concert I'm telling stories, not just playing music, not just
playing a solo, but every song is a narrative. For example, take "The African
Cookbook": the melody is North African, the rhythm is found in different
parts of Africa, but particularly south of the Sahara, that irresistible 6/8
rhythm. Within that 6/8 concept Benny Powell, the trombonist in my band,
might play a spiritual, Talib Kibwe (TK Blue), the saxophonist, might play
a calypso, I might do some other stuff . . . Alex Blake and Neil Clarke, the
rhythm section, we're always challenging them, we're always challenging
each other.

Someone might ask me why I like a certain song more than other songs,
but I don't really have an answer for that. Take a piece like "Little Niles." I
didn't play that piece for three years after I wrote it; I thought it was a sad
tune. Willie Jones, my drummer at the time back in the '50s, used to beg me
to play "Little Niles," and it later became a standard. Even sometimes when
you first compose a piece you don't recognize its worth. Like, for example,
if I want to record something I may pull out some tunes that I haven't
played in a while. Maybe it's certain songs that just stay with you, which
I discovered in Duke, regardless of all the songs he wrote. When you'd go
to hear Duke there were certain melodies of his that stayed with you when
you heard the Ellington band play them. When you'd go to hear Monk you
knew you were going to hear certain songs, but those pieces are so strong
they're structured so beautifully, just a perfect composition . . . whether it's
"Round Midnight" or "Take the A Train," those pieces are timeless.

When I wrote "Nice Ice" I was not as heavily involved with Africa as I later became, I was a pianist writing waltzes. I wrote a lot of songs about children. "C. W. Blues" was written for my eldest daughter Cheryl—a spiritual blues for her. "Pam's Waltz" was for my daughter Pamela, "Little Niles" was for my son Azzedin, and later on I did a piece called "Penny Packer Blues" for my youngest daughter Kim. She's an actress, very active, very dynamic, so I wrote that piece for her. The first recording I did with Melba Liston was seven waltzes for children, because I've always been interested in children. Since then I realized that I've become like a storyteller. My compositions have always been more about spirituality, important people in my life, and places than about technical aspects of composition, which I don't really dwell on. So what I try to project to our audiences is that we are an African people and we have many stories to tell.

I don't really determine what I'm going to play in advance of a performance; rarely have I prepared a set list. It's a combination of the piano at the venue, the temperature, and of course the audience. The audience is all individual people, yet when we come onstage they become one and you've got this mass of humanity radiating their vibrations back to us. It depends on who's on the program as well. One night in 2005 we were playing a concert in Guadeloupe, and a Senegalese kora master named Lamine Konte opened the concert. There was also an African dance company from Paris on this same festival, and they were all sitting in the audience. So I said, "OK, I'm in Guadeloupe, Lamine Konte is here, the dancers are in the audience, what's the message I want to convey, what's the first song going to be?"

I started with "The African Cookbook," because it has a 6/8 rhythm and you'll find that rhythm all over the continent of Africa, and as I said it's a great rhythm that people really relate to, you can dance to a 6/8 rhythm whether you're five years old or a hundred. Lamine Konte played a lot of things in a 6/8 rhythm during his performance. I wanted to play "The African Cookbook" first of all because it's a tune that emphasizes that we are a global people and this cookbook is a *musical* cookbook: whether it's reggae, hip hop, bossa nova, ska, the Guadeloupe rhythm known as Gwo-ka . . . it's all African. Then after that opening piece I wanted to change the tempo, get into a different kind of mood. So it's a combination of sending different messages, different kinds of mood . . . but it all depends on the audience; it's something that you feel, it's a magic that I can't explain, certainly not in technical terms.

I knew I was going to end that Guadeloupe concert with "Blue Moses," and I knew we were going to play "The Shrine," because I wanted that audience to hear some music that would take them somewhere. When people say to me, "You've taken us on a trip," that's exactly what I want to do, take the audience on a global trip of African culture to realize that we are all the same people. That is the real message. The thing that has been destroying us as a people is that we've been so cut off from each other as a people: she's Senegalese, he's American, that one over there is Jamaican . . . There's tremendous separation of our people. All kinds of audiences—European, Asian, etc.—always say to me, "You've taken us on a trip." I say that's what I want to do. When they leave a performance I want them to feel not that we've played such virtuoso solos, but that we've taken them all over Africa through our music. When people leave our performances they'll have a greater respect for Africa, more respect for us as African people. They will see that we're not just a facsimile. That's why many times I'll play "Caravan." Why would I play "Caravan," it's not even my tune? I play it because that was the first song I learned to play about Africa, and Duke was playing that for fifty years.

Lamine Konte, who is part of a family of master musicians of Senegal, told me afterwards that he had heard many jazz musicians trying to connect their music with African music but in his mind there was always a disconnect. He had never heard us before that night, but he said his mind was blown by our performance because we truly connected to Africa with our music. He said when he went back to his hotel room that night, all night long what he heard from our performance was in his head. He felt we have been able to make that connection. The reason is simple, because I have lived among African people and experienced magical and seemingly supernatural things. I didn't tell him that, but I know that's the reason, because the tendency in the West is to just jump in and play *about* Africa, not play *with* Africa. Even up until now there are things about Gnawa music, for example, that I don't know. That's very important to keep in mind, because this is Africa we're talking about and you may think you know, but you don't know anything.

One of the first pieces I ever wrote was "Loose Wig," during my trio days in the early '50s with my original Berkshires trio of Sam Gill on bass and Willie Jones on drums. It was just a piece saying somebody was a little crazy, her wig is loose, she's out to lunch . . . When I wrote that I was going through a period of being heavily influenced by Basie, Nat Cole, Ellington, Monk, Fats Waller . . . which inspired a combination of writing about family or writing music about incidents I experienced, or friends, or about particular events. So obviously somebody I met was crazy! Before "Loose Wig" I wrote a piece called "Under Blunder," inspired by being stuck in a subway in the tunnel under the East River. All the passengers were going nuts, and this was way before Bin Laden. You know, with the river flowing on top of the tunnel people were quite uneasy being stuck down there.

Probably the tune I wrote that is most closely identified with me is "Hi Fly," a takeoff on my height. I wrote that during the time I lived on 13th Street in Manhattan from 1957 to 1967, which was the first time I lived in Manhattan. I had an incredible six-room apartment for $75 a month. Down there we were also in contact with a lot of musicians in the area, people like Sam Rivers, who had his loft Studio Rivbea further downtown. A lot of piano players used to hang out at my apartment, like Tommy Flanagan and Barry Harris, who came from Detroit, Ray Bryant, Sadik Hakim from Philadelphia, Bud, Monk . . . This apartment became a kind of melting pot. A lot of guys came from other cities to New York and they would settle in that area of Manhattan. "Hi Fly" came out of that environment.

I figure "Hi Fly" must have come from a rhythm I heard in African drumming, though I'm not certain about that. "Hi Fly" was not only based upon a rhythm, but also what was happening on 13th Street in Manhattan. The greatest cover version of "Hi Fly" was by Cannonball Adderley and the band with his brother Nat, Bobby Timmons, Louis Hayes, and Sam Jones on a live recording they made at the Blackhawk in San Francisco. They got the right tempo, captured the right spirit of the piece like nobody else. Another favorite rendition of my music was Freddie Hubbard's version of "Cry Me Not," which was a piece I later renamed "A Portrait of Billie Holiday." Melba Liston wrote the arrangement for Freddie and it was a masterpiece, just incredible the way he played it.

Thinking of Freddie reminds me of the *Blue Moses* recording for CTI on which I play electric piano. Freddie and Grover Washington were exceptional on that record. That was the only time Grover and I played together, and after that whenever I saw Grover he would talk about that record date and thank me. On *Uhuru Afrika* that solo that Cecil Payne takes on "African Lady" between the soprano voice of Martha Flowers and the baritone voice of Brock Peters, where Melba changed the tempo, was another memorable interpretation. I also recall Booker Ervin playing "Portrait of Vivian," the piece I wrote for my mother, at that Monterey Jazz Festival performance we gave in 1966. That's one of the greatest saxophone solos . . . I would put that solo alongside any other tenor solo. Booker literally cries on the tenor saxophone.

When I think about that particular performance I also remember Ray Copeland's solo on "Berkshire Blues," and Big Black's congas on "Afro Black," a piece I wrote for him. On that concert we did with the Boston Pops, Big Black shook up the whole symphony orchestra with his solo on "Afro Black." Afterwards all the string players came and looked at his hands they couldn't believe he'd played all those drums. I've had a lot of wonderful moments with musicians playing my music. Those are some that stand out in my mind.

Jon Hendricks wrote lyrics to my tune "Where" and sang it with strings with the London Philharmonic, and it was just beautiful. Eric Dolphy and Ron Carter playing "Where" is also a beautiful rendition. I was really pleasantly surprised when Carly Simon recorded my song "Pretty Strange" and did a good job with it. Mel Tormé sang "Hi Fly" and it wasn't his thing, it was unusual for him, but he loved it. Betty Carter sang a nice version of "Berkshire Blues." I've been fortunate that there've been a number of artists who've interpreted my music, like Max Roach, Abbey Lincoln, Oscar Pettiford, Panama Francis, Dexter Gordon, Art Blakey, Bobby Hutcherson, Gigi Gryce, Johnny Coles, Phil Woods, Ellis Marsalis, Winard Harper, Stefon Harris, and others.

I wrote "The Healers" as a dedication to the masters—whether you're talking about Monk or Ellington, or a master musician going back to ancient Africa, perhaps to Egypt or Senegal. The piece is about those masters that teach us about music, and they develop a certain dimension, a certain power in music, and we look up to these people as healers. They set the natural laws, they guide you in what direction you should go. Ellington not only produced great music but also kept the history of his people alive. Most of his compositions were historical documents of the struggle of our people, whether it was "A Drum Is a Woman" or "Black, Brown and Beige." Ellington was the epitome of what you should do as a musician, as a composer. Whatever Duke wrote you could always hear the blues underneath, which was symbolic of black people.

I remember once Cannonball Adderley introduced one of my tunes on one of his live records by talking about how I was known for writing waltzes. I always liked waltz rhythms, even from those silly European movies about the seventeenth and eighteenth centuries where they were waltzing. My first memory of a hip waltz was Fats Waller's "Jitterbug Waltz." The waltz form really came together for me when I heard a calypso singer named MacBeth up in the Berkshires. He played some of those African-French melodies called quadrilles, calypso-style, and I had never heard a waltz swing like that before. Dizzy was doing waltz time as well, like that wonderful arrangement Walter Fuller did for Dizzy's band of "Lover Come Back to Me." I think 3 and 6 was just a very natural rhythm for me and somehow I tied up the ¾, the waltz rhythm.

Competition is not the correct description, but at the same time it is a good word to describe what was happening in terms of composition of this music back in the '50s and '60s. There was so much great music being written during the time I was growing up—Ellington, Waller, etc.—not to mention the great standards like "Stardust," "Body and Soul," "You Go to My Head," "Yesterdays" . . . all those great pieces that were standards. And then there were my peers who were constantly writing great stuff, like Horace Silver, Jon Hendricks, Hank Jones, Bobby Timmons, Wade Legge, Benny Golson, Art Farmer, Gigi Gryce . . . there was a lot of inspiration to compose because everybody was writing and doing it so wonderfully. Gigi Gryce was a very important example for us, because he had an all-black publishing company. Gigi took care of the business and he would always tell us never to sell a song, never . . . So from that kind of inspiration a lot of great songs were being written, and I suppose I was in that wonderful movement.

Gigi Gryce was a real warrior, but he dealt with a lot of racism. He tried to get all of us to protect our music, but the establishment didn't want to deal with that, so a lot of pressure was put on Gigi. For example, when we wrote "Uhuru Afrika"—and Gigi eventually played on the record date— I published that through my own company. I had to deal with the head of Roulette Records at the time, a guy named Morris Levy. He wanted a certain percentage of the publishing, higher than normal. Gigi said no, no, we've gotta have our songs in our own publishing companies. So Levy, who also owned Birdland, said, "You guys are never gonna work Birdland again, forget about it"; he put the freeze on. As a result of this kind of thing Gigi had a lot of pressure on him all the time and he just retired, just kind of vanished off the scene. At the end of his life he was teaching junior high school, then he died rather mysteriously. Some people felt certain entities had it in for Gigi because he was always propagating his beliefs to musicians about owning their own music, which was kind of unheard of back then. There was speculation among musicians that he was actually killed. I'm not sure about that, but I dedicated a tune to him called "G Blues G," which I renamed "Kucheza Blues," which he soloed on for the *Uhuru Afrika* session.

When I was coming up it was forbidden to play like somebody else, you just shouldn't sound like somebody else. The only person that got away with that was Paul Quinichette, who they always said sounded like Lester Young, yet Paul actually had a different sound from Prez, so they called him the Vice Prez. The whole key is that you've gotta have your own program even though we all get our sound from someplace. Duke and Monk were my great influences as composer-pianists. There was a time when I played standards: don't forget my very first recording was a Cole Porter program. I was playing standards as a trio before I started playing my own music. Then the whole African influence came into my music, which was the direction I wanted to go in after so many influences. Hearing Dizzy and Chano Pozo really cemented the whole African direction for me.

Dizzy had this incredible bebop orchestra, which to me was the most original orchestra sound after Basie and Ellington because they, along with people like Lunceford, had the big-band sound sewn up. Dizzy had the first really original-sounding big band after those giants; his music was very complex. Pieces like "Things to Come" were so advanced. But when I first heard Chano I was hanging out with George Russell and Max Roach. George was living with Max in Brooklyn at the time, when he wrote "Cubano Be Cubano Bop" for Dizzy's orchestra. When I heard Chano Pozo with that modern orchestra, for me it was complete, because it was like going back to Africa. Chano was Cuban, jet-black in complexion, he was truly an African brother playing that African drum, and that really inspired me. From that point on I started working with hand drums in my bands. Then the great Cuban drummer Candido came on the scene, and we worked together for almost three years in the early 1950s. I met Candido in the Berkshires, and he replaced Chano in Dizzy's band when Chano was killed. So I was working with this great Cuban drummer in my trio and the music was getting more and more into Africa.

From the time Big Black played with me in the mid-1960s in my sextet with Ray Copeland, Lenny McBrowne, and Booker Ervin I've worked with hand drummers. When bebop hit in the '40s and '50s a lot of the trap drummers tended to play very loud, they didn't work with the brushes too much like they used to. The way I play I just loved the way the hand drums complemented my playing. I certainly wasn't the first in that respect. Erroll

Garner used percussionists, so did Nat Cole, so it wasn't an original concept. One thing about hand drums is that you usually don't get drowned out. That's why I give McCoy Tyner a lot of respect for playing all those years with the great Elvin Jones. Elvin used to come to the Five Spot when we were playing there and he loved to play with me. He'd ask to sit in, and man, I couldn't hear nothing I was playing.

## Portrait of a Session

Thinking about Dizzy Gillespie, I guess he and I came full circle when he played on "African Sunrise" for the *Spirits of our Ancestors* record. This record was another opportunity to work with Jean-Phillipe Allard at Verve, who had produced my portraits of Duke, Monk, and the portrait of my own music. That series of three records made in just three days was so successful that Jean-Phillipe wanted me to make another recording. In the back of my mind I wanted to do another big project, like *Uhuru*, but not with the same kind of big band. So I started thinking about the music and what songs I wanted to record. At this time Melba Liston was disabled and in a wheelchair from the stroke she'd suffered in 1985. But I knew I needed Melba to write the arrangements on this recording. So I went to see her and I told her she was the only person who could do this. She looked at me like I was crazy, as if to say, "Fool, can't you see I'm in a wheelchair?" She obviously wasn't in a position to consider writing for such a project, or so she thought. Fortunately her Aunt Thelma, a wonderful sister who was Melba's caretaker, was a computer specialist. Melba began studying the computer and learned how to write music with the computer.

I had an all-star group in mind to make this recording: Pharoah Sanders, Billy Harper, Dewey Redman, Idris Muhammad, Jamil Nasser, Big Black, Azzedin Weston, and my regular band members Benny Powell, Talib Kibwe, and Alex Blake. And I also had a very special guest in mind as well. Meanwhile Melba was working on the arrangements. I told Jean-Phillipe the lineup I wanted, he agreed, and the recording was scheduled for May 21 and 22, 1991, in New York. Melba came in from Los Angeles, so everything was set. But I had one problem: I wanted to have some African traditional music on the record, and considering my experience with the Gnawa, that sound was what I wanted. So I contacted several Gnawa masters in Tangier. It was arranged to have seven Gnawa, from Tangier and Casablanca. They were supposed to meet up in Casablanca to get their visas.

Unfortunately this was during the Desert Storm war with Iraq, and the American consulate wasn't granting any visas, especially to people from Islamic countries. I was visiting Morocco at the time and we went to the consulate in Casablanca with all the Gnawa musicians and met with an American woman who was in charge of processing the visas. She was extremely insulting to the Gnawa, a really terrible person. For example, she questioned one of the Gnawa, a young guy who was married to a European woman who I think was twice his age. This consulate woman had the audacity to ask him, "How come you married this woman twice your age?" Obviously this visa process wasn't working, but unfortunately it was too late to try contacting the State Department in Washington.

So these poor guys had to go back home, and I didn't know what I was going to do about that part of the recording. Luckily Pharoah Sanders knew one Gnawa who lived in Oakland, California, named Yassir Chadly. I also contacted another Gnawa living in New York, a guy named Hassan Hakmoun, but he told me he wanted to play his original music. I told him I didn't want his original music, I wanted a traditional piece, plus he wanted me to speak with his lawyer. So I said, "Man, just forget about it" and I brought Chadly in. Chadly sang a traditional Gnawa piece on the session, with my son Azzedin playing the Moroccan karokob and Jamil Nasser playing the bass.

The extended piece for the date, which had been commissioned in the '80s by the Jazz Institute of Chicago for a Chicago Jazz Festival concert performance, was titled *African Sunrise*. It was written specifically with Dizzy Gillespie and Machito in mind. For that festival Melba conducted the performance and we played her arrangement of *African Sunrise* with Dizzy, Machito's band, Johnny Griffin, Richard Davis, Art Blakey, and me. The performance was outdoors in Grant Park, but the weather acted up and there was a lot of wind and rain. Dizzy arrived very late to the performance, so there was really no time for a rehearsal. When it came time to hit, the winds came up and blew some of the music off the stage, so it was kind of a crazy scene. But we got through it.

Back to the recording session: my Moroccan friend Jacques Muyal, who was close to Dizzy, called and said, "Hey, Randy, why don't you have Dizzy play [*African Sunrise*] on the recording?" Jacques also told Jean-Phillipe, "Hey, man, you gotta have Dizzy" on this session. Jean-Phillipe kinda panicked and said, "No, Dizzy wants too much, too much money." But Dizzy agreed to a very reasonable fee. Dizzy was actually supposed to hear the piece before playing it with us, but when it came time for the recording session he was scheduled to fly to California. While we were rehearsing the piece in the studio Dizzy came by to listen to it, on his way to California. Somebody said, "Dizzy, while you're here why don't you take out your horn?" This was already a very special occasion, because Melba did the arrangements and she was in the studio that day, so it was a reunion between these two old friends. To see Dizzy and Melba together that day was really special.

Dizzy took out his horn and played the piece—after hearing it a couple of times. This was intended to be strictly a rehearsal, he was supposed to record the piece later. But he was so moved by the arrangement that he took out his trumpet and played. We wanted to do another take, just one more. But the next thing I knew he was packing up his horn. I said, "Diz, man is everything OK, are you all right?" He said, "Yeah, man, but I gotta go." So he cut out. Luckily when we played it back it was perfect, a perfect solo, just like that, one take. That was Dizzy for you.

Recording session for *Spirits of Our Ancestors*.
From left: Randy, Dizzy Gillespie, Melba Liston. *Photograph by Cheung Ching Ming.*

# Recording the Gnawa Project

When I first connected with the Gnawa in Tangier in the late '60s I remember Abdullah el Gourde talking about how one day he wanted to get all the elder Gnawa Maalams (or masters) together to do a recording before they passed away. It took us until September 1992 to finally realize that dream. Again I approached Jean-Phillipe Allard, who always seemed open to my ideas, and told him I wanted to record the Gnawa masters, but I wanted to record them in Morocco, and I also wanted to make a solo piano record in Morocco. He agreed with both ideas and asked for all the details. I was in Morocco at the time and Abdullah came to Marrakech, my grandson Niles was with us, so was my friend and liner note writer Rhasheedah McNeil. We spent weeks making the arrangements. We took three weeks traveling around Morocco selecting the masters, even going down to the Sahara. Finally we assembled everybody in Marrakech for a recording session at the La Mamounia Hotel. La Mamounia is one of the most famous hotels in the world; it's the hotel where people like Churchill and Roosevelt used to stay in Marrakech, a fantastic hotel with the most elaborate Moroccan designs.

La Mamounia actually had seven concert grand pianos on site; they also have a jazz room and a room for chamber music, plus many big ballrooms. I met with the hotel director and told him of our plan and asked if we could record in the hotel. He said, "No problem, let's look around." I told him I needed a space with absolute quiet, since obviously this wasn't a true recording studio with soundproofing. He took me around the hotel, we went down some stairs and found a huge ballroom that was completely silent, with no outside noises of any kind. Then he showed me all of the pianos and I selected a really wonderful Steinway.

I had met an engineer in Paris named Vincent Blanchet who had invented a very different kind of microphone which was shaped almost like the human ear. He was anxious for us to use this microphone for recording, so I had Jean-Phillipe make that connection and Vincent came to the recording session. In addition to the Gnawa masters, Jean-Phillipe, Rashida, and Niles, Ellen Barlow came down to do a radio interview for the "Afro Pop" radio series produced by her brother Sean; she came to interview the Maalems.

The recording was on September 17, but we brought the Gnawa together three days early to plan. Some of them hadn't seen each other for thirty, forty years. It was fascinating talking with them and hearing them exchange stories. For the session we asked each master to perform his own original piece, from the eldest to the youngest in order. I played piano on only one song, "Chalabati." Needless to say this was a very powerful, spiritual recording session. Then the following night, with the heavy spirits of the Gnawa still in the room, I made my solo piano recording that was called *Marrakech in the Cool of the Evening*. The Gnawa CD was eventually nominated for a Grammy in 1996, which blew my mind.

## Making Khepera

The 1998 recording session for the record *Khepera*, which I produced this time along with the good brother Brian Bacchus, was quite different from my other recording sessions. In addition to my regular band of Alex, Neil, Talib (TK), and Benny, I added Pharoah Sanders, my old friend Chief Bey on African drums, and Victor Lewis on trap drums. We also had as a special guest a young Chinese woman I'll tell you about shortly.

The great Chiekh Anta Diop was the inspiration for this recording. He was one of the true masters of our planet. He was a Senegalese man, a historian, Egyptologist, scientist, nuclear physicist, linguist, and all-around visionary from a village called Caytou. I wrote a piece for *Khepera* dedicated to him called "Boram Xam Xam," which in Wolof (the pre-colonial language of Senegal) means a man of very high integrity. I had read his book *Civilization and Barbarism*. Important historians like John Henrik Clarke, Ivan Van Sertima, and Wayne Chandler all speak of Diop as the high master.

At the time I met Diop he was living in Dakar, teaching at the University of Dakar. In 1985, when I was in Dakar, luckily I got Diop's telephone number the day before I was supposed to return to New York. I felt I really had to see this man because he's one of the high priests for me. So I called him and ironically he had just come back from Atlanta the previous day after being honored at Spelman College. When I called I said, "Dr. Diop, you don't know me, but I am one of your admirers, I am a student of your work. And I wonder if I might have an opportunity to see you before I leave."

He said, "Randy Weston, I know your music," which completely shocked me. He invited me to come by the university at 11:00 the next morning. Unfortunately he spoke mostly French, and my French is minuscule. I went to his office at the university and turned on the tape recorder, and he spoke for one hour, then he showed me his laboratory, which was like something out of those early Frankenstein movies. After encountering Diop I told myself I had to compose some music for this man. But it took a combination of things for *Khepera* to happen, plus the passage of some years.

I wanted to write some music that was kind of ritualistic. Years later, when I was in Atlanta playing a solo piano concert, a young Chinese woman came over to me after the concert and said, "My name is Min Xao Fen and I'm a musician. I played with Mor Thiam on the concert. I play an instrument called the pipa." She described it as a two-thousand-year-old instrument. She told me that when she heard me play she had never heard anyone play piano like that before. She wanted me to hear her play the pipa, and as it turned out she was living in Brooklyn after moving there from San Francisco.

When she stopped by my house with her pipa and began playing, her music really touched me. Then a bell went off in my head. Back in 1967 in Rabat, at the Conservatory of Music, the professor of music was a man I believe named Mr. Agoumi. I went to visit this man after playing a concert and I spotted a huge piano in the conservatory. When I asked where this unusual piano had come from he said it was from China. I didn't even know the Chinese made pianos. He told me that once he had visited Peking and he heard a Chinese traditional orchestra and saw some instruments that were just like traditional Moroccan instruments. And he remembered that the people living in southern Morocco look Chinese and their music resembles Chinese music. So when I met Min Xao Fen I played some of this southern Moroccan music for her and she said, "That's Chinese music," and I said, "No, that's African Chinese music," and her mind was blown.

I had also read Wayne Chandler's articles. He's an anthropological photojournalist, following in the tradition of J. A. Rogers by projecting our history through photographs. Wayne writes about ancient Africans coming to China and influencing the Chinese through the Shang dynasty. When I told Min about this she got excited about her African heritage. She started bringing me books on the history of Chinese musical instruments. I got a book at a library in Baltimore through a friend of mine that was written by a guy named Kai Si Chang, a Chinese expert on the Shang dynasty who taught at Harvard. Through all of these different books, in Chinese and English, we kept seeing this African presence in the Shang dynasty.

Chiekh Anta Diop made all of these connections in his early works. If I hadn't met Min all of this might not have come together for *Khepera*, a term I learned from Professor Yaalingi Ngemi, a Congolese man who lives in Harlem and who translated Diop's book from French to English. He taught a class at the African Poetry Theater and I kept seeing this term "Khepera" on some fliers he was passing out. I asked him about this word because it was speaking to me for some reason. The word itself has many spiritual meanings because ancient Egypt has a lot of complexities. But basically it means transformation and regeneration, which is what happened to our people; think about it, we've gone from colored, to Negro, to Afro-American, to African American. But the reality is that we are all African people. So Min played on *Khepera* and it was a wonderful session.

## Min Xiao-Fen, Chinese pipa master

*Min Xiao-Fen*: I met Mr. Weston in 1997 when I was invited to play a concert at the Hickman Student Center at Morris Brown College in Atlanta. Mr. Weston played a solo set that evening. I have never heard such beautiful music before as Randy Weston's music. In his hands you are deeply moved by African culture and musical spirits—strong, deep, and mysterious. Listening to his music, I imagined Chinese ink painting, with brushstrokes or little touches on the paper; you will see the ink spreading in different directions, slowly changing the patterns and shading layer by layer . . . together they are making a harmony. Randy's music is like this.

Mr. Weston invited me to record a duet, "Shang"—the first Shang Dynasty goes back three thousand years—for his album "Khepera." The theory for this piece is how Africa and China are connected. Trying to find an answer, Mr. Weston and I went to the Guggenheim Museum and did research, such as reading Chinese history books. Although there were no particular records discussing this connection, we found some traces and similarities between the two cultures. About five thousand years ago, our Chinese ancestors were making music during their work, using sorcery, primitive dancing, and poetry to serve their lives. They were offering sacrifices to the gods, hunting, raising livestock, and farming; they used clay and animal bone to make instruments, like flutes. The first instruments, created about five thousand years ago, made of clay, were called the "xun" and reminded me of the African ocarina—the similarities of the pentatonic scales for both African and Chinese music are present. There are definitely some connections between the two cultures—Africa and China.

## 16

# THE AFRICAN RHYTHMS QUINTET

I've been fortunate to have my music played by some truly stellar musicians, going all the way back to my very first record dates with my homeboy Sam Gill on bass, then having the distinct pleasure of Art Blakey's ancestral beat for my first trio date. Today bandleaders just don't seem able to keep a band together and build any kind of longevity, mainly due to lack of work and because all the young guys want to be bandleaders. That's why I am so thankful about having kept my African Rhythms bands together for so long. And when I say bands it's because for a number of years now through business necessities I've been able to play concerts in every context from solo piano, duo with Talib, trio with Alex and Neil, through the sextet with Billy Harper. The members of my quintet have been with me the longest. I know I'm not Art Tatum, Talib Kibwe (TK Blue) is not Charlie Parker, Benny Powell is not J. J. Johnson, Alex Blake is not Jimmy Blanton, and Neil Clarke is not Max Roach, but put us all together as a quintet and we have this *thing*—we're a true family on the bandstand.

## Alex Blake, bass player

Alex Blake is one of the most unusual bass players I've ever heard; he's been with me the longest. I first heard Alex when he was working with Dizzy Gillespie at the Village Vanguard in the '70s. I had taken Ruth Ellington down to the club to hear Dizzy and I had never heard anybody play a bass like that, I couldn't believe Alex's technique. He was sixteen years old at the time, which made it even more incredible. Unfortunately somebody had given Dizzy some bad food that didn't agree with him that night and he got very sick, they had to take him to the hospital, and he almost left us. So that really stayed in my mind, not that I forgot about Alex, but he wasn't on my mind as much as wondering if Dizzy was going to recover, which fortunately he did.

Randy Weston's African Rhythms.
From left: Benny Powell, Alex Blake, Randy, TK Blue (Talib Kibwe), Neil Clarke.

Alex, Thelonious Monk Jr., my son Azzedin . . . they're all around the same age and came up together musically. It was my son who urged me to get Alex Blake in my band, so I called him for a gig we played at the United Nations for the anti-apartheid committee. Alex gives me that *rhythm*, it's in his blood—we share a Panamanian heritage—and I have to have a strong rhythmic concept in my music, maybe because I always wanted to play the African drums. I put those rhythms into the piano. Probably that's why I was so interested in people like Monk, Tatum, and Ellington . . . people who were very rhythmic in their concept. So Alex was just perfect for my music. That very distinctive rhythmic sense is precisely why I used to love playing with Ahmed Abdul-Malik much earlier and Sam Gill before that. Alex and I have a way of going in and out; there was a period when we didn't see each other for years, then all of a sudden we'd come together to play again. Somehow we spiritually connect on a high level.

On nearly every recording I've made with Alex he'll create a rhythm that I hadn't originally intended to be in a particular piece, which will bring another color to the composition. He doesn't get credit as a composer, but in a way he's a real composer. For example, my tune "Saucer Eyes" was just a regular 4/4 rhythm. But Alex took that tune and played some other kind of rhythm on the piece when we recorded it for the album "Saga" and gave it more depth for me, gave it more meaning. He's ideal for my music, because he just automatically creates sounds and rhythms that fit right into my music.

## Alex Blake

*Alex Blake*: I met Randy in 1967 when I was sixteen years old. I knew his son Azzedin from when we played in a band called Natural Essence, with Buddy Williams, Onaje Allan Gumbs, a cat named Rashid on saxophone, and Thelonious Monk Jr. But at that point I had never really heard Randy's music. I remember one night when I was playing with Dizzy Gillespie and Randy came down to the Vanguard. After I met him I became curious about his music, but it wasn't until his *Blue Moses* record on CTI that I really checked him out. I was a little over eighteen when Randy first called me for a gig. After that we didn't work together again for a long time. In the meantime I worked with McCoy Tyner, Clark Terry, and then Freddie Hubbard.

When I really checked out Randy's music it was incredible. His music was different from anything else I had ever played with anybody. Back then everybody's music was pretty much either straight ahead, or commercial. That was when fusion music was starting to happen, and I was doing a bit of that. Randy's music had a different element beyond everybody else's music. I couldn't really put my finger on that difference, but it felt like elements of Africa and South America. Since I was from Panama, I heard certain elements in his music that reminded me of music that I'd heard as a kid in Panama. So a lot of the rhythms he played were right up my alley. Everything he played related back to

Africa. When I started working with Manhattan Transfer in the '80s I would get occasional calls from Randy for gigs when we were off, and every time I played with Randy I came out feeling musically and spiritually refreshed. Randy's writing incorporates Africa and a kind of spirituality within the music that was just entirely different than anything else I had ever played. We could play the same music two weeks straight and it would always be fresh.

The first time people hear Randy's music I think it blows their mind, because they're expecting something else and the music sort of puts them in a trance. It can be so different for his audiences that it may take them a minute before they actually clap, because they're thinking, "Wow, what was that!?" And from that time on they're hooked. I've had people after a performance say, "I heard you guys for the first time and it was so different," they went out and bought his whole collection. Randy has had so many great players work with him, but I really feel so connected to his music that it is a part of me, partly because I'm from Panama and the rhythms are right there, I just feel it. Playing with Randy is an adventure; each tune takes you on this journey, an adventure through the continent of Africa.

One of my most exciting experiences working with Randy would have to be my first encounter with the Gnawa, which happened sometime in the late 1980s. We went on tour and he had these Moroccan musicians with him. Randy kept telling me about Abdullah el Gourde and the instrument he played, the guimbre. The first time I saw the Gnawa play it totally blew my mind, it was like an awakening into other rhythms that I had heard, but never really played quite like the Gnawa played them. When I heard Abdullah play the guimbre I had never heard a concept quite like his, because he plays it like a bass. I approach the bass a little differently anyway, but this took me on a whole different path of approaching the instrument. The way I play the bass is very rhythmic and the way they play is totally rhythmic. I really learned a couple of things from Abdullah. Randy had told me, "I can't wait for you to hear these guys." He was absolutely right, I was hooked.

Of all the records I've made with Randy the *Saga* date stands out. When we were rehearsing for that record I told Randy I had various ideas about that music, and he was so open to my ideas he agreed to incorporate them. Everybody in the band sort of contributed to that date, not that we didn't contribute to any of the other albums, but *Saga* was a lot different from anything else I had done with Randy. *Saga* was like a journey for me, from the ideas we put into it to the opportunity to record with Billy Higgins, it was an incredible experience.

I left Panama when I was seven years old and I hadn't been back to my country in about forty-five years, until I went down there to play on a festival with Randy in January 2006. That first time returning to Panama was as if I was going to Africa for the first time. My heart was racing when we landed, because I hadn't been back in so many years. As soon as we got off the plane we were whisked off to have lunch with the president. Then at the concert the audience response to our performance was incredible. Listening to Randy's music was something the Panamanians could relate to rhythmically and melodically, and their response was overwhelming.

I think of Randy Weston as the highest of masters because he's tried to tell the story of a continent and a people, the history of a people, the culture of a people. This man has sacrificed his entire career to tell a story about the continent of Africa. Randy is an entirely different piano player because of his approach to the piano and his concept in playing his music and where it comes from. I thank God for giving me the time and experience of working with Randy, because it's been the greatest experience of my life to work with him. There are two great people on this planet: my father and Randy Weston. Randy's been one of the major influences in my life as a human being and as a player.

## Talib Kibwe (TK Blue), saxophonist and flutist

I believe I first heard Talib Kibwe (TK Blue), the saxophonist in the African Rhythms Quintet, playing with the South African pianist Abdullah Ibrahim. My father was very sick at the time, but he loved music and I said, "C'mon, Pop, let's go hear this guy from South Africa." Then a while later I ran into Talib when I was playing in this club that was run by a drummer named John Lewis, downtown next to the Bottom Line. The gig was just piano and bass, with Don Pate playing bass, and one night Talib came by and asked to sit in. When a musician asks you to sit in you have to use your instincts because sometimes fools will say that, get up on the bandstand, and kill everything. But there was just something about Talib that I had a good feeling about his request. He came up and played with us and I liked his playing right away.

The gig didn't pay much but our meals were part of the deal. When we finished the set Talib ordered some food. The waitress was from the Ivory Coast, a really nice sister who only charged Talib half price for his meal since he'd sat in with us. But the club owner went off, screaming at this woman, threatening to fire her, it was unbelievable. But that was the beginning of my long relationship with Talib Kibwe. We eventually played all over the world, and for years he's been my music director, the straw boss of the band. I trust his instincts, musically and otherwise, implicitly.

## Talib Kibwe (TK Blue)

*Talib Kibwe*: My first knowledge of Randy Weston came in 1972 while I was a student at NYU. A teacher I studied with named Kaliq Abdul Raoof invited me to a gig at the East cultural center in Brooklyn. He said his group was opening for "Ramsey Lewis"—or so I thought he said. I went expecting to see Ramsey Lewis and it was Randy Weston, not Ramsey Lewis who was playing that night. Randy's music completely overwhelmed me. It was just he and Azzedin on drums and his generosity showed up right away, because in the middle of their set this brother got up and started playing the flute, walking toward the bandstand, and Randy just waved him on . . . it was James Spaulding.

Randy impressed me so much musically because of the stuff he and Azzedin were playing. My consciousness about music was so limited at that time, and to see a duo playing, and these cats going from one tune right into another, playing medleys, all kind of swerving in and out of keys . . . That kind of presentation knocked me out because they were like one; I had never seen anybody play with that kind of closeness. The whole evening was just magical, but I didn't meet Randy that night.

In 1978 I was working with Abdullah Ibrahim, who was still known as Dollar Brand. We had a gig at Ornette Coleman's place called Artists House down in SoHo, and Randy came to the gig along with Colette, who was managing him at the time, and his father. I was introduced to Randy and I was struck by how proud he was to have his father with him, introducing him to everybody in the band. In between my first encounter with him at the East and meeting him in '78 I became even more aware of his greatness through his *Blue Moses* record. At the time I was heavily into that CTI Records sound, so I liked George Benson, Freddie Hubbard, Stanley Turrentine, Hubert Laws, and Grover Washington . . . that whole crew. To see this *Blue Moses* record on CTI with Freddie, Grover, and Hubert in the band, I said to myself, "This cat Randy Weston's gotta be a giant!" Then when I turned around and spotted him in the audience at Abdullah Ibrahim's gig it really knocked me out.

My next encounter with him came around 1979, early 1980, when he was performing a benefit at the Brooklyn College branch on Jay Street, where they used to have a lot of jazz performances. I had my piccolo with me that evening, and when I saw Randy backstage he remembered me. I asked if I could play a song with him and he said, "No problem, do you know 'Hi Fly?'" He was playing the gig solo, and I came up to play "Hi Fly" with him, on piccolo, the first time I played with him.

Shortly after that I asked him if I could sit in at his gig at John Lewis's place Syncopation, because we'd had a nice feeling from that concert at the college. I played "Little Niles" with him that first night, and the vibe was so nice he asked me back the next night. I came back Wednesday and he asked me back again the following night. On Thursday he said, "Look, man, I can give you a little bit of dough so why don't you just finish out the week"; and that was how I started working with him, in 1980.

My next contact with Randy came shortly before I moved to Paris in '81. He was doing a gig at Reverend Daughtry's church in Brooklyn, and Randy called me to ask if I would come play the concert with him. He had Peck Morrison on bass, Scoby Stroman and Chief Bey on drums, and myself. Back then he was still living between Brooklyn and Annecy, France, and since I was moving to Paris he said, "Look, man, here's my number in Annecy, let me know when you're coming to Paris." So when I settled in Paris I contacted him and he asked me to join the band since we were both living in Europe. Our first gig was in '82, opposite Wynton Marsalis at the San Sebastian Jazz Festival in Spain; it was me, Randy, and Muhammad Ben Fatah on percussion. That's when we really started touring a lot.

My being Randy's music director kind of evolved organically. With our small ensemble gigs there really wasn't much to discuss, because everybody knew the music. Maybe with our quintet dates I might make some suggestions, but when we got to the larger ensemble performances that's when he chose to delegate that responsibility to some-

one else. One thing that facilitated my becoming Randy's music director was Melba Liston's failing health. In 1985 we really began doing
more big-band or ten-piece engagements, and Melba was so ill it kind
of fell on me by default to assist him in that capacity.

Randy's musical philosophy is about a concept. When he performs
it's very rarely about stringing a bunch of tunes together. A lot of
times we don't even know what he's going to play, especially in small
groups because he never discusses a program beforehand, he just kind
of moves the way the Creator has guided him. Larger performances
have to be more program-oriented, and in that case we have to discuss
tunes, personnel, arrangements, soloists—things of that nature.

I have hundreds of cassettes of various gigs we've played since the
early '80s, and I remember on so many occasions when he would play
some standard or some tune that you rarely hear him play and the
way he would play it would be completely incredible. I remember once
playing in Spain when Dizzy died, that night we were playing trio and
Randy went into a whole medley of tunes that Dizzy had played, like
"Kush," "Con Alma," and others. He meshed them all together in a
medley and my jaw was wide open. When he finished Dizzy's tunes
he went into "Hi Fly" and I was still mesmerized. He played the "Hi
Fly" theme twice before saying to me, "Hey, man, you gonna join us or
what?" I was still in a trance from that Dizzy medley.

Observing Randy's relationship with Melba Liston was really special. Melba knew things intuitively. I remember when we made Randy's
record *Volcano Blues* there was one arrangement where Melba had me
on the flute but I wanted to play saxophone, so I played saxophone on
the solo, but in the end I didn't dig it and I wished I had just played
the flute like she had originally written, because she knew my sound
and she knew what would work, she knew that tune was better on
flute than saxophone. She was like Duke in that regard. Their relationship was very special, like Duke and Billy Strayhorn, a lot of telepathy,
unspoken things, nonverbal contact and communication. There was a
lotta love there, you could see they had a lot of history between them
and Randy never had to tell her anything about what to write, she just
knew.

In January 2004 we played Randy's commissioned piece *Ancient
Future* for Jazz at Lincoln Center. One segment was called "Kom Ombo,"
the third part of that suite. I had written the arrangement, but Melba

came to me in a dream the night before the first rehearsal and she said, "You've gotta change something." I woke up and I was messed up! So the next day at rehearsal I'm going through the whole arrangement and when I got to "Kom Ombo"—which is an ancient city in Nubia—I realized there was this one passage in my arrangement that had one section that was going to repeat four times, and I thought, "Wait a minute, that's a bit redundant," so I changed it to make it more interesting and it made sense. The people at Lincoln Center said, "Oh, man, we already gave the music to the copyist." I said, "I'm sorry, blame it on Melba." So they made the changes and I'm glad, because it made much more sense. Melba and Randy had a very, very special relationship.

There are also a lot of funny stories from my years playing with Randy. Once we arrived at a theater in Algeria to play a concert and the presenter had a two-foot piano onstage for Randy to play, a child's piano for Randy, who stands 6'7". Randy and I took one look at that piano and we said no way we're going to play a concert with that. At one point I went backstage for something and I spotted a crate with a nine-foot grand piano inside. I told the guy Randy would have to play that, and the guy objected because that new piano didn't have any pedals on it. Long story short, Randy played the entire concert without pedals. In another city in Algeria we were playing and the piano seat broke during the middle of the gig. Randy went from playing straight to playing from a tilted position.

I remember a concert in Switzerland and the guy presenting the concert brought a huge joint backstage and insisted that purely as some sorta ritual everybody in the band had to smoke it with him. So everybody took one hit and we went out to play the concert and the music just disintegrated. We started off really playing together, and by the second tune one of the guys had froth on his mouth. My reed got so dry . . . The only one who was together was Randy. The bass player was lost . . . The next day in the paper there was a review of that performance that said it was "the greatest concert ever!" in Bern, Switzerland; "Randy Weston and his superb orchestra . . ." We laughed about that one.

Another time we played in Tunisia, and there was a big article on the front page of the newspaper with the heading "Randy Weston, the Uncle Tom of African American Music." People from abroad often don't know the connotations of certain terms we use and things we know between us. So the writer who wrote the article thought Uncle Tom meant somebody of high standing. Otherwise it was a great article, all in French, that said "Randy Weston played superbly . . . fantastic . . . and he uplifts black culture." But he had that Uncle Tom reference in the headline. We cracked up when we saw that.

I remember once in London we were standing outside on the sidewalk in front of the venue where we had just finished playing, and this British cat, a street beggar, walked up right in the middle of a heavy conversation we were having. He stuck his head right up in the conversation and said, "Hey, got a few quid?" We ignored him and just kept talking, and he looked at Randy and said, "You black Sambo." Randy said, "Man, I'll punch you out." We had to hold Randy back from knocking this guy out, it was the only time I had ever seen Randy really angry. After he cooled down Randy said, "Man, I haven't heard that term 'Sambo' in a long time . . . that guy brought one outta the archives," and we laughed about it.

It's been a blessing playing with Randy. People look at stuff from different angles . . . I'm out here hustling like everybody else, trying to promote my own career, making a living at what I do and just trying to get to the next level. A lot of people have said to me, "Man, you've been playing with Randy for twenty-five years, aren't you tired of it, or aren't you embarrassed by that?" I'm proud of the fact that I've had an opportunity to play with somebody for twenty-five years on and off. I've seen from an inside perspective someone go to that ultimate level of masterhood. When I listen to Randy from 1980, even going back to when I first heard him in the '70s, I hear his whole development. What he does with a tune now is a lot different from what he did with a tune back then.

What I mean by the difference is the lines of demarcation; whereas he might have played a standard or something in the early '80s where you can hear where 1, hear where the A, and the bridge are . . . but now his playing is on such another level of music that counting is no longer necessary; 1 is no longer necessary, key is no longer important, tempo is no longer important . . . He might start it off fast, might go slow, might go to 3, and might have odd meters . . . all of that becomes unimportant because it's just a sound. I've watched that evolution from the inside, his going from a great pianist to a true master. It's very rare that you have that opportunity to work with someone for that length of time. I don't think there's anybody out there that does what he does. All the great masters of the piano play Monk or Duke tunes, but with Randy there's no more bar line, no more tempo, no more meter; it's beyond the realm of classifications of music, where it really becomes pure art.

## Benny Powell, trombonist

Benny Powell and I have the same spirit. When I met Benny Powell he was in the Merv Griffin television show band in Hollywood and he was playing all these big shows. He was drugged and felt like he was in a rut experiencing the same old racism out there in California. We talked one day when he was back in New York for a visit and we realized that we were in tune with each other. To play this music well the musicians have to have a certain pride and a certain respect for each other and the music, that's very important. I've worked with musicians that don't have that and it doesn't work. Benny Powell has a carload of pride and he's got such a beautiful sound on that trombone. Until he joined the band the only brass I'd used with any regularity in my small groups was trumpet; Benny Powell changed all that.

*Benny Powell*: I can't even remember when I first met Randy, because people like him are so comfortable you don't meet them, you encounter them, because the first time you meet them it's like you've known them for years. The first music of his that really struck me heavy was *Uhuru Afrika*. What stands out about that piece was the orchestration and the fact that all my friends are on the record, including Clark Terry. During the 1970s I lived in California working in the Merv Griffin show band. My daughter was growing up at the time, and I used to come back east to check on her and satisfy my New York jones, because when you live in California you live in another zone, and environment shapes a lot of your experiences.

I remember the first time talking with Randy at length way back when the musicians union was on 42nd Street. I ran into him one day coming from the union office, at the subway stop at 42nd Street and 8th Avenue. We talked, asking each other the usual questions, and I told him that it was OK out in California but I wasn't getting the same inspiration I got in New York. I mentioned the fact that everything seemed so white in California because I was operating sorta in a white world in that television and studio scene; there weren't too many black musicians around. I felt fortunate to be working at all, but somehow there was nothing out there for an African American musician in the studios. I realized why—the business wasn't set up for me to be out there playing in their stuff; it was through civil rights activism that I landed out there in the first place. I told Randy about one circumstance when I did a movie date. Movie call was typically about 9 or 10 in the morning, and I remember coming out into the street at one point and just being shocked by the bright sunshine against the white buildings and stuff, almost being hit over the head by this whiteness. I said to myself, "This is not really where I want to be . . . although I know forty musicians who would cut off their right nut to be where I am."

So I talked with Randy and said, "If you ever need a trombone player"—and I knew he didn't use trombones that much—"I admire you and your music and I certainly would like to work with you." The first time he called me they were playing the Spoleto Festival in South Carolina in the late '70s and he wanted me for that. But I had some dates booked with George Wein's concerts in Europe. He understood, but after I hung up I said to myself, "Damn, this is like telling someone you're drowning, they throw you a life raft, and you throw it back!" Culturally I was drowning in California, although I played with Bill Berry's big band and stuff; I wanted somewhere I could grow in a small-group setting. There were only two black guys on this film date in a full orchestra, Buddy Collette and Earl Palmer, and I said to myself, "I should find some way to get out of here." I told Randy about that and as soon as he threw me a life raft I threw it back!

When I finally joined the band in the early '80s I asked Randy, "Where's the music?" He said, "There is none . . . I've never used the trombone before." I said, "Well, what am I supposed to play?" He said, "Find some pretty notes and play them." Randy is so much like Basie he doesn't realize it. When I first played in his band I worked very hard to get Basie to say, "Yes, Benny, you're hired." But Basie was kinda quirky, the more I asked him the more evasive he got. Randy never tells you what to do, he leads by example. When you see him hit the stage his shoes are polished, he's well-dressed . . . and so was Basie. In their treatment of the guys neither of them let little things get them bent out of shape.

We played someplace in Jamaica with Randy, and when we got finished there was no food for the band—as a matter of fact no food and no bus. They had taken us to the gig but they didn't come back for us. At that time all the restaurants were closed but someone found some sandwiches. I pay attention to the little things and Randy waited until everybody got a sandwich before taking his. I'd worked with Lionel Hampton and he was the exact opposite, a very self-centered man. He would have eaten four sandwiches, then asked, "Anybody want a sandwich?" Randy makes the smallest guy feel big just by talking to them as a person. Randy very seldom admonishes anybody, never for notes or anything; he never admonished anybody who didn't deserve it.

If I had gotten a chance to play with Randy earlier I think I'd be a much better musician. Randy has made me a better leader as well; I've learned that you don't have to belittle people. Before Basie I was with Lionel Hampton, and he didn't give a damn about belittling anybody, or even making people feel good. Playing with Randy has broadened me as a person, because some of his finer points have nothing to do with music, more to do with him as a person. Playing with Randy has given me more confidence in myself. There's joy and pride in being part of Randy's band, he's made every gig very interesting. Randy's band is perfect for me because sometimes I have to forget about playing conventional notes and I'm trying to play elephant or other animal sounds on the horn. For Randy's music that's excellent; as he said: "Find some good notes and play them, but let your spirit play them. Your spirit is what gives you the freedom to fit in any music."

## Neil Clarke, African percussionist

Neil Clarke came to the band through Talib. Although Neal is from Brooklyn and doesn't live too far from my house, I never knew Neal before he came to the band. I had developed a concept of playing for the children at Rev. Daughtry's House of the Lord church in Brooklyn, which is the church where we had my father's funeral. My first time playing with Neil Clarke was at that church when we were doing benefits for the children in the 1980s.

*Neil Clarke*: Life is funny, although the first time I played with Randy was in the mid-'80s at Reverend Daughtry's church; my connection to Randy actually goes back to maybe '74, '75. I had come back to New York from school in Boston, where I'd met a lot of musicians from sitting in on that scene. Steve Berrios and I became friends; he was kinda like a mentor to me. Steve called me up once and said he needed to borrow a conga drum for a tour he was doing. He had opened up some doors for me, so I said, "Yeah, sure." Ironically that's when Steve was going on tour with Randy. So my drum actually went with Randy before I did.

Before I joined Randy's band I was in awe of him, because for me it was the best of both worlds. Because of the instrument I play, from the beginning I was aware of Africa and the rhythms coming out of Africa, being a drummer. Olatunji's record *Drums of Passion* was probably the first recording of African music that I was aware of, besides Afro-Cuban stuff. And the other side was jazz, the whole heritage and realm of jazz music. It was just the whole idea of the improvisational process and the level of musicianship that took. As I was aspiring to be a better musician, jazz was a very attractive form of music to me, so it was just a matter of finding the opportunities to participate in jazz. At that time there were only certain artists and certain types of music where the instrument I play was invited, but I always felt I could play all of it.

Randy Weston is a jazz giant, well known in the mainstream and a well-respected jazz musician who turned his attentions and his music to Africa and African elements. So he was perfect for where I wanted to be as a musician. To play music on that level, where African sensibilities are not incidental, they're the core of the music . . . that was ideal for me.

I finally joined his band in 1991. They had recorded Randy's *Volcano Blues* record, and there was something going on with the mix of that recording that wasn't clicking, something in the rhythm track. During the mixing Talib called me and they asked me to come in with some percussion instruments, to make a contribution to try and bridge that gap. I went to the studio with a bunch of percussion instruments, listened to what was happening, and made an assessment of what I could add to kind of bridge the gap between what was happening and what was not happening.

Right after that Randy was going on tour with the Gnawa in Great

Britain. At the time I was working with Harry Belafonte, who I had been with for about thirteen years. We had just finished up a tour, and Harry let the band know that we were going to be on a break, because he had a film project and there wasn't going to be anything happening for a while. Randy called and asked if I was available to make this tour with the Gnawa in Great Britain.

At the time I wasn't at all familiar with Gnawa music, but working with Randy and the Gnawa was kind of a dream come true for me. Coming up I had been exposed to many different dimensions of African music. I had studied with Ladji Camara, the first djembe drummer to come to the U.S. in the '50s; I studied Guinean musical forms with Ladji. I had worked with probably the premier African dance group in New York, the International African American Ballet. I had been working with Letta Mbulu and had done several tours of Africa with her. I had also worked with Miriam Makeba and had played salsa. So the scope of African music I had played was very broad. For me to be with Randy and the Gnawa was just an opportunity to explore another dimension of African music.

Randy's music is organic. You sit down with Randy and he'll say, "OK, I want to play this tune," and his book is so vast, he has so much stuff in his book, all these great tunes. He'll pull them out when we're sound checking or at a rehearsal for a particular gig, and it will be something he wrote thirty years ago. He'll give you a tune and say, "This is how it goes." and then somewhere along the line he'll tell you the story of the tune and then it becomes a whole 'nother thing. There's a story behind all of his tunes, and when you learn the story then your approach to playing the tune becomes one of a storyteller.

Just to show you the power of Randy Weston, one time we were in Morocco and we had just finished playing the Sacred Music Festival in Fes. The day after the concert I was going to spend some time with the Gnawa musician Abdullah el Gourde, so I caught a ride to Tangier with Jaap, Randy's road manager, and a German cat who had done the sound. We were driving from Fes to Tangier, driving through these little towns, and I'm sitting in the backseat. At one point the driver was driving too fast as he hit a speed bump, and the brakes screeched. There was a cop out in the middle of this square, and he heard the brakes squeal. He looks over and sees these two European cats in this car with me in the back, so he flags us over to the side. I was like, "Oh, boy, here we go . . ." The cop walked up and looked us over and asked for our papers, so we pull out the passports and hand them over, ready for this cop to take us through some changes.

The German driver starts talking and tells the cop we were just coming from playing the Sacred Music Festival in Fes, and we're with Randy Weston. When he said "Randy Weston" the cop stopped, looked up, and repeated "Randy Weston." The cop stoops down and looks at me in the backseat and says, "Randy Weston, huh?" The cop closed the passports, handed them back to us, tipped his hat, and said, "Have a nice day." This is not the capital we're in and we're not some diplomats, this is a beat cop in the middle of Morocco in some small town. We mentioned Randy Weston and it just flipped the whole thing.

As for my favorite recording date with Randy, I would have to say *Zep Tepi*, which was the trio with me and Alex. It was exciting because being with Randy has given me the opportunity to explore dimensions of my musicality, opportunities that I have never really gotten anywhere else. For him to use a percussionist instead of a drummer, to put me in the position where I'm the drummer, is challenging. We're playing tunes that are in many ways structured in a western kind of format—piano, bass, and drums—although they have an African sensibility. So it's given me the opportunity to really explore a lot of different things and challenge my musicianship to fulfill that role, satisfy what Randy is seeking, and still exercise my creativity.

The way I've adapted to that role as a percussionist, the first thing is I'm not deferring to somebody else for the demarcation in the arrangement. When you're playing congas in a Latin ensemble you're playing in a section. The core of a jazz group is generally piano, bass, and drums, and you'll find the drummer and bass player are locked in synch and the percussionist is kind of like playing along. With Randy that's the role I'm playing, the drummer's role, and I'm keeping the time, I'm laying it down. I've added cymbals and play them in the same way that a drummer would play them, with my hands instead of sticks. I've combined instruments by combining the congas with the djembe with the cymbals with the tambourine, so I can get the full range of sound.

I think Randy is right up there with the other luminaries, the giants, the trailblazers. Randy always says he wishes he could have been there the first time an African touched a piano. It's obvious that the African dimension is very important to him. He has explored that to a degree that is beyond most if not all. He has established himself by his compositions, but then he's gone into some uncharted waters. Many people have composed tunes with an allusion to Africa and the African element, but to actually take the time to immerse yourself so you have a functional understanding of those elements and then exercise it from a knowledgeable perspective is remarkable. Randy stands out because he's gone in the direction of Africa. That's been controversial because of the state of the world politically; it might have even been detrimental because of all that Africa evokes and represents; but that's Randy Weston.

## Postscript

What's great about these four musicians is they know how to interpret my music, they understand what I'm trying to say. They understand that for me it is more than music, they understand that my music is a message for our people. I've worked with other musicians who could really play, but they don't have the same mind-set, they don't have the same interest in the ancestors. This is not a band per se, this is a family of black people who are proud of their tradition and realize they have a responsibility not to be stars, but a responsibility to inspire, to help uplift our people through music. That's the foundation of a band. We have a message that other bands don't have. When we're on the stage with Gnawa, the Gnawa are not in the background. When we have traditional people on the same show we're going to come together and show the people that these musicians represent our ancestors.

The Creator brought this group of musicians together, without question. A good example: back in the '90s Benny Powell was very, very sick, he had just gotten his kidney transplant and was in the hospital in New York, sometime in February or March. We had a gig in Atlanta in August, and I could have gotten another trombone player, but something told me Benny Powell was going to do that gig in August. He told me, "I'm going to be there," and he was there, for his first gig after his kidney transplant he was there with us. When Benny picked up that trombone he transformed the music completely. He had to be there, and I wouldn't have thought twice about getting another trombone player. When you're in tune with the ancestors they send you these messages to let you know that you're not doing this stuff by yourself.

## 17

# THE AFRICAN QUEEN

In 1994 I met my African queen. I was in Paris to play a concert with the Gnawa and I was staying at a hotel near an interesting-looking African shop called Saga, which I had always meant to check out, but each time I passed by I seemed to be in a hurry or on some deadline. Even though I passed by every day, it took me a while to finally go in this shop, but somehow the Creator finally directed me there.

## Fatoumata Mbengue-Weston

*Fatoumata Mbengue-Weston*: I was born in Senegal to a great family of eleven siblings. My grandfather was a spiritual Imam; very well known, everybody went to see him for their problems, he was the man every-body sought for advice. I'm the oldest of eleven children and I was the first of my family to leave Senegal. I left Senegal after I got my degree at the university in Dakar. Then I came to Paris to finish my graduate degree in accounting. I remained in Paris because of school and the opportunity to have more of the world open to me, because from Paris you can travel all over the world, whereas from Senegal it's a little bit more difficult.

When I got my graduate degree in France I went to London to work for two years for an African bank. After that I came back to Paris and I couldn't find work, so I decided to open an African shop. I wanted the shop to look nice and reflect the beauty of all Africa. I had things from Mali, Côte d'Ivoire, from Ghana . . . and all of that was like African unity, and I tried to put that unity into my shop, which I called Saga.

Like Randy always says, it was written that we were going to be together. One day four people from Morocco came into my shop and one wanted to buy a hat. As we were talking about hats he told me they were going to play a concert that night with a man named Randy

Fatoumata
Mbengue-Weston.

Weston, and asked if I knew this Randy Weston. I said no, I don't know him. So they invited me to the concert that night, "We're playing tonight, you come." I said OK and asked them to please leave the name of my daughter Khadija at the venue too, so she could come. We went to the concert and the music was so, so strong, with the Gnawa and Randy, and Johnny Copeland . . . it was just fantastic! When the Gnawa played I saw a woman in the audience go into a trance. I thought to myself: this music makes people go into trance, just like in my native Senegal. It was a major new experience for me in Paris.

At the end of the concert, when I saw this guy Randy Weston stand up from the piano onstage, I thought, "My God, he's a big man!" This was really the first time I saw him. He wore beautiful blue and he looked like a god. I thought he's so beautiful, this man . . . After he played all I could think was "Wow, I've got to meet this guy." After that performance the Moroccan guy I had met earlier at my shop named Mbarek Ben Outhman said OK, come on backstage, we're going to introduce you to Mr. Weston. I told them yes, but there were too many people backstage. I told my daughter Khadija, "Listen, let's go, this is crazy, there are just too many people backstage." Plus we had a long trip home because the concert was outside Paris, in the suburbs, and we had to go back to Paris, where we lived.

The next day I saw this guy Randy Weston. I found out later that my shop was not far from where Randy was staying. I saw him walking by on the street, the same man from the concert. I said, "That's the guy again!" And I'm looking and he's going, going down the road . . . and he disappears. I thought maybe he'll come back. Maybe when he comes back by here he will come and see the shop. He never came back that day. I just saw him once because there was another way for him to go back to the hotel, so he took the other side to go back to his hotel. Three months later he came back and I saw him walking past my shop and I thought, "That's the man again!" The next day I was in the shop doing something and he walked in and said, "Aha, an African shop!"

He said, "Hi, how are you?" I said, "You know, I came to your concert the other night." So he just started small talking about various things, looking over the things in my shop. He said "OK, give me one of these, and one of those, and that . . ." He's buying, he's buying, he's buying. He asked me where I was from, blah, blah, blah. The next time he came back to Paris he came to the shop and asked me if I made clothes. I said, "Yes, I have a tailor and can have them made, and he asked if I would have some clothes made for him, because he really liked to wear African clothes. And that was that. That's where we started, with business. Later I had him over to my house for dinner.

The first time I traveled to the U.S. with Randy, in 1996, we went to an event for John Henrik Clarke, and I was amazed when I saw all these black people dressed in African garments. I said to myself, "Wow, these are the people who are the other half of me, the people who left Africa!" From Randy I know the African Americans, I truly discovered African America through Randy. Also his music is Africa; when I first heard his music I heard kora, I heard balaphone . . . I heard everything African. I hear all that in his music, and he's the only one I hear that in his piano playing; and that's what I get from Randy Weston.

She had everything African you could imagine in her shop: statues, beautiful cloth, cards, jewelry, a window full of beautiful African things—giraffes, seven-foot-tall statues . . . all kinds of beautiful things. She also had clothing there but nothing that would fit a big man like me. After I started going by the shop fairly frequently she arranged for her tailor to start making clothes for me because I was already wearing African clothes, but Fatou just took it to another level. I was so inspired and so attracted to her that I learned that Saga—the name of her shop—signified the African family in the Wolof language of Fatou's native Senegal, and that became the basis of my record Saga: the African family.

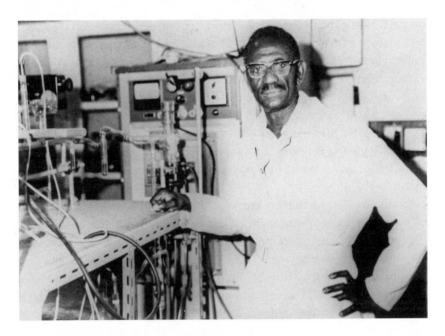

The great Egyptologist, scientist, and historian Cheikh Anta Diop in his lab at Cheikh Anta Diop University in Dakar, 1985.

My first time in her shop I bought a bunch of things and we talked quite a bit. When I found out she was from Senegal I got excited and asked her if she knew much about Cheikh Anta Diop, one of my heroes. But she really didn't know much about Diop. Sometimes you can live in a country and have a giant in your midst, but it takes somebody from someplace else to come and tell you how great they are; that happens to all of us. Fatou had heard about Diop but she didn't realize how deep he was until I told her how inspired I was by his work. I gave her Diop's book on African civilization. I had been to Senegal in 1967 and I told her about my experiences in her country.

I knew I just *had* to keep going back to her shop; this is a truly beautiful woman and I was very attracted for many reasons. I was like, "Wow, she's fantastic!" I went back to the shop to see her, then she started having her tailor make new African clothes for me: shirts, vests, and whatnot. The next time we played Paris with the Gnawa, she came to the concert and I met her daughter Khadija. Finally she invited me to her house for some food; the usual thing that happens with a man and a woman. Our relationship just steadily grew every time I went to Paris. We found that we had the same interests, she loved the music, and it was great also because through her I had contact with Senegal, and met all of her family and friends from home. In Paris or wherever I go I always try to find our people, whether it's Afro-Cuban, Afro-Caribbean, African Mississippi, whatever . . . I always try to find our folks. I had already been in touch with many Africans in Paris. I had met Mr. Amadou-Mahtar M'Bow, who had been the director general of UNESCO for thirteen years, and we became good friends. He's a very important man in Senegal. So Fatou and I had many things to talk about, many things in common. I just kept visiting and our relationship grew from there.

Fatou is well aware that my music is part of the struggle and the struggle of our people is very important to me. I feel like I'm a cultural warrior, fighting 24/7 to liberate our people from this maddening racism because it's such an evil system. What racism has done to our people . . . what it has done to my parents . . . what it has done to Fatou's people is what makes it such a monumental struggle to overcome. In a way I could just be a musician—and it certainly is difficult enough just being a musician—but I'm also an activist, I'm an Africanist, and I'm very much involved in the struggle, which makes it doubly hard. The other side of the coin is Fatou is African, so she appreciates and understands what I'm trying to accomplish. I told her right away, "Baby, you're with a soldier," and a soldier's life is not the same as an ordinary life. I think our relationship is beyond Fatou and me; we're a very ancient people, and I really say that with all seriousness.

One reason Wayne Chandler's book *Ancient Future* is so important to me is that he has such a unique way of breaking things down. A lot of the other important Africanists and scholars I've read and admired, like Diop, Chancellor Williams, John G. Jackson . . . man, those brothers' writings are so heavy that you need ten dictionaries to decipher their stuff. But Wayne breaks it down in plainer terms and he emphasizes the holistic approach to black folk in his book. Wayne emphasizes the seven principles created by Tehuti which set the basis of civilization. And one of those principles is that nothing happens by chance, everything that happens is already designed in the universe, which is preordained.

So it seems that with everybody I meet there's a correspondence between everything on the planet. We don't necessarily always pick up the vibrations, but we're all corresponding with each other. Consequently I knew that I loved Fatou, but at the same time I know that our relationship goes back . . . way, way back before this. I know we go back thousands of years,

I know this spiritually just by looking at her. And that was really proven to me when we sailed down the Nile River in 2001.

We traveled down the Nile and went to Nubia—land of the original Egyptians, the black Egyptians—from Aswan down to Abu Simbel, which is where you see some incredible, ancient monuments. I knew then that it was not just a matter of meeting this beautiful woman at her shop in Paris, but I knew that we had another destiny. One thing I didn't have in my life was an African woman. Right away Fatou and I just *connected*. I've learned so much about Senegal and about the Wolof people from her. I've eaten their food and learned much about their culture. By the same token she's learned from me about African Americans and our struggles, our greatness . . . so we have this constant and very wonderful exchange.

Back to our spiritual journey down the Nile. I had been invited to attend a conference on Sufism, on Sufi singers from the Nile River, in an Egyptian town called Gourna, which is right near Karnack, one of the great, great cities of ancient Egypt. Karnack is just unbelievable, just overwhelming. This conference was organized by a Belgian woman who has an art gallery in Paris. Her concept was to bring these Sufi singers from the Nile region to this little village about two hundred miles south of Cairo, each one to perform on a different night for one week. The purpose of this was for the people of the village to come and experience this, because with most festivals of this nature the people who should be able to hear the music can't afford to pay. That's one of my criticisms of the Fes Festival of World Sacred Music in Morocco, and that's all too typical of such events; the common man cannot afford to attend these events. Unfortunately we found it was the same in Egypt. This woman invited me to attend this event and Fatou traveled there with me.

We spent a week at this conference and it was beautiful. These Sufis—one or two of them were blind—sang these Sufi songs from the Nile River. They were chosen to sing from different places along the Nile. They all sang in Arabic, singing the old text of the Koran, and it was really beautiful. Following the conference we wanted to go to Nubia, the original black Egypt, which you get to from Aswan by traveling south. That's where they flooded one of the most valuable monuments, which sits under Lake Nasser, unfortunately. They've restored some of these monuments, but they displaced a lot of black people to build the Aswan Dam, which is the same thing they did when they built Lincoln Center in New York, and so many other places; that's nothing new—they used to call it urban renewal.

We arranged a ride with a guy named Ramses who had a funky taxi but with a lot of legroom for me. He drove us from Gourna to Luxor, then to Aswan. It's about three hours by car, but you have to have a military escort, because bandits wiped out some tourists in Luxor several years ago. We drove to Kom Ombo, an ancient Nubian city, to have lunch, walk around, and stretch our legs a bit. The police escorts generally picked up caravans of tourists from each hotel who wished to go in this direction. When we got ready to get back on the road the driver Ramses said, "Oh, man, forget that police escort," and he just sped off down the road. When we got to Aswan we checked into a hotel. All this time I was hearing the call of Isis, the original spirit goddess of Egypt. Spiritually speaking, there's no words to describe it, it's like music, I can't describe this call. While we were in Gourna we met the woman who is the head of the Palestine Liberation Organization in Paris, a woman named Shadid Hassan. She was Arafat's representative in Paris and she came down to be a part of the conference. Leila wanted to make this trip to Nubia too, but she wanted to fly down, go to the temple of Isis, and come back the next day. I told her I was sorry but we wanted to go down the Nile and spend a few leisurely days just checking things out, we didn't want to just go down and come right back.

The next morning Fatou and I asked how to get to Phillae Island, to the temple of Isis: how do we take a water taxi? The people we asked said, "Well, you go down to the river and you see the Nubians, they control how you get to the island." So we walked down to the river and there were merchants selling all kinds of things. These brothers were jet black, most of them wearing white. Their boats are like sailboats, only some of them have little motors. When they saw us they started shouting and gesturing, they all wanted us to come on their particular boat, so we had to pick one guy with a boat.

Backing up a bit, before I left on this trip I knew two people at UNESCO in Paris: one a Nigerian I've known for twenty-five years, the other is Amadou-Mahtar M'Bow from Senegal, the secretary general of UNESCO who I mentioned earlier. He's the same man who had put together the plan for UNESCO to build a silk trade in China and to rebuild Abu Simbel. I went to each of these men to ask them for some Egyptian contacts, but they didn't give me anything before we left. I knew one guy in Egypt, Salah Ragab, a musician who has a big band in Cairo that recorded once with Sun Ra. Otherwise nobody gave us any contact names. Anyway, we got to Phillae Island and we got off the boat where there was Isis's magnificent temple, with huge walls covered in spiritual writings. Isis is the original Madonna; she, Osiris, and Horus, that's the original trinity, way before Christ, way before Christianity and Islam . . . this is the original. Fatou and I looked at this temple in amazement, we were walking around blown away, and we were the only black folks there. All the other people there were white tourists, from Italy, France, Spain . . . we were the only two blacks. It was so funny because the other tourists were watching us at the same time we were watching the statues.

At one point we sat down on a rock to rest and a brother walked over to us. He asked whether we were enjoying ourselves. I said, "Yeah, very much so, we're very happy to be in Egypt." This gentleman introduced himself as Shazly Aly-Abd Elazem, the inspector of Phillae. This brother really hooked us up. He introduced us to the head of antiquities in Egyptian art, and two hours later he took us to the Nubian museum to meet the head of this most incredible museum in Aswan. This place was all about black culture, pre-Egypt, the original pyramids, a beautiful museum. All of a sudden we were meeting all these top people, just like that . . . the power of Isis.

We had such a wonderful time on that trip that we went back two years later. This time we didn't go down to Abu Simbel, we just stayed in Aswan. The previous trip we had gone to Phillae Island, but not further south. This time we were determined to travel further south down the Nile. We arranged for a boat; we didn't know what kind of vessel we were going to get, and Fatou was nervous about that. But no worries, it turned out to be a beautiful boat.

We sailed down the Nile seeing all these incredible sites. We met the captain of the boat, a guy dressed in a djellabah and wearing a turban. These guys know the Nile blindfolded. We saw all these incredibly powerful images, enormous monuments, amazing antiquities, some of which were partially eroded. When we got to the southern city of Nubia, where they have great temples, we saw the astounding monument of Abu Simbel. We disembarked and went to our hotel to have lunch—Fatou, Shazly, and myself. We were sitting at a table having lunch together and telling Shazly what a good time we were having, but he was upset because he couldn't go with us, he had to work. He wanted to go with us to make sure we knew where all the sites were, that's his specialty.

We were sitting there, casually talking with this guy, when all of a sudden out of the blue a voice comes out of me: "Hey, Shazly, I want to marry this woman!" Fatou is looking at me all wide-eyed, she can't believe what she just heard come from my mouth. Shazly looks at me and says, "What are you talking about?" I said, "Listen, man, I want to marry this woman and I want you to arrange this for me." He said, "OK, but I've never done this before." Meanwhile Fatou is in total shock. We were so overcome with these images we'd seen it was like we were in another world. We were still so high from this experience and what our ancestors had created. You read about these antiquities in books and you may see them in movies, but the sheer height of those enormous columns, with spiritual writings all around them, it's mind-blowing.

Anyway, Shazly agreed to arrange this spur-of-the-moment inspiration. Fatou agreed but was still in shock. Shazly returned that evening and said, "OK, now tomorrow you'll do this, this, and this," explaining our various preparations. He'd never done this before but he was arranging this marriage. This whole process took three days. The next day he took us to see where our wedding was to take place, in a little Nubian village maybe twenty minutes outside Aswan. When we arrived there right away the women of the village took Fatou and created henna decorations on her feet and hands. The men took me to another room and started talking to me about the sanctity of marriage. That night the women took Fatou to another room and dressed her up completely in Nubian garments for the occasion. Meanwhile they took me to Shazly's brother-in-law's house and wrapped a traditional white turban on my head; they wear a lot of white there. Shazly said, "OK, now listen, we're gonna go and have photographs made . . . you're Nubian now! These people don't know you, so when you go with them I want them to know that you're Nubian, that way the price of the wedding photographs won't be as high." This was starting out like something out of a movie, if you could just imagine this scene.

We got out of this guy's car and I still didn't see Fatou yet and she couldn't see me, until we got ready to take the photographs. So there we are, looking like a Nubian couple, all dressed up for our wedding. We go to the town to take the photographs and it's a big place, all lit up with people standing on the side looking at us. Now remember, we don't know any of these people except for Shazly. I looked over at Fatou and whispered, "Show biz." I grabbed her arm and walked in with her. I was thinking to myself, "Man are you crazy!" We really aren't supposed to speak with these folks because remember, we're supposed to be Nubians and the moment we would've opened our mouths to speak I was afraid they'd know we weren't Nubians . . . or so we thought. Anyway we took the photographs, but all the time they knew we weren't Nubians.

While we were taking the photographs Shazly said, "Listen, man, I've arranged for you to pick out the wedding jewelry." We went to this wonderful jewelry store and I found out that Nubian gold and silver still exist, which is what Egypt uses today. We each chose a Nubian gold cartouche, which is an oval shaped piece of Egyptian jewelry with our names written in gold or silver and worn on a necklace. We picked out our jewelry and Shazly said, "OK, we're going to have your wedding at such and such a time. We're going to pick you up." I'm figuring there's going to be about four or five people at this wedding at most, because nobody really knew us in this town.

When they picked us up to go to the wedding ceremony site, we pulled into the village, and it looked like the whole village had turned out for our wedding. There were literally hundreds of people there to witness our wedding. They had taken two chairs and fashioned a throne for Fatou and me and had placed them on a platform. When we got out of the taxi all the musicians started playing. It seemed like the whole village surrounded us. They took us to a big courtyard and sat us on this throne. We're sitting there looking all around at people hanging off the roofs, the place was completely packed. They had a band playing, they were serving food, and meanwhile Fatou and I are sitting there mystified. It was the most amazing thing, This went on for hours. They brought out a cake and the whole thing. For the ceremony they spoke, they sang songs, the whole bit. The Nubian wedding ceremony is not the western-style ceremony, it's a spiritual marriage with nothing written, no license. Part two is when you're supposed to complete the written ceremony with the license, like in the West, where you sign papers and you're legally married. What we had that day was a spiritual marriage.

It was an amazing scene; there were folks of all ages. The place was mobbed with people. And here we are sitting on this throne, this Brooklyn dude and this Senegalese woman, and our minds are completely blown. I truly believe Isis brought us together in Egypt. When I sat at that lunch table with Shazly I had no plan to marry Fatou in a Nubian village, any more than I could tell you I had a plan when I wrote "Little Niles." I might have had an idea—with "Little Niles" I wanted to write a song for my son— but I didn't know it was going to happen. I get these messages, and to me that's more true than anything else because it's not something that we could discuss in normal levels of conversation, it's deeper than that. I truly believe Fatou was chosen, we were chosen to be together.

## 18

Playing with Randy Weston we don't play gigs . . .
we have adventures! —BENNY POWELL, trombonist

## THE ADVENTURES OF RANDY WESTON

As a creative musician you can stay in the jazz world all your life: you play clubs, you play festivals, you play clubs, you play festivals in an endless cycle . . . and that can be your whole life, which can be a great life. But when the music ventures out of that arena, when it goes into the spiritual realm . . . when it travels to Africa, to Asia, plays in churches, shrines, temples, goes to nontraditional places, when the music offers you opportunities to perform in unusual settings, or if it is a festival with a more spiritual meaning, your life as a musician is enhanced well beyond that typical cycle. Most of my music has always been directed toward an emphasis on African people, so I tend to play places where people are more open to that, not necessarily the usual haunts.

As a result, some of the traditional jazz venues don't hire me because of that particular interest. My music is based in African culture; that doesn't mean that an Asian can't play this music well; it doesn't mean that a European can't play it well. The point is that this is our culture, it's not just music . . . and it's our way of life. I think because of that direction I've had to try and open up other areas in which to perform our music. Whether it's in the Berkshires, Kyoto, or Marrakech, it's that cultural dimension that Benny Powell experienced that inspired him to make that statement, some things that you do not normally find in the jazz world. As a result of this philosophy and the fact that my music has not always been seen as accessible on the regular jazz circuit, I've been fortunate to be invited to play in some nontraditional places, often under what some might consider unusual circumstances.

I'd like to perform more, but on the other hand I'm working all the time. I'm not frustrated because I know I've been fighting a very entrenched system all my life. I see cracks in the wall. I see recognition of Africa coming from places that didn't happen years ago, I see the beginnings of that on a wider scale with Barack and Michelle Obama, so I see the spiritual change. I see the recognition of myself on the African continent. Whenever I play the piano that is a great moment, wherever it is; just to sit at the keys and work my hands to make music is a wonderful thing.

I come out of the influence of great people like James Reese Europe, Ellington, Max Roach, Monk . . . people like that. My history is of a man whose life is dedicated to working for black people; so when you're in that arena a lot of the less culturally advanced people who want to control the music, they will not hire you. Of course I love to play the clubs; I'd love to play anywhere. I feel wherever we go we give the same message, we give the maximum. No matter where we play we give 100 percent. I had to go that route to survive. I've been privileged; being shut out of certain traditional music venues just means that I have to find other ways to survive, and sometimes that means taking unusual trips, playing in unusual places, for audiences that are not the usual jazz audiences. It seems the Creator had another plan for me. Who else among jazz musicians spent seven years living in Africa like I did? Who else experienced what happened to me in Japan? It's a matter of value and what you want to do while you're on the planet. I think it's kind of a mystery. I have no control over that, all I try to do is make sure that what I'm doing is real, make sure it's respected by our people, and make sure that I get the message of the beauty of our people across wherever I go, wherever I perform, to whatever audiences I encounter.

## Japan 2001

The city of Kyoto is the spiritual center of Japan, where many of the country's most famous temples and shrines are located. One of the most renowned of those shrines is Kamigamo Shrine. There's a gentleman in Kyoto named Tetsu who has a café called Lush Life. At his place the only beverage they serve is coffee, they have strictly jazz LPs, and the place is frequented by true jazz enthusiasts. They formed a group of people there who decided to organize a very special concert. This group of people consists of students, painters, writers, printers, businessmen, and women representing many different professions, all deep into the music. One member of this group owns a very famous restaurant in Kyoto which has been favorably reviewed in the *New York Times* for its artistry with Japanese food. This man has a very close relationship to the Kamigamo Shrine.

Somehow this group of people got the idea that they wanted to have a concert in the Kamigamo Shrine and also in a nearby Buddhist temple, and a third performance at a jazz club. They chose me to make these performances because they wanted to have music that was of a spiritual nature. The shrine is sixteen hundred years old, and they had never had a piano there before. Mine was to be only the second music concert ever to be performed there. The Buddhist temple is 680 years old and they've never had a piano there before either, so this trip was really unprecedented on several levels. Certainly these encounters broadened my spiritual horizons, as I came to experience these deeply spiritual people and places.

My friend Michiko Imada, a Japanese woman who lived in Brooklyn at the time and speaks English, came with me to be my translator. When we arrived at Osaka, the airport closest to Kyoto, two gentlemen met us, took our bags, and drove us straight to this little café called Lush Life. This whole group of enthusiasts was there to welcome me. We had some coffee and they showed me some of the many jazz LPs they had. I found a wonderful LP I had never seen before by Oscar Pettiford on which Gigi Gryce had written an arrangement of my tune "Little Niles." These people were just wonderful and only one of them spoke English, a woman named Keiko who had arranged my contract. Before I left New York I called my percussionist, Neil Clarke, and he urged me to have a purification ceremony while in Kyoto. I remembered that, so upon my arrival that was one of my first requests, to have a purification ceremony at the Kamigamo Shrine.

Backing up a bit, there was an interesting prelude to this trip. There's a woman in New York named Reiko who I've been going to for years for shiatsu massage at a spa on 57th Street. She's a very spiritual woman, and she's friends with a young woman in Japan who plays music only for the royal court of Japan. Reiko told me that when she was last in Japan—before I made my journey—she had shown this young woman my photograph. She said this woman suddenly started crying for no apparent reason, burst out in tears saying that I'm the one, I'm the person that's due to come to Japan. Reiko didn't know what that meant, but when she found out I was traveling to Japan she told me this story.

Reiko told me I should be sure to see her two friends, this young musician woman and also another spiritual woman. She gave me a long list of things to do while in Japan and she suggested I eat at three particular restaurants in Kyoto. This young musician, named Iya, plays a particular kind of traditional music purely for the emperor and the royal court. During my visit Iya and the spiritualist woman Shigeko Kurokawa traveled from Tokyo to Kyoto, which is maybe a three-hour trip by bullet train. They called me and invited me to have lunch with them. Michiko came with me and translated because the spiritualist spoke no English and Iya spoke only a little English.

## Michiko Imada

*Michiko Imada*: The spiritualist woman had studied and done research on the importance of this particular day, the 6th of October 2001; according to her it was the day for another future to be revealed. This was the day of Randy's concert at the shrine, and she said even the people who organized it didn't realize it, but that was a very important day—the beginning of all the spiritual forces coming together. She told Randy he was chosen to open the door of this spirituality and that was why he was in Japan. She said, "We need somebody to open the door for another future," meaning the new future, the new world; "We need somebody to open the door." She said Randy was the key person to open the door. She gave me a piece of paper listing the locations of two shrines and the Buddhist temple.

When Randy and I were in Kyoto we were staying at a hotel that was inside this pyramid, and she explained that this too was something meaningful. She explained that Japan is like a compact version of the world, and many things are going on in the world today, but this is the time for somebody to open the door to the new world and she said Randy is the one to do that. She told Randy he was in the middle of this pyramid and that this was very symbolic. I told her Randy was interested in having a purification ceremony and she said he must do it before the concert, that it was very, very important to have it then. She said so many things but she couldn't explain everything.

The next day we went to Shikoku Prefect to a jazz club. Randy played for about eighty minutes straight even though his concert was only supposed to be forty-five minutes each set. The club owner came to me—he didn't speak English—and told me that Randy's contract was for two forty-five-minute sets, but since he played eighty minutes it was OK with them if he didn't play a second set. So I asked Randy if he knew that he had just played for eighty minutes the first set. He said he didn't realize that. I think because they didn't speak English he didn't speak, he just played. It was incredible! Randy played some Duke Ellington. At Kamigamo Shrine he played his compositions, mostly spiritual. Randy always has a lot of energy; everybody was really concentrating because Randy's playing was so colorful. At the club I asked Randy if he would like to play the second set. He said, "Yes, I have to play 'Blue Moses'!"

I had told Mr. Sano, one of the organizers, that Randy wanted to go to a hot spring, because the Shikoku Prefect is very famous for the hot springs. So after the concert, at midnight, Mr. Sano drove us to the hot springs, which were open twenty-four hours.

The next day, the 8th of October, we went to another city in the same prefect. When we got to the Buddhist temple the first thing I wanted to know was where the piano was, because I had never seen a piano in a temple. Finally I found the piano, and it was in front of the most important place in the temple. I couldn't believe it: 180 people attended the concert, and they were expecting 150. Everybody had to remove their shoes and sit on the floor. Before the concert two priests did a Buddhist reading. After the reading Randy started his concert and everybody felt like this was more than just a concert, it was a spiritual thing.

A British woman named Gil Melle, who teaches English in Japan, had made all the arrangements for this to happen, and it took over a year for this trip to come together. My first concert was at the Kamigamo Shrine. This particular shrine is on the United Nations UNESCO list of very important world monuments. When we arrived it had already been arranged for me to take the purification ceremony. Wherever I go I request to hear traditional music, so I asked Gil if she could arrange that as well.

*Michiko Imada*: Gil arranged for Randy to hear traditional Japanese music, in a traditional building with a Japanese garden. Five or six musicians came to play for him, playing instruments like the koto and shakuhachi flute. This place was kind of like a museum, a traditional Japanese house with a traditional Japanese garden.

The next day we had to leave, but the priest at the temple asked me if Mr. Weston wouldn't mind meeting the kindergarten children, so about four classes of kindergarten children came the next morning. Randy played "Congolese Children" and "Kasbah Kids" for them. The children were so excited; they wanted to take a picture with him. He took photos with three or four classes.

The day before we left, October 10, these people organized a big party for Randy. One woman, a pianist, had some of Randy's CDs, like *Spirits of Our Ancestors*, but she had never heard Randy before these two CDs. She was so impressed by Randy's CDs and she said she dreamed of seeing Mr. Randy Weston one day. For her he's the highest person. When she heard Randy was coming to Kyoto she started practicing the piano on one of his tunes, and she learned "African Village, Bedford Stuyvesant" note for note. She didn't want to touch Randy because for her it's like he's a god. I brought her over to Randy and I was pushing her to please sit down next to him. She told me an old story about why she was so impressed with his music. The first time she played his two CDs she got some feeling from him, so she practiced "African Village, Bedford Stuyvesant" a thousand times so she could play it for him.

When I first visited Japan I felt vibrations like Africa, but I couldn't understand why; it wasn't the architecture, it wasn't the people . . . It's hard to describe the feeling. The Japanese people are very warm; they're very giving like Africans. It was something mysterious, this feeling, like a certain tune. It reminded me of when I went to Holland, and my son and I were walking down the street, and I said, "Man, this place looks familiar." Then I realized it was the Dutch architecture and the Dutch were the first ones to colonize Brooklyn, and Brooklyn is a Dutch word. So it's experiences like that. In Japan it's that spirit that reminds me of Africa.

I went into the shrine that day and there were various priests in residence. They conducted a purification ceremony for me, in essence taking out the evil spirits by reciting old Japanese texts, invoking certain sounds, certain tones devoted to purifying the body. It was an amazing experience. They gave me a precious element to place in my house when I returned for inspiration and protection. Following the ceremony they invited me to meet the head priest. I talked with him and he said he was very happy to have me in the shrine as an honored guest. He told me their shrine is a thousand years old and he emphasized that they'd never had a piano there before. Then I was taken to the room of the performance, which was an incredible space. They had placed a Bösendorfer Imperial piano for my use

Randy at
Shinto shrine
in Kyoto, 2006.
*Photograph by
Wataru Nakamura.*

on a stage they had arranged, just slightly elevated from floor level. Around the stage they had arranged mats for the audience to sit on.

At my sound check they had a great photographer take shots of me. Just prior to concert time a gentleman took me to a very famous restaurant, very chic, very private, so I could change my clothes and relax before the concert. They had expected maybe 200 people for the concert and 280 arrived, completely filling up the room, sitting on mats very close to me and the piano. When I rehearsed I kept my shoes on, but nobody wears shoes in these shrines—the tatami mats on the floor are made of bamboo and they can't take dirt or the pressure of shoes—so they put my shoes by the piano because I had to walk shoeless to the piano. So when I got to the piano and got ready to hit I suddenly realized that I certainly couldn't put my shoes on now, nobody else had on shoes. My first ever concert without shoes was at the Kamigamo Shrine.

That night I played two sets with an intermission. I never realized how emotional the Japanese people are until I glanced out into the audience and spotted a number of people crying during the performance. I played my usual repertoire: "The Healers," "Blue Moses," "Little Niles" . . . I didn't play anything particularly new. People came up to me after the performance and they were so happy, they seemed to really *feel* what I played, it was an incredible experience. Later on they told me that at the end of the concert there was one particular man who was still sitting there even after everybody had left. Some people walked over to him to see if he was OK and asked if they could help him sit up. They had to physically lift him up and take him out of the concert room. He said the music had overwhelmed him so much that he couldn't move his legs. Michiko told me that after three songs the spiritual woman I mentioned earlier burst into tears of happiness.

The following day we were picked up at the hotel for the drive to the next performance, in a town I had played three years before that, where some of the people who had come to the shrine concert had heard me the first time. I was going there to play in a small club called Koln. We arrived at the club about 3:00 p.m. Since our hotel was a bit further away they arranged for me to go to a nearby Japanese retirement home to get a couple of hours' sleep before the concert. When we arrived at Koln the place was packed with about seventy people. I was supposed to play two forty-five-minute sets but I was so energized by the previous day's experience at the shrine that I played eighty minutes during the first set before I even realized it.

The next day was the Buddhist temple concert. When we arrived at the temple I met the priest, and we stayed in the temple living quarters that night. The priest informed me that they planned on conducting a Buddhist ceremony before I played the piano. Viewing pictures of this temple is mind blowing, because the place is over 680 years old, and as with the Shinto shrine, they had never had a piano in the temple either.

The priest spoke no English, so he talked with Michiko and explained that for the pre-concert ceremony they were going to sound the bells, and then they were going to display certain colors and make certain sounds. They explained that they would give me a signal to start playing. There were about 180 people there that night and once again it was an incredible experience, with people crying and getting very emotional. After the concert they took us to have a special dinner.

At dinner there were a lot of young men sitting around a long table with the priest at the head of the table. One of the organizers of the concert told me that the priest played the trombone. I didn't pay that much mind, since people are always telling me they play, but after about an hour of food and conversation someone mentioned musicians and the priest said, "Oh, by the way, these men are all musicians and we have a big band that plays jazz." They showed me photographs of the big band and gave me a CD.

The next morning they brought about a hundred kids between four and six years old to the temple to meet me and hear me play. They took photographs, and I really enjoyed playing for these children. After that we returned to Kyoto to prepare for our flight home. The night before our departure they threw a big party for me. Everybody I had met and all those who were responsible for this journey came to the party, and I autographed many t-shirts, posters, CDs, and the like. The next morning they came, said goodbye, and took us to the airport, and it was truly an incredible experience from the moment we arrived until the moment we left.

## Gil Meller, Japan trip coordinator

*Gil Meller*: One of the many subtleties of Japanese society, which is deep-rooted in their turbulent history, is that most people do not think of themselves as individuals but rather as part of a wider concept such as family, neighborhood community, geographical area, or interest group. Most Japanese people seem to feel more comfortable existing with the support of their group and contributing to the function of the group. Inability to relate to a group can cause utter misery. It is this psyche which has brought together a number of artists, writers, musicians, and other individually creative people who simply drop in at a particular coffeehouse irregularly to catch up with news of others from the "master" manager and his wife, who are the catalysts that enable things to happen and problems to be solved. The common factor for all these people is the comfort and excitement they derive from listening to jazz. This is why the seemingly loosely associated people who go to Lush Life Jazz Coffee House are called the Lush Life Family. When necessary the commitment of the members of this family functions with the loyalty that one could only expect from blood relatives.

From the inception of Randy's visit in October 2005, as with his first visit four years before, everyone took on tasks related to their specific skills, all coordinated from the coffeehouse by the respected master Tetsuya and implemented by Michiyo, his wife. The inspiration and enthusiasm come from the love of the music and the respect for the musician. Respect is a very important part of the psyche of the Japanese, especially for a person of whose skill they are in awe. It takes many serious, dedicated years to learn a skill from a Japanese master of any art or craft, and someone who has achieved true mastery is almost godlike. Randy Weston is respected in this way. So grateful were the members of the Lush Life family that Randy was prepared to come to Kyoto and play for the limited fee they could afford, and many happy meetings were held to generate ideas for the best way of enabling Randy to feel comfortable and rested, and for the family members to show him some of the treats unique to their culture. Especially after their meeting with him four years earlier, the deep love from the emotional Japanese heart was not only for his music but also for the person. It is this motivation that enables everyone to happily work hard and pay their own way to achieve a perfect visit with the selflessness and thoughtfulness of a Japanese group member. They all wanted to give in every way they could in return for the pleasure of the music and the company of Randy. Such is the power of music. Two weeks before the concert all the tickets had been sold out, leaving many applicants disappointed.

On Sunday morning, the day of Randy's concert, he went to the shrine offices to meet the Guji, the head priest. In his room Randy noticed a framed certificate showing that Kamigamo Shrine is designated by the United Nations World Heritage Committee as a historic site requiring protection for the benefit of humanity. After taking tea with the Guji, Randy went to the inner part of the shrine for a prayer and a blessing; what looked like a large paper dish mop was ceremoniously waved over Randy's head. Then Randy went on further into the normally inaccessible part of the shrine to pay respects to the god and to drink blessed sake from a small dish offered by the priest.

After that, Randy's piece of mind was respected in preparation for the evening's concert, while the family continued to work on preparation tasks at the shrine. Even in the green room, a curtained-off entrance balcony at the side of the hall, Randy's privacy was strictly respected. Meanwhile Mii chan, a well-known radio personality who had come all the way from Okinawa to Kyoto, where she used to live, specially to introduce Randy's concert, was keeping the audience entertained. Finally the music that they had all been waiting four years to hear was about to start, introduced by the ancient shrine gagaku music to remind us that we were in a shrine in Japan. I hope that the feeling Randy had from the audience that night was of hushed admiration and deep enjoyment. For the Lush Life Family it was the glorious fulfillment of all their efforts, and they all hugged each other with tears and relief. Michiyo Chiki-san especially, who had coordinated the arrangements and the finances and carried the worry of the responsibility in her head for months, could now relax. While some of us were taken to a small restaurant with Randy after the concert, most of the family was hard at work again gathering the cushions, clearing and sweeping up the hall, and taking down the gateway they had constructed, and dismantling all the sound equipment. Finally they all joined us and the party was relaxed and happy.

## A Brooklyn Canterbury Tale

Zeyba Rahman, who lived nearby in Brooklyn and worked for years with the World Music Institute and as U.S. liaison to the World Sacred Music Festival in Fes, Morocco, contacted me in 2003 about performing with Gnawa musicians at a conference of spiritual leaders from all over the world . . . at the Canterbury Cathedral. That sounded really intriguing, and I suggested that we bring Abdullah el Gourde and two of the Gnawa brothers from Tangier. Playing for the archbishop of Canterbury—that's like another world. I went on the internet with Zeyba to see what the cathedral looks like and learn something about its history, because I had never been there. I saw how all the kings and queens of England had been baptized at this particular church, and I saw the image of Thomas Becket, who was killed by King Henry V. With all that history in mind I quickly agreed, and we left New York for London on October 6.

Zeyba had arrived earlier, and she met me at the airport with some people from the church. We drove about two hours to Canterbury, which is southwest of London. Canterbury still has the atmosphere of old England. The two-day conference of these spiritual leaders was on the subject of world poverty and how the spiritual leaders of the world have to more seriously focus on relieving poverty across the globe. I stayed at the Chaucer Hotel, named after the author of the *Canterbury Tales*, a copy of which was in each room. That evening I was taken to meet some of the spiritual leaders gathered there for the conference.

The final day of the conference was our performance, and we were supposed to play in a crypt, which felt a bit strange to me. I had the same impression of a crypt as most people: it's a grave, a place where Dracula and those cats reside. The actual crypt for our performance was something like one might imagine, because it was under the cathedral. But their definition of a crypt is simply a still place. We were performing opposite an English choir and a Japanese flutist. The tuning of the Gnawa stringed instrument—the haghouje, or what some people call the guimbre—has a lot to do with the temperature in the room, and the spirit of the place. As you can only imagine, this place was kinda strange in that respect: all the ancestor archbishops were buried there, so you can imagine what that was like. Abdullah couldn't get the haghouje tuned properly with the piano for some reason. So one of the other Gnawa grabbed it and finally wrestled it in tune with the piano.

At concert time they assembled all of the spiritual leaders in a semicircle around the performance space; this was not a public concert. We played forty-five minutes—three or four solo piano pieces, then I played with the Gnawa. Afterwards an Indian gentleman, a high spiritual leader who is director of a major association in New Delhi that concerns the Hindus and Muslims and efforts at bringing them together, was the first one to come up to us after we finished playing. He said, "You have to come to India!" I knew they had never heard any Gnawa in that place before.


## Opening the Grand Library of Alexandria

As I said, I have not always been afforded opportunities to perform at some of the more traditional jazz clubs and festivals. On the other hand I've played my share of unusual gigs and venues. Right after the Canterbury Cathedral performance Fatou and I went to Egypt to perform at the grand opening ceremony for the major new library they've built in Alexandria. My good brother in Cairo, the musician Salah Ragab, arranged this trip. Fatou and I always visited him whenever we went to Cairo. He knew that they were getting ready to open this huge library in Alexandria and he arranged for me to perform at the opening ceremony.

Alexandria is maybe three hours northwest of Cairo by car. This new library is historic, because it's reputed to be the biggest library in the world and it's located on the original site of the great library that was burnt down by the Romans centuries ago. Salah knew my immersion in Africa, and he sent me a fax suggesting I get in touch with the conductor of the Egyptian symphony, Sherif Mohib el Din, who was in charge of the music for the grand opening ceremony. I sent him a few CDs, we talked back and forth, and to my great surprise he said yes, they wanted me to come. Although this was a major event in the history of Africa the western press doesn't pay any attention to those kinds of things, so I was surprised that they'd want a musician from Brooklyn to perform on this grand occasion. And besides that I had no previous contact with the Egyptian government, so the invitation was all the more unexpected.

Fatou and I arrived in Cairo on October 14 for the event on the 16th. There were no other artists there from either North America or West Africa. They had Arab Egyptians and some South African musicians, an artist and his wife from India, and the other artists were European. Numerous heads of state were there: President Hosni Mubarak of Egypt and his wife, President Jacques Chirac from France, the queen of Spain, the president of Greece, and assorted diplomats from all over the world, so you can imagine the security was deep.

Norwegians had contributed heavily to the building of this library, and I had to coordinate my performance with a Norwegian conductor. Everything was very tightly programmed. They had a small string orchestra, and every artist was scheduled to play for three minutes; I played five. The great Nigerian writer Wole Soyinka was the only brother who spoke at the ceremony. Accompanied by the bassist James Lewis, I played "The 3 Pyramids and the Sphinx," which I had sent to this Norwegian conductor in advance so he could coordinate it with whatever they were going to perform on the rest of the program.

Jaap Harlaar, who manages my web site and is my road manager whenever I'm in Europe or Scandinavia, had sent my music to the Norwegian conductor, who really didn't want us to play "The 3 Pyramids and the Sphinx," or at least that's what he told Jaap in advance. But when I met him at the event not a word was spoken about it and they had "The 3 Pyramids and the Sphinx" listed in the program. As I said, the event was very tightly programmed and we had to have three rehearsals. At the end of the event they had three or four thousand children from all over Egypt sing, which was very moving. My performance was beautifully received.

One of the more interesting aspects of this event is that they really concentrated on Alexandria, the Greeks. Alexander started the original library in this part of what is now Egypt. So the ceremony was really about Alexander, not about what had happened *before* Alexander. In a way, by playing "The 3 Pyramids and the Sphinx" we represented Egypt pre-Alexander. We later learned that this event was broadcast all over Egypt and afterwards people stopped us in the street to thank us because we were the only ones who really played anything that was really about Egypt. It was quite an experience—and again, another spiritual trip . . . from Canterbury to Alexandria!

## Celebrating a Giant

In African tradition you celebrate the death of someone, not the birthday. One of my true heroes, the Senegalese genius Cheikh Anta Diop, whom I had the great fortune of meeting in the flesh years ago on a trip to Senegal, passed on to ancestry on February 7, 1986. I learned that in 2003 they were going to have a big celebration of Diop and I had some free time, so I just *had* to be there. I contacted Royal Air Maroc regarding some things I wanted to do with the Gnawa of Morocco, and I subsequently arranged a trip to Dakar, since that airline also flies to Senegal. I flew from New York to Casablanca, spent the night there, and then flew to Dakar. It seems these kinds of connections are very magical, mystical, and quite wonderful. I arrived in Dakar the week prior to the celebration: I couldn't be there for the actual day, because I had to play at Alabama State on the 7th.

Fatou met me at the airport and then we hooked up with this wonderful guy Kisito Diene, who owns a nightclub called Jus 4 Us. It's a wonderful club, which they call a jazz club but which actually features more traditional Senegalese music. It's an outdoor place with a huge bar and a library. It's kinda like a house made into a club. Before I arrived Fatou had contacted a woman named Marietou, who had been quite close to Cheikh Anta Diop. As the story goes, Diop was traveling the villages of Senegal when he spotted Marietou and told her father that he wanted her to come with him—and this just goes to show the respect, reverence, and trust in which Diop is held: her father was honored and she went with Diop. He subsequently taught Marieto many things from his wealth of knowledge. I had actually been hoping to do a concert in tribute to Cheikh Anta Diop, and Marietou was an excellent contact to make that happen.

Diop has more than one son in Senegal, but I've become acquainted with one particular son, a doctor named Masamba Diop. He works with an organization called SOS and sometimes travels with Senegalese patients on trips to Paris for medical treatments; he's constantly on call internationally, particularly between Senegal and France.

I had also become acquainted with Cheikh Anta Diop's wife. Madame Diop is a French woman who met Diop at the Sorbonne, which they attended at the same time. She's a very brilliant woman. The word got out through Fatou on my arrival that I wanted to do something to celebrate this man, and the family was pleased. I explained to them my history of meeting Diop in Dakar in 1985, how I had read his books before then, and how deeply he had inspired me. So this club owner Kisito and I decided that we were going to perform this tribute at his club.

Everything had to be done within the four or five days that I would be able to stay in Senegal. We also decided to host a symposium on Cheikh Anta Diop at 5:00 p.m. on the day we scheduled the tribute concert. The idea was to invite various African Egyptologists and professors who had studied Diop's work or knew of his work to speak. Everyone would read a paper or talk about Diop, and then at 10:00 p.m. I would play and the great Senegalese drummer Dou Dou N'Diaye Rose would bring four of his sons to play with me. It was truly going to be a night to celebrate Diop.

While there in Senegal I was also compelled to visit the village of Caytou, where Diop was born. It's a very small village, where he is also buried. Fatou and I were lucky, because Diop's son Masamba arranged for Diop's chauffeur, who coincidentally had been with Diop when he died, to go with us, and Kisito drove. The four of us made the three-hour drive from Dakar to Diop's ancestral village of Caytou.

It was a wonderful trip, because the chauffeur told us things about Diop that were very personal, and about how dedicated Diop was to his people. The trip was going smoothly until we drove through a village along the way, and all of a sudden here comes a horse crossing the highway in front of us. And Kisito is driving too fast, like most of my brothers in Africa. We slammed into the horse on my side of the car. Luckily Kisito had shatterproof glass in his car, or I'd have been in trouble. The car was smashed but the horse got up and just walked away.

When we finally arrived in Diop's home village and visited Diop's gravesite we were kind of surprised that this great man wasn't buried in a more elaborate setting. A European woman had set up two huts in the village, of which one was designed to represent a library of Diop's books and the other was supposed to be a school to teach the children how to read and write.

But when we went inside the library hut all we saw was dust all over Diop's books, and we couldn't understand why it was so poorly maintained. We were surprised, because we felt the family or the world should do more for this great man. They told us that Diop's family had wanted to build a pyramid for Diop in this village, but the village chief wanted to build a mosque and they never settled this difference. How Diop came out of that humble village to be one of the most brilliant men of the twentieth century—or any century—is amazing.

That evening in Dakar we had the symposium, and different people came and spoke about Diop. Meanwhile we had searched all over Dakar to find a proper piano, and the only one we found was really sad. We brought this piano to the club anyway, but they didn't have a microphone or sound system, so I ended up playing the electric piano. Dou Dou N'Diaye Rose and his four sons played percussion with me. The MC, a brother named Moktar, introduced Dou Dou N'Diaye Rose, and this is what Dou Dou said: "Tonight I'm going to present you Randy Weston. He's my brother and we've known each other a long time. I never play with anybody just like that, meaning anybody can't just come to me and ask me, 'Dou Dou can I play with you.' I love to play with Randy Weston, because he's a brother who knows what he's doing. I'm going to play with him, and to tell you the truth we didn't even rehearse, but you'll see we are going to cook for you a new cuisine that will prove to you that jazz comes from us."

The club was packed with people for our performance. The night before, I had seen Dr. Charles Finch, along with twenty people from Atlanta, some of whom were doctors who were traveling to a village in Senegal to study traditional medicine. Dr. Finch was there that night, and I was really delighted to see him. It was a very, very spiritual night. We played "Borum Zam Zam" and "Portrait of Cheikh Anta Diop." It was really just rhythms, color, and sound because I had this electric instrument and the sound wasn't that great, but it was a very spiritual evening. The most beautiful part for me was when they introduced a singer, a sister who was a griot with a powerful voice. She sang in Wolof—the ancient Wolof. She gave the whole history of Cheikh Anta Diop, starting with his grandfather and his father, going way back. Then we played again to conclude the evening. I also got a chance to hang out with Fatou and her brothers. So that was Senegal—special as always.

## 19

# ANCIENT FUTURE

## Anatomy of an Extended Composition

Many times I've written music about trips or places of cultural importance that have inspired me. I've been blessed to write new music conveying a number of places and images over the years. That was definitely the case when I wrote an extended new composition for a performance in January 2002. Todd Barkan commissioned me to write this piece through Jazz at Lincoln Center. I've known Todd since he owned the old Keystone Korner club in San Francisco. He's a pianist himself and he always picked the best artists to play his place. I remember one year at the Keystone Korner he put me opposite Cecil Taylor for one week and Anthony Braxton for another; that was pretty wild. In 2001 Todd contacted me about writing a new piece and he asked me if I would consider featuring the fantastic violinist Regina Carter.

Wayne Chandler's book *Ancient Future* really had a profound impact on me, not only for its content but for what it represents. We live in a world where there are so many untruths, and when you run across real truths it can be very powerful. Wayne's book is really about the beginnings of spirituality, the beginnings of religion, how it came from Africans and how spirituality was in its purest state. I was so moved by the book—and I really love that title, *Ancient Future*—that I wanted to write some music based upon this text. The title means that for us to be strong, creative, and spiritual we must go back and pay homage to our beginnings in Mother Africa, that's where we have to focus. Chandler talks about the ancient Egyptians, the Nubians who created a whole concept of civilization. At the same time, as Wayne's book insists, we must bring these ancestral principles into the future.

While writing this commissioned music I developed several themes based upon the two trips Fatou and I made to Nubia and Egypt. On those two trips, as always whenever I travel to Africa, I was looking for the old people, the elders. There are very few young people I'm in contact with for wisdom or knowledge, with the exception of those young people who know these things and are in tune with the elders, of course, because it's the elders who make Africa what it is, since it's such a continent of tradition and contrast. To really know Africa you must reach the elders, and they'll tell you what's happening.

The first theme I wrote was titled "Kom Omba," which is an ancient Nubian City; I just love that name, and we visited that very old city on our travels. Another piece was about the Nile River, which obviously made a huge impact upon me; I named my son after the Nile. The Nile was so important in creating the first civilization in the Nile Valley. It was the first cultural highway, and it was the place where there was so much exchange between the south and the north, the Nubians and the Egyptians.

To perform this suite, in addition to the African Rhythms Quintet I brought together three string traditions, represented by Abou M'Boup. a kora player from Senegal, Min Xao-Fen of China on pipa, and Regina Carter of America on the violin. I put these three strings together to demonstrate that it was African civilization that came into China and helped give China its civilization, principally during the Shange Dynasty; Africa and China were the two original great civilizations.

I wanted to make that wonderful transformation from the kora, which is a very ancient instrument coming out of West Africa via Egypt, and how the kora and the pipa of China were a marriage of strings. Regina Carter represented how Africa has spread to the United States and how she's taken this violin in another direction. The basic idea was to have these three instruments come together, celebrating the ancient and the modern together.


## Regina Carter, violinist

*Regina Carter*: It's inspiring to hear that with all of Randy Weston's life experiences and musical journeys, he seems to maintain the enthusiasm to seek, learn, and share. Randy's compositions and productions always seem larger than life. Clearly he has ingested all these melodic and rhythmic styles from the continent and proved to us all that music is just one language. The very first rehearsal for this concert was with only Benny Powell, TK, and me going over the horn lines. It was difficult to grasp how the music would sound without all the other instruments. Although the lines seemed simple by themselves, this rehearsal with just the three of us proved to be important once the full band came together. All of the lines, harmony, and rhythms made Randy's music breathe and move in a way that if I wasn't secure in my part I'd be pulled into someone else's space.

Although I had heard Abdou M'Boup on several occasions, this would be our first time playing together. This was my first time meeting Min, and my first introduction to the pipa. I had no idea what to make of the whole collection of musicians and instruments Randy had assembled for this concert. Some of the sounds were new to me, making me feel the excitement of a child discovering something new. Once I became more familiar with the music and could get out of my head and off my part, the experience of Randy's music reminded me of the feeling I get when I'm floating in the sea, with the waves pushing and pulling, but trusting that I haven't traveled too far from safety.

Randy is such a gentle giant with a beautiful soul. His compositions have many layers, each playing an important role, with many stories that everyone can relate to. It's extremely important for me to be able to find my personal groove within a piece of music, and Randy's music definitely offered that. There was so much joy in the music and excitement from the audience; it felt more like a celebration than a concert.

> "Ancient Future" explores the similarities—and differences—shared by cultures and music from around the world. It reminds me how the world has become smaller. Wherever you come from, music has no boundaries. We should always respect that.
> —MIN XIAO-FEN, pipa player

In my search for a kora player I went to a Senegalese restaurant I often frequented called Kuer N'Diaye, on Fulton Street in Brooklyn, which unfortunately has since closed. There I heard about Abou M'Boup. Min Xao-Fen had previously recorded with me on my 1998 album *Khepera*. At that point I only knew Regina by reputation. The purpose of the three strings was to make the audience stop and meditate—to take a figurative trip. Usually at a concert it's very rhythmic and very active, very up-tempo; that's not a criticism, because I do it all the time myself. But in this case I wanted the audience to take a contemplative trip with these strings, to transform them, so they would kind of leave the earthly world when they heard these in-

Min Xao-Fen playing the pipa. *Photograph by Cheung Ching Ming.*

struments alone and together. Min told me later that she heard from the Chinese consulate and they knew she was playing this piece with me at Lincoln Center and were quite pleased.

I have to pay a very special tribute to Talib Kibwe here, because he put his heart and soul into making this commissioned concert happen. He not only wrote the arrangements for me—for the first time, because before that it had always been Melba—but he also got the band together to rehearse and make suggestions. Talib and I talked at length about the initial concept behind *Ancient Future.* He was key to the success of this piece, not only as musical director but also for those other things that people usually don't get credit for.

# Talib Kibwe (TK Blue)

*TK Blue*: First Randy played me three different pieces from the overall work on the piano. I notated what he played: melody, harmony, and rhythm. I read the book *Ancient Future*; then I wrote the arrangements based on my long relationship with Randy, the inspiration I received from Wayne's book, the specific instrumentation, and the featured guest artist Regina Carter.

"Kom Omoba" has an AABAA form. I felt that the piece needed a shout chorus to feature the horn section with Regina. After I wrote my initial chorus I thought that was cool, but there was something missing which I couldn't quite figure out. That night Melba appeared to me in a dream and said she was proud of what I was doing but I had to change something on the second A section (with four A sections, things can get a little dull if you don't change it up a little). So the next day I added a different part to the second A section, which repeats in the fourth A section. It gave the horns something a little more involved to play and it gave the piece a bit of cohesion.

I'm very happy with the results, and Randy was thrilled when he heard it the first time and gave me his nod of approval. He said that Melba would have been proud of me. I feel this is a monumental work—which was actually recorded and broadcast by the syndicated radio program "Jazz Set" with Dee Dee Bridgewater, and I hope one day it will be released on record.

I added Billy Harper on tenor saxophone to the quintet because he's certainly one of my favorite players, but Billy could only make the first of our scheduled two nights. For the second night I thought it absolutely had to be Cecil Payne as guest saxophonist, because even though Cecil has experienced vision problems, we grew up together and his baritone playing remains so great. We also wanted somebody to play jazz trap drums in addition to our regular percussionist Neil Clarke, so I got Lewis Nash, because he played with us when we did the second concert of "African Sunrise" with Arturo O'Farrill's orchestra in Chicago. Lewis played so beautifully that night that I knew he would be right for *Ancient Future*.

In the beginning of the piece I wanted to depict the sound of the planet earth itself, because in western teaching everything is focused away from the earth, there's no real appreciation for the earth except for the farmers and people who actually work the land. The whole idea behind this piece was to depict creation itself: how there was silence, then vibrations, increasing vibrations. And then after that, when the earth is created, Abou M'Boup would represent the first musical instrument and almost the first sound after the birds and Mother Nature, the original orchestra. So we had Abou create the first sound, the sound of earth on his instrument. Then he would start playing a Senegalese theme about a master, and from that point Min joins him on pipa. That meant symbolically China joined Africa, the two of them played together; and then all of a sudden here comes Regina to join them with her genius. So we have the West, China, and Africa all together, represented by these three strings.

After the three strings made their entrance the piece evolved into a call and response between them, which is the foundation of black music all over the world. For me this was like opening African civilization to the audience through this work. And I'm sure my friend Danilo Perez had much the same feeling about Panama with the commissioned work he performed to open the program.

Talib was our arranger, but in a different way from Melba. She was the utmost professional when I met her; she knew more about music than I did when we met. When I met Talib he was just coming into his own, developing over the years by playing with other people and by playing with me; so I've been able to witness the evolution of Talib Kibwe. When Talib told me that story about Melba coming to him in a dream and solving an arrangement mystery for him it blew my mind. Because of all these elements coming together so beautifully those two performances of *Ancient Future* were really very successful.


## Further Adventures

In October 2005 I returned to Japan for another beautiful journey. Once again I performed a special concert in the Kamigamo Buddhist Shrine in Kyoto. Prior to the concert the head priest sent some other priests to the shrine to perform a ceremony. I had to kneel down, and these priests began reciting verses designed to in essence remove the evil spirits. They took a staff with a white cloth attached to it and they rubbed that cloth over my head to prepare me for that evening's performance. The head priest told one of the young men to bring me a special piece of wood, which was shaped like a long sliver from a tree branch. The translator told me that the head priest wanted me to sign my name on this piece of wood. But he instructed me to sign my name across the entire piece—so I had to stretch out my name to make it fit. After I did that the translator told me, "Mr. Weston, this piece of wood is going to be placed on the roof of the shrine ten years from now, and that's why they needed my signature—so that I would be in the shrine forever." I was honored. They had the Shinto priests play their traditional music, with flutes sounding very high notes, to welcome me before I played my solo concert.

I made a similar ceremony when I later performed at a Shinto shrine in Tokyo. The woman I had been getting shiatsu treatments from for years had relocated back to Tokyo, and she arranged for me to perform at this other Shinto shrine in town. This shrine is in an area of Tokyo that was being rehabilitated; it seemed to be a haven for many different artists. When I arrived at the shrine for this concert they once again performed a similar preparation ceremony. And just as in Kyoto, they had an ensemble of Japanese traditional musicians perform prior to my solo piano performance. However this time they had set up the musicians in the staging area, directly behind where I was seated at the piano, preparing to play. And when they began playing those flutes in that high-pitched way, because of my hearing problems I was really suffering from their closeness and those piercing sounds. But what could I do? I certainly couldn't be rude and cover my ears to block the sounds. I just sat there grinning, listening, and hoping they wouldn't go on for too long.

I made it through, and following my performance one of the shrine officials told me that if this concert had not been a success his generation would be cursed, and three generations after that. He said that's how important my concert was. Success to them was how the people reacted to the concert; the audience was very happy and it gave them a spiritual lift, gave the other artists encouragement, and was apparently further impetus to restore that part of Tokyo. As they say, music is a healing force. I think when the Japanese hear these rhythms it seems to reach them very deeply.

## My Eightieth Year

In 2006, when I turned eighty, I knew it would be a special year. I wanted to do something at 651Arts, the arts presenting organization in Brooklyn whose presentations of my work have always been special for me. I hadn't performed for them for a while, not since the collaboration with the Gnawa in September 1999 at Lafayette Presbyterian Church. We made a record called *Spirit! The Power of Music* that night, and it was another special 651Arts concert. And before that had been the revival of *Uhuru Afrika* at the Majestic Theatre in '98, so my 651 concerts have really been high points in my career, thanks to good sisters like Mikki Shepard and Maurine Knighton. I got the impression from many folks that when you turn eighty that's a year you're really supposed to celebrate, so I was ready for that.

Fatou and I went over to 651's office above the old Majestic Theatre on Fulton Street, which is now the Harvey Theatre, to discuss some ideas. We met with the executive director Georgina Pickett and the managing director Anna Glass. We talked about how rare it was for me to perform in Brooklyn, and they began planning right away. Finally they got back to me and said the only time they could schedule a program would be in January, but my birthday wasn't until April. So they said let's start celebrating your eightieth in January. It was their idea for me to do an evening of solo piano, followed by an evening with the band plus guests. It soon occurred to me that I had never played a solo piano performance in Brooklyn before. Funny, but the closest I ever came to playing solo in Brooklyn was when I was a little boy playing for the church ladies with my mother, and the church ladies telling me I should be playing God's music, don't play the devil's music.

Those turned out to be two tremendous evenings in Brooklyn, at the brand-new auditorium at Long Island University. The night of the solo concert they arranged audience seating right on the stage, surrounding the piano; it was really intimate, with large plants surrounding the stage. For the band performance Gil Noble was there as MC, and I had Min Xao Fen, Abou M'Boup, Billy Harper, Candido, the regular members of the quintet— TK Blue, Benny Powell, Neil Clarke, and Alex Blake—in the band, and Yaa-Lengi Ngemi spoke to the audience about music from the Congo. They had a beautiful birthday cake shaped like a piano at the after-party, and it was really special because this was in Brooklyn, and it was marking my eightieth year.


## Panama, January 2006

For several years I had been bugging the wonderful pianist Danilo Perez, asking him, "Man, when are we gonna go to Panama, my father's homeland, and play your festival?" As it turns out, a Panamanian friend of mine named Carlos Russell invited us to a luncheon in New York for Panama in early January. Carlos is an activist who has lived in Brooklyn for a long time; he was also a good friend of my father. The luncheon was at an Asian restaurant in Manhattan where the president of Panama honored Carlos for his work on behalf of Panama in the U.S. A lot of Panamanians had left their country, but now the mood of the current regime was for the expatriate Panamanians to come back to help rebuild the country. There were people at this luncheon from all over the Caribbean, and they all knew Carlos. They had a big-screen television there to show a video which featured the president of Panama giving Carlos a wonderful medal and talking about how they wanted to do more for the black people of Panama.

The next morning I got a call from my agent Maurice Montoya, who said, "You're going to Panama, Danilo called!" This was certainly ironic. Later Danilo called me and said he had wanted to bring me there previously but not until things were right, when everything was organized for me. Danilo runs a beautiful festival there every January. I called Alex Blake right away, because Alex had left Panama when he was about seven and hadn't been back since. The gig was set for my trio with Alex and Neil. When we landed in Panama City Fatou immediately said she felt at home there, and when she says that she means it feels like Africa. We were picked up and went directly from the plane to the White House (that's what they call their presidential residence too) to visit President Espino.

When we arrived they had a scrumptious buffet lunch and the president welcomed all of us. Rubén Blades, the great salsa singer who was a cabinet minister there, welcomed us as well. The son of Mauricio Smith, the great Panamanian flute player, was there representing his father, and the saxophonist David Sanchez was there along with other artists. The president made a speech saying that jazz is the music of Panama, they love jazz. They told me that since my father is Panamanian I was automatically a Panamanian citizen, I could have dual citizenship. I was really excited to hear that and eager to get my Panama passport.

To begin that process, the next day a piano player took Fatou and me to Panama's national archives. We saw pre-Columbian archives from the eleventh, twelfth, and thirteenth centuries, which was fascinating. I gave them what information I could, which only amounted to some minimal information about my dad and my cousin Frisco. They took down the information and later got back to us asking for more.

The Panama Jazz Festival was a real family affair for Danilo: his mother was right there taking care of some of the business of the event; meanwhile his father socialized with all of the artists, his wife played saxophone with his band, and their children were always around. We played three concerts during the festival and I did a master class. The Panamanian saxophonist Carlos Garnett, who I knew from his days in New York, was there and played with us on one concert. The last concert we played there was free, and the plaza in Old Panama City was packed. They had an ensemble playing classic Panamanian music, dressed in traditional clothing.

When we performed, the people seemed to really know the rhythms; I cannot tell you how long it had been since I received that kind of reception of my music. It was like they were asking with delight, "What kind of music is *this*?" But it was *their* music, they felt the spirit of the music, and they responded to the music. It had never happened like that in Jamaica, Trinidad, or other places in the region. It was like the old days in Harlem and Brooklyn, that kind of wild response. And for sure Alex Blake is now a superstar in his homeland; they had never seen anybody play a bass like that in Panama. Since Alex had left Panama when he was a boy, no one there knew him as a bass player. Panamanians who knew his father came from everywhere to see Alex. It was like we were all truly home. Everybody was telling us, "You've got to come back, you're a Panamanian now." I was also so deeply moved by Danilo Perez, he treated me royally. He told the audience, "Randy Weston we owe a lot to you, you've paved the way for young people to follow," and he kept saying that. Panama was fabulous, like being home.

## Journey to the Heart of the Blues

A few weeks after we had left Senegal on that trip to honor Diop I got a call at the end of March from a guy named Ed Silvera and a professor named Marvin Hair down in Mississippi. They asked if I'd like to come down to Mississippi Valley State University and be in residence for a week at the Delta Research Center in Ita Bena—the home of B. B. King. I accepted right away and told Fatou that we were gonna go down to the *real* soulville, the Mississippi Delta. So we made the trip, and there we were right smack in the Delta. As usual Fatou was intently looking all around, checking out the scene, seeing those familiar faces from home, and then we got a weeklong lesson in the blues. They were doing research on the blues at this center and had a young poet there who writes and recites his work about the history of the blues. He and I were the two artists-in-residence on this occasion. The bluesman Corey Harris, who once collaborated with the late Senegalese master bluesman Ali Farka Toure, had preceded us there by a week.

For my presentation, I took one of Fatou's DVDs of Ali Farka Toure to show the people that the blues really is music directly out of Africa. Then I talked about the blues, and the poet and I did a duo together. During the week they gave us an amazing tour of places where all these Mississippi blues men and women had played. They took us to the house where the blues master Robert Johnson had lived. We saw the cotton fields for the first time in our lives; we saw how black folks were exploited in the South. Ironically, now the Europeans are paying thousands of dollars to come to the Delta and stay in a former slave shack, "roughing it," to have that experience. The state of Mississippi is creating themed kiosks all along the highway, and each one will have the name of a blues artist. We visited one of the graves of Robert Johnson; they say he may have three or four gravesites. It was out there, man . . . shaped like a huge guitar. We met the mayor of the very small, notorious town of Money, where Emmett Till was murdered. They took us to the store where the incident started and they took us to a spot where they're going to build a huge monument to Emmett Till.

During my research for this trip I realized I have written over forty blues, something I had never considered before. I never thought of looking at my compositions to see how many blues I've written. I gave them a list of these blues. They told me they want to create a Randy Weston room at the university. I kept telling them, "Man, I don't play the blues; I'm from Brooklyn, New York." They said, "Yeah, you play the blues." The cotton fields made the biggest impact on us; we were really moved and pained at what one people could do to another people. But I also felt proud that the same people who could withstand that kind of pain could produce a Louis Armstrong, a Thelonious Monk, or whomever. I spent my actual eightieth birthday down there on April 6.

In June 2006 I proudly received an honorary doctorate from Brooklyn College. I owe a lot to Robin Kelley and Ingrid Monson for writing beautiful letters to the college on my behalf. It was quite an occasion; all three of my daughters, Cheryl, Pamela, and Kim, were there, as was my cousin June from the Jamaican side of the family; plus Fatou and Khadija were there as well.

It was a heartwarming occasion, and my mother's spirit was in the house, because I remember when I was ten years old she worked as a domestic, making about $15 a week. I wanted to help her so much and I insisted on giving her money when I could. She got me a little job passing out fliers at Brooklyn College. So during the ceremony my mind flashed back to that time, and I sure wished my mama could have seen this—what a miracle. The playwright Woody King and the pianist and bandleader Arturo O'Farrill were also honored, and we all kept hugging each other back and forth.

## Russia

July 2006 in St. Petersburg was the first time I had ever played in Russia. When we arrived there we found that poor Alex had left the key to his bass case in Milan. But the Russian officials at the airport insisted on opening that huge bass case to see what was inside and take photographs of it before they would let him in the country. He had to go through a lot of changes with that bass, but everything turned out OK, and the people were just beautiful. We played our trio concert in a big open park in St. Petersburg. Jaap Harlaar, who was traveling with us as road manager during this tour, said it was the greatest audience he had ever experienced. The people were just incredible; they treated us like rock stars.

I asked to see the museum of Aleksandr Pushkin. The Russians were taken aback by that request; they said that was the first time an American musician had asked about Pushkin. I know Pushkin was Russia's greatest poet. They were thrilled and took us to this museum to see his whole history, from his black Ethiopian great-grandfather on. St. Petersburg was a city I'd always wanted to visit, because it is the cultural center of Russia. The people were exceptionally kind and they really loved the music. I felt the real strong cultural spirit of the Russian people.

## Rwanda

I had never traveled to East or East Central Africa before 2006. Our trip to Rwanda was connected to Morocco, believe it or not. There's a man in New York named Abdul Kabir Abbadi I've known for at least twenty-five to thirty years. He was formerly at the UN, knows all the ambassadors, and is a real diplomat himself, though he's actually a journalist. He's involved in the organization called World Culture Open (WCO), which is independent of but affiliated with the UN, from my understanding.

The purpose of WCO, an international organization concentrating on peace and healing through the arts and culture, is to bring the arts to the world. On June 5 my friend Abbaddi arranged for me to meet the woman in charge of WCO, Dr. Grace Lee. She's a Korean PhD who is the head of one of the major Buddhist organizations in New York. I met Dr. Lee and Abbaddi at the WCO office on East 26th Street. Dr. Lee is a very warm, charming, and passionate woman. She told me all about the organization and said they were scheduling missions to Rwanda in 2006, Ghana in 2007, and Beijing in 2008. She said they knew about my work and would like for me to be one of their cultural ambassadors. I asked what that meant and she said they wanted me to do what I do normally do, play music and speak. They even gave me a certificate designating me as a cultural ambassador. This all sounded very interesting to me. She wanted me to go to Rwanda that August, since this was already June, and there was very little time to make that happen.

I told her there had to be some money involved, because the trip would require a ten-day stay and they wanted the whole quintet to make the trip. So I told Dr. Lee the musicians would come as cultural ambassadors in their own right; in other words our collective purpose would be to come and make a spiritual and healing contribution to Rwanda—all of us, not just me.

I had two meetings with Dr. Lee and a third meeting which included my attorney Gail Boyd. I had told Gail about the WCO and she had agreed to go to Rwanda with us. She didn't come to the meeting officially as a lawyer or as a manager: she really came because she wanted to know more about the WCO organization, plus she was free to go to Rwanda between the 4th and 14th of August. Because of my other travel that summer I didn't know the conditions as things developed and I didn't know we had an actual agreement until the very last minute.

Fortunately Gail and her assistant Alexis were on top of things there in New York, because there was supposed to be a press conference which I couldn't attend due to travel, and TK Blue couldn't be there either. There was also supposed to be a meeting to settle the final arrangements, which I also couldn't attend. So everything was kinda disorganized, to put it mildly. Gail and Alexis drew up the contract; luckily that part was taken care of in my absence. I called the guys in the band and asked them if they'd like to go to Rwanda, because Rwanda is a place that some people would be reluctant to go due to their notorious genocide back in the '90s. When I spoke with Benny he said, "What are the dates, let me get back to you." When he did get back to me he said, "Man, listen, can I help people [by making the trip]?" I said, "Yeah," and he said, "I'm ready." Just those few words said it all.

The band left from New York on August 3 via Washington, to Rome, to Addis Ababa . . . to Rwanda; it was a crazy itinerary. Fatou and I left from Paris on August 4 via Addis Ababa to the Rwandan capital of Kigali. We all arrived at basically the same time and we were all wiped out from travel. Dr. Lee met us there at the airport and the U.S. embassy provided our transportation. They took us to the gorgeous Hotel Intercontinental; it's quite modern, decorated with the Rwandan colors, and blends in harmoniously with the landscape. Rwanda is a very beautiful country, with all the houses rising up the mountainside; it's quite a panoramic scene. We checked in and saw that all the hotel personnel and the guests were black. That's pretty different from our usual hotel check-ins in other parts of the world, to say the least. We had a beautiful room, and all the food was delicious.

There was a lot of confusion when we got there about transportation, pickup times, and the like. But having dealt with Morocco I was used to that; what else is new? We had our first performance the day after we arrived, in a big stadium. I've always disliked performing in stadiums, that scene is just so impersonal and too big. But this stadium was really nice; there was a lot of green grass and flowers. Most stadiums are very cold in appearance, but this stadium wasn't like that at all and was full of people that evening. The president was going to be there, so the place was crawling with soldiers and security. As sometimes happens in such situations, somebody hadn't taken care of business, so we couldn't gain entry for the longest time. There was a big crowd just milling around, trying to enter this place. I've had this experience before; I've never played in a stadium where there wasn't chaos, which is one reason I don't like them. But this was actually the best stadium I had ever played in.

Finally I was able to communicate and get a soldier to clear the way for us to get in. The stadium was packed, but the interesting and sad thing about Rwanda is that there are very few old people, since so many of the elders lost their lives in the country's various conflicts. Everybody is young all around: the soldiers, the police, the government ministers—all young people. When it came time for us to perform I had to play on a Fender Rhodes electric piano, which I knew in advance, so I wasn't surprised. So I said OK, for the opening I'll play it because I know Africa and sometimes you just can't get a decent piano there. Then, as big as I am, they had me sitting at this electric piano in what amounted to a lawn chair. And Fatou just *knew* that thing was going to collapse under my weight.

We played "African Village Bedford Stuyvesant" and the audience was fantastic. But they only gave us fifteen minutes to perform because they had different ensembles, dance companies, and other performers on the program. There were artists there from South Africa and other parts of the continent. This particular evening was all part of a festival called FESPAD, an African dance festival which has been going on for six years. World Culture Open collaborated with the festival, and it was all broadcast on Rwandan television. The audience responded beautifully to our music. But we only had time to play that one tune, and then we went back to the hotel. Playing such a short time was disappointing.

My responsibility as cultural ambassador representing WCO was to meet and interact with various ministers of culture around Africa, and particularly those from Central and East Africa. There was hardly anyone there at the conference from West Africa, and from other parts of Africa just one woman from Algeria and a representative from South Africa. Funny thing was that this was a roomful of African diplomats, and I was the only one wearing African garments. These ministers were supposed to present a proposal on creative economic development, because the whole purpose here is to engage the artists to help encourage the Rwandan people to utilize their arts and culture for economic development. Rwanda lost nearly 1.5 million people during the genocide in the '90s, and they were still in recovery.

All the ministers spoke about how they could assist creative economic development, and give new energy to Africa through technology and art, to encourage the people to make a living producing their own native art. I talked about an African village project I had planned in the '70s to establish a cultural base for all of us from the West to come and study Africa and its history and exchange our musical ideas with Africans. Throughout the day there was a woman sitting next to me wearing jeans. I didn't know who she was, and whenever she participated in the discussion she was quite aggressive, but in a pleasant way. And that morning I had forgotten to put my hearing aid in, so I was a bit handicapped. Most Rwandans speak English and some French, as well as their traditional language which is similar to Swahili but not quite.

This woman who'd been sitting next to me starts talking about the Rwandan children, the families, AIDS, poverty, and whatnot, but I still didn't know who she was, though I knew she wasn't one of the ministers. It turned out she was one of the leading AIDS doctors in Rwanda; she represented Rwanda at the big global AIDS conference in Toronto in June 2006.

When I spoke I talked about what I usually speak about—the importance of the music, how we have long wanted to establish a base of African music in Africa, where we can come to rest and create, and where the elders will be taken care of, all in true African tradition. After I spoke, this woman in jeans, Dr. Agnes Binagwaho, leaned over and said, "I want to talk to you." So we had breakfast the next morning. Her plan is to develop a foundation for street children. She said in Rwanda you have two kinds of children: the ones who are victims of genocide and those who are victims of AIDS. There were also two European women at the meeting who work with these orphaned children.

That same afternoon we were in her office and she was busily typing on her laptop, all the while talking with me, Fatou, and Gail. She didn't know it at the time, but she was essentially providing a true purpose for the African Rhythms foundation we're working to establish. In essence this new effort was going to be called Street Schools and was going to raise money to help these children. That inspired me as an ideal direction for my own foundation; it gave us a goal. The good doctor left for the AIDS conference in Toronto the following morning.

The next thing I knew, later that afternoon some other Rwandans I had met before gathered a group of fifty children from two organizations in Rwanda. Gail and I and the American embassy all chipped in some money so we could buy a big meal to feed these fifty children at the French consulate, where we were going to do a concert that night. Dr. Binagwaho had previously introduced us to the guys to arrange the children's transportation and the food. These children ranged in age from maybe five to sixteen, and the food was arranged buffet-style.

The band and I went to each table to meet and talk with all these children, who basically all spoke English. I went up to the front of the room and talked to them all about where we're from, why we were there, why we were in Rwanda, and how we know about suffering; but, I added, you are our children and we want to do everything we can for you. One little boy told me that his mother, father, and entire family were destroyed in the genocide. He said, "All I want to do is go to school, can you help me?" Each one of these children talked about education; they weren't begging us for money, they were all talking about how they wanted to go to school. It was so emotional that we were nearly all in tears.

I thought about how spoiled we are in America, we have so much abun-

dance that we never use and these kids have nothing. Finally the food arrived and we served the children. One remarkable thing was you could
hear a pin drop in this room with these fifty children; not at all like it would
have been in New York, where there would have been chaos. Everything
seemed connected: from my meeting earlier that summer when Gail and I
met with Laura Greer at the Apollo Theater to plan an event there for February for my foundation, to meeting the AIDS doctor, to connecting with
these kids. When we met at the Apollo we discussed having a benefit for
some cause but we didn't really know what our purpose was, we didn't
have a theme. Suddenly meeting these children gave us an instant cause:
assisting their desire to be educated.

I thought about my "Congolese Children's Song" and thought I'd change
that to "Rwandan Children's Song"; maybe contact someone like Jayne
Cortez or one of my other friends to write some new lyrics—same melody,
just change the name and the lyrics. After the kids ate we were to play a
concert for them and an invited audience at the French embassy. We played
a couple of numbers, then I asked each musician to walk out and talk to
the audience about their instrument for a few minutes. Benny Powell stole
the show. He took out his trombone and did one of those New Orleans
parade rhythms, then he started singing "When the Saints Go Marching In"
and everybody joined in. It was magnetic—like Louis Armstrong was right
there in the room.

Then we brought the kids onstage and started singing "Rwandan Children's Song" based on the original lyrics, substituting Rwandan for Congolese children. It was so spiritual, and we realized instantly that these children would be the focus of the foundation. For one of these children to go
to school, including room and board, was only $200 a year.

Our next performance was at the Hotel Intercontinental in a room with
a good piano. The concert audience included five of the ministers from the
earlier meeting, and they really enjoyed it. We said, "This is your music, but
this is also the future." There were a lot of Rwandan people in attendance
and some Europeans as well. Considering the music and the personality of
the Rwandan people, we totally felt at home. The day we left there was a
guy at the hotel desk writing us a note when we were checking out. This is
the same guy who had persistently been requesting that we play "Salt Peanuts," which I finally did on the piano. It turns out this guy was very close
to the president of Rwanda. He told me he was so moved that he's now
our number 1 fan, that they were going to make me an honorary citizen of

Rwanda, that we have no idea what our music did for them. It was just that kind of trip.

There was more than a little confusion throughout the trip, but I knew from my experience with these things that you have to remain above that and concentrate on the important things, like those children. The entire trip was tremendously moving and gave Fatou and me some real direction for our foundation. We planned to perform that benefit concert at the Apollo. Those Rwandan children would be a beneficiary of our efforts on behalf of the foundation; they have really given us a purpose.

The musicians are the keepers of history. When you hear Louis Armstrong you can envision New Orleans at that time—we're the keepers of the history of our people. I think we're coming back to who we should be; in other words black music should support black people, support African people, whether its children, seniors, or whoever. Our music is much deeper than Birdland or some festival, our music is how our ancestors survived slavery. Rwanda is one of the worst tragedies in the history of the world, especially in terms of black people killing black people. But those people gave us every reason to care very deeply.

*Fatoumata Mbengue-Weston*: When we arrived in Rwanda we were all excited because after '94 and the genocide, none of us really knew what exactly happened in Rwanda. For me being an African, I wanted to see these people. I really felt the vibe of what had happened; these people were walking, talking, smiling, but something else was happening inside them with all that death and everything. After the initial chaos of that stadium scene we really started to see the beauty of the Rwandan people—through the dance, how they treated us, everything was perfect.

After Randy met with the AIDS doctor she told us, "I've got the right man for what I want to do." The way Randy talks about Africa really convinced her; she could see that this man does not lie about Africa; this man doesn't try to say "I'm an African" falsely. When he says that it feels genuine to Africans; she had never heard an American talk that way about Africa. We want the children of Africa to have a future. In Rwanda they are on the street and the streets are very dangerous for them. I was crying because for me as an African going to Rwanda was very painful. But it was a wonderful trip

*Randy*: The year 2008 was extraordinary. My partner Abdeslaam from the African Rhythms Club passed away in January, so we traveled to Tangier in February to pay our condolences to his wife Khadija. Then we went to Dakar,

Senegal, to once again celebrate the death of Cheikh Anta Diop. Africans celebrate death dates because you know what a man has done in his life, so you celebrate those accomplishments by honoring the day of his passing.

*Fatoumata*: In Africa when you're alive they celebrate your birthday, but when you die you are no longer in this world so now you have to celebrate the day of a person's passing; it's like the beginning and the end. When you're alive you celebrate the beginning of your being in this world, when you die you celebrate the date of your death because you can't come back.

*Randy*: We gathered with the family of Cheikh Anta Diop to travel to his home village where he was born, Caytou, north of Dakar. On this occasion they were going to build a mausoleum for Cheikh Anta Diop as a historic UNESCO site. So we got on a bus for the drive to Caytou. But the bus driver obviously didn't know how to drive very well. Next thing I knew we had skidded into a ditch.

*Fatoumata*: We had a police escort for this bus and we drove up to a traffic cop directing the traffic like a ballet; our bus driver was just about to hit this traffic cop, so he swerved and ran into a ditch trying to avoid hitting this traffic cop.

*Randy*: We've just started this trip; we're not even out of Dakar yet. So Fatou jumped out of the bus and said, "Here we go again," just like during our 2007 trip to Diop's village, when our driver was going too fast and hit a horse.

*Fatoumata*: The Minister of Culture was in the back of an SUV making the trip, so I grabbed Randy and said, "Go with that SUV, I'll stay behind in the bus."

*Randy*: So we arrive in the same village as the year before, with all the dignitaries and whatnot. They have this incredible square, which on this occasion held the minister of culture and other dignitaries on one side. On the other side were mostly women with all the families, all the different colorful garments, a sizable crowd of people. When we finally got seated Fatou is sitting next to the guy who is supposed to be the organizer of FESMAN, which is the next black arts festival of Senegal. I'm sitting next to him and the minister of culture is in the middle. And then there were different speeches about Cheikh Anta Diop, everything spoken in French. The minister got up and introduced me to the crowd as a great friend of Cheikh Anta Diop and asked me to say a few words. This was a big shock, totally unplanned. Meanwhile I'm sitting in this chair and the chair is slowly sinking into the ground. I could see Fatou and I knew she was thinking, "Oh, no, here we go again." So I grabbed the microphone, and Fatou said she had never heard me speak such great French before. I told them how I met Cheikh Anta Diop, how he was a great man, and how highly he is regarded in America because he told black people who we are. When the ceremony was over one guy came up to me and wanted to give me a wife and a house!

*Fatoumata*: I said, "House, yes, wife, no."

*Randy*: In May 2008 a Professor Amine at the University of Tetouan in Morocco, just east of Tangier, decided to honor me and my great friend the Gnawa Maalem (or Master) Abdullah el Gourde. It was a fantastic and unusual occasion for Morocco because it was a week of tribute events for two black men. We received recognition I didn't think we would ever get. Coincidentally there was a crew there from PBS filming a documentary on Morocco, so I did a special concert for them on film. That was not only a big shock because of them honoring two black men, but also because when I arrived in Morocco in the '60s Gnawa music was not considered important at all; remember, back then they thought of the Gnawa as strictly street musicians. So for us to be honored in a North African country was an exception.

## The Year of Obama

The year 2008 was also very important because I got to meet Barack Obama when he spoke at the Brooklyn Marriott. I've never been one to get excited over politics or politicians, but that night I really sensed something special in this brother. If you look at life as the ancients did—and I always try to imagine that by what they wrote: the ancient Egyptians, the elders, and the things they wrote and how those people saw the world—they don't see the world the same as people in the West. People in the East are a much older civilization and they have a much deeper concept, so for me Obama is a prophet sent by the Creator because we've lost our way. For so long we have not had the kind of leadership like we had with giants like Paul Robeson, A. Philip Randolph, Marcus Garvey . . . people we were inspired to follow. But today a lot of our leaders have gotten away from the culture.

All of our ancient leaders, all of our elders, they knew the importance of music and art, painting and poetry, and writing . . . The leadership of today has gotten so far away from the culture. So for me the Creator has sent Obama to bring us back. As I've said, and as my father taught me—Africa is the past, Africa is the present, Africa is the future. I think that Africa created civilization, became very big, people started turning against each other, Africa went all the way to the bottom, and everything else stemmed from that: the slavery, the bad leadership in Africa, the bad leadership wherever. But I think that now we have to go back and Africa now is the future. Obama's father being from Kenya makes it even more incredible. If he was just an African American like Jesse Jackson that would be fantastic, but this man's father is from Kenya. So for him to arise at this time is God's way to give us the inspiration for him to influence us to be better people in whatever we do, to be better citizens of the world.

# CONCLUSION

## Randy Weston . . . Philosophically Yours

Africa, the cradle of civilization, is my ancestral home, the home of my spirit and soul. Africa has always been part of me, Africa has always been deep in my psyche from childhood, and I knew I'd have to go there sooner or later. In 1961 I finally did, and again in 1963—both times to Nigeria. Then my sextet and I toured those fourteen countries in West and North Africa in 1967, and later that year I went back to stay. So many memories . . .

For me the most compelling aspect of African culture—North, South, East, and West—is its music, magnificent in its power and diversity, with the "true drums"—African Rhythms—always at the heart. The music of no other civilization can rival that of Africa in the complexity and subtlety of its rhythms. All modern music, no matter what it's called—jazz, gospel, Latin, rock, bossa nova, calypso, samba, soul, the blues, reggae, even the music of the avant-garde—is in debt to African Rhythms.

The rhythms came from all over Africa. I knew the rhythms were African, but I didn't realize how universally African they were until the 1967 tour. Africans in nearly every country we visited claimed the rhythms as their own, as typical of Ghana or Gabon or Upper Volta or Morocco; each African country has its very own traditions.

Most of my compositions are about African people or involve African themes. Every concert and even in my day-to-day conversation I'm speaking about African people. I am an Africanist in every sense of the word because of my immersion in African Rhythms, the realization of which came directly from my mother and father and goes all the way back to ancient African civilizations.

I have visited many countries, performed for thousands and thousands of people, and I am blessed to have the power of music—given to me by God—to spread our history, our creativity, and our music. And I've been very fortunate that my audiences have received that sincerity and spirit so warmly.

The music is so varied that we still have no real idea what African music is. I do know this, though: when an African touches an instrument, whether that African is a diaspora extension like Louis Armstrong or a master healer from Morocco, that instrument becomes an African instrument. When a person is touched by African music, from his skin to his soul, that person has become Africanized. Perhaps this is the true meaning of universal—something seemingly foreign that touches you and reminds you of your deepest self. In Africa I discovered what the true purpose of a musician is. We are historians, what some Africans refer to as griots, and it is our purpose to tell the people the true story of our past, and to extend a better vision of the future.

I am very proud to be a black man. I'm very proud of my tradition, of my past, of my parents and my ancestors, and I'm very proud of our home continent Africa. We of African ancestry have a tree, at the root of which is African music with its infinite variety, and we have our masters—Art Tatum, Duke Ellington, Charlie Parker, John Coltrane—and from this trunk we spread out into branches and tributaries. But we are all part of the same tree, and we are all involved with each other in a continuing evolution. I'm convinced that we are only an extension of African civilization, and all our music is really African music.

African music is based on rhythm—the kind of rhythm that makes people move, because our music is music to uplift the spirits. In the African tradition the audience and the music are one—there is no separation between the two. So when you perform for a black or African audience and you are in tune with them, the audience becomes part of the performance, and they will in turn convey certain responses to you so that it becomes a complete experience.

The truest test of our success as musicians is to maintain our basic traditions, to maintain our historical and our visionary concepts of the music into the future. The whole notion of "old" music is utter nonsense, because there is no such thing as old music. Time is eternal, so you will hear melodies and rhythms that have existed for thousands of years and retain the spark of spontaneity. I think that if people got away from that concept of "modern music" and really got to the music itself, they would be checking out the 1927 Duke Ellington band—that's some way-out stuff. It's no accident that Duke called his band the Jungle Band in the twenties, because Duke himself was always trying to capture the soul of black people. And if you listen to Ellington, from his early work all throughout his career, you can always hear the spirit force of Africa.

The mission of my music is to reach the people who are in tune, be they black, brown, beige, red, yellow, or white. I also hope to reach the teacher, who will teach it to the kids. I want to influence the people who know, who will get to the people as messengers to carry forth these traditions.

I feel that the reason why I'm on this earth, the reason why God has given me this time on earth, is to try to project a heavy spiritual message about who we are, what we have done, where we are going, so we will be able to absorb all things African, including vital forces like music. To play my music—that is my greatest success of all. My music is eternal, because God has given me a gift which I project into the piano. My message in music is unity for our people, to be proud of who we are and what we have contributed to the world. This music will live forever, and that is my success.

I call my music African Rhythms in an effort to convey to all who hear me or read about me that however they may label my music, or whatever my nationality, they must understand that my music is solidly rooted in the music of Africa. Years ago I decided to call my music African Rhythms because Africa is the common denominator, the nucleus of our music. When I give a concert for children I'll play an African traditional melody, I'll play the blues, and I'll play a spiritual, and I'll do it in such a way that the kids will hear it's all the same music, the same source.

Gospel music, the blues, and especially the highly diversified music known as jazz are a special contribution of the American black people to the culture of America and the world—a unique combination and adaptation of African musical sound, rhythms, melodies, patterns, and harmonies utilizing European instruments, musical forms, and melodies.

Music is the sacred art and God has given us the gift of music for communication. African musicians throughout the world are the griots of the present day. But theirs is the vision not only of the past and present but of the future. In a way, musicians are truer griots than those using the spoken word, because their language is universal and not subject to debate about "meaning" or "connotation." Music speaks to the heart, from the heart; its rhythms are the rhythms of life itself. I just do my best to try and spread our message everywhere in the world so we can all have pride in Africa and African people. We come from a very, very high civilization and it's no accident that we're playing this music.

Those of us who have been given the gift of music by the Creator have a responsibility, a spiritual responsibility to enlighten ourselves and our brothers and sisters about the true role of the African musician in ancient times and up to today. Only truth can strengthen us, guide us to make our real contribution to world civilization—and to the universe, and to our Creator.

Music is our only real universal language. I've traveled to many parts of the world, and though I could not always speak the language, I was able to communicate with people through music. Music is a sacred art; music can give people inspiration in their battle for freedom. You can't kill music because music is life itself. And music is something that is very spiritual—and though it has its mysteries, it is a unifying force.

> Link ourselves with our past
> And our true ancestors
> to free our minds and spirit
> to use all our creativity.
> We are simply an extension of African civilization,
> another branch of the Mother tree
> and underneath the roots,
> the foundation,
> the spirits of our ancestors
> who have given us the Rhythms and Sounds
> to survive and create
> no matter how high the barrier.

## Yaa-Lengi Ngemi, educator

*Yaa-Lengi Ngemi:* African music goes back to the period of time that the Ancient Egyptians, who were Black, called Zep Tepi, or First Time. Zep Tepi, in the sacred language of ancient Black Egyptians called Medu Neter (hieroglyphics), or the language of the gods, refers to the time of the Beginning, the Time of Creation, when gods and goddesses walked and talked with the first humans, the Black man and the Black woman on this earth. In this context Randy Weston has been able to transcend the routine dimension of music for music's sake and he has reached the spiritual dimension of that Ancient African music. One has to listen with spiritual ears in order to penetrate the higher nature of Randy Weston's African Rhythms; for in doing so one can feel and experience that African spirit that speaks through the sounds of the ancients. The instrument does not make the music, the spirit of the music maker makes the music, and gives the music that higher spiri-

tual dimension. This African music maker—Randy Weston's spirit—
has reached that ancestral high level of becoming endowed with the
gift of making the music that reaches that high dimension, that takes
us forward and back to Zep Tepi, and every one that has ears to listen
and hear is blessed by his music.

> Rhythm is the secret
> the beginning and the end.
> African Rhythms have found its way into
> the hearts of many.
> Many are feeding their souls
> and curing their wounds with its glory.
> —PAPA OYEH MACKENZIE, as told to Randy Weston

Before the music comes pride as a black man; if I didn't play music I'd be
fighting for the black man. Music has been a way for me to convey that
struggle; I've been gifted with the power of music. But before the music
came a tremendous pride mixed with anger at what racism has done to my
people. That foundation comes from growing up in a segregated, racist society; growing up among people who were considered a "minority." I knew
these people were not better than me, so I grew up spiritual but angry. I use
the music as a way to unite our people. I use the music to say that we can
develop a language that you can't steal, because when we go back to our
tradition you can't steal the spirituality of Africa.

Number one is God, Mom and Pop . . . and that's it. Sometimes I eat very
badly and may not take proper care of myself, but I think it's a mental thing
also, that you don't let numbers decide how you feel and what you are. If
you think old you become old. Of course there are some things I can't do
now that I did twenty or thirty years ago. I think it's important to be happy
to reach an advanced age, unless you're physically ill, of course. It's wonderful to be able to make that transition, getting old is not a drag for some
people. I see the beauty in age: age is experience. I've had so many wonderful experiences in life and with luck I've become old.

I was in the Army for three years, in Okinawa for one year, been in dangerous situations where there were bombs, booby traps, and street gangs
. . . a lot of things have happened that could have wiped me out. Longevity
is a combination of things, but I think you really have to believe it's coming
from the Almighty. I have been protected to a certain degree; before he

died my father said, "You are protected." And after being around the elders I truly believe that the ancestors play a very important role in what we do with our lives. So when I'm on that stage, Duke Ellington is on that stage with me, as are Monk, Mom and Pop, Billie Holiday, Diop, African civilization . . . they're all there. So it's not just Randy Weston, it's these collective spirits.

God has given me a gift which I project into the piano. My message in music is unity for our people, to be proud of who we are and what we have contributed to the world. This music will live forever and that is my success.

# DISCOGRAPHY

*(compiled by Jaap Haarlar; asterisk (\*) indicates original composition by Randy Weston)*

*Zep Tepi*, Random Chance 7020267 (CD), New York, December 2006

    Randy Weston, piano; Alex Blake, bass; Neil Clarke, percussion

    "Blue Moses"*
    "African Sunrise"*
    "Berkshire Blues"*
    "Route of the Nile"*
    "Ballad for T"*
    "Portrait of Frank Edward Weston"*
    "Hi-Fly"*
    "Tamashii"*
    "The Healers"*
    "Love, the Mystery of" (Warren)

*Live in St. Lucia*, Image Entertainment ID2982RW (CD),
St. Lucia, April 2002

    Randy Weston, piano; Alex Blake, bass; Neil Clarke, percussion;
    Talib Kibwe, alto saxophone, flute; Benny Powell, trombone

    "African Cookbook"*
    "The Shrine"*
    "African Sunrise"*
    "Little Niles"*
    "Three Pyramids and a Sphinx"*
    "Blue Moses"*

*Ancient Future/Blue* (2 CDs), Mutable 17508-2, New York, 2001

    Randy Weston, piano

    "Ancient Future"*

"Roots of the Nile"*
"Kom Ombo"*
"Bambara"*
"Portrait of Oum Keltoum"*
"Ballad for T"*
"Isis"*
"Blues for CB"*
"PCN"*
"It Don't Mean a Thing" (Ellington)
"Body and Soul" (Green/Heyman/Soer)
"Double Duke Pt 1"*
"Out of the Past" (Golson/Hendricks)
"Double Duke Pt 2"*
"Come Sunday" (Ellington)
"Sketch of Melba"*
"Penny Packer Blues"*
"Earth Birth"*
"The Last Day"*
"Lagos"*
"Blue in Tunisia"*
"Mystery of Love" (Warren)
"Ellington Tusk"*

*Spirit! The Power of Music*, Verve/Gitanes 543 256-2 (CD), Sunnyside
SSC 3015 (CD), Brooklyn, N.Y., 24 September 1999

Randy Weston, piano; Alex Blake, bass; Neil Clarke, percussion;
Talib Kibwe, flute, alto saxophone; Benny Powell, trombone; Gnawa
Master Musicians of Morocco (M'Barek Ben Othman, percussion,
vocals; Ahmed Ben Othman, percussion, vocals; Ahmed Saassaa,
guembri, vocals; Abdellah El-Gourd, guembri, vocals; Abdenebi
Oubella, percussion; Mostafa Oubella, percussion)

"Origin"*
"Receiving the Spirit Pt 1 and Pt 2"*
"Haghouge & String Bass" (El-Gourde)
"Chalabati" (traditional)
"Who Know Them?" (El-Gourde)
"El Wali Sidi Mimoun" (traditional)
"Lalla Mira Pt 1 and Pt 2" (traditional)

*Khepera*, Verve/Gitanes 557 821-2 (CD),
New York, 23–25 February 1998

Randy Weston, piano; Alex Blake, bass; Neil Clarke, percussion;
Talib Kibwe, alto saxophone, flute; Benny Powell, trombone;
Victor Lewis, drums; Pharoah Sanders, tenor and soprano
saxophones; Chief Bey, ashiko-drums, vocals; Min Xiao Fen,
pipa, gong; Melba Liston, arrangements

"Creation"*
"Anu Anu"*
"The Shrine"*
"Prayer Blues"*
"Niger Mambo" (Benson)
"Mystery of Love" (Warren)
"Portrait of Cheikh Anta Diop"*
"Boram Xam Xam"*
"The Shang" (Weston/Xiao-Fen)

*Earth Birth*, Verve/Gitanes 537 088-2 (CD), Montreal, 4 July 1995

Randy Weston, piano; Christian McBride, bass; Billy Higgins,
drums; Orchestre du Festival de Jazz de Montréal; Melba Liston,
arrangements

"Earth Birth"*
"Pam's Waltz"*
"Babe's Blues"*
"Little Niles"*
"Where"*
"Hi-Fly"*
"Portrait of Billie Holiday"*
"Berkshire Blues"*
"Portrait of Vivian"*

*Saga*, Verve/Gitanes 529 237-2 (CD), New York, 14–17 March 1995

Randy Weston, piano; Alex Blake, bass; Neil Clarke, percussion;
Talib Kibwe, alto saxophone, flute; Benny Powell, trombone;
Billy Harper, tenor saxophone; Billy Higgins, drums

"The Beauty of It All"*
"Loose Wig"*
"Tangier Bay"*

"F.E.W. Blues"*
"Uncle Neemo"*
"Lagos"*
"A Night in Mbari"*
"Saucer Eyes"*
"The Three Pyramids and the Sphinx"*
"Casbah Kids"*
"Jahjuka"*
"The Gathering"*


*Volcano Blues*, Verve/Gitanes 519 269-2 (CD),
New York, 5–6 February 1993

Randy Weston, piano; Wallace Roney, trumpet; Talib Kibwe, alto
saxophone, flute; Benny Powell, trombone; Teddy Edwards, tenor
saxophone; Hamiet Bluiett, baritone saxophone; Ted Dunbar, guitar;
Johnny Copeland, guitar, vocals; Jamil Nasser, bass; Charles Persip,
drums; Obo Addy, percussion; Neil Clarke, percussion; Melba Liston,
arrangements

"Blue Mood" (Robinson)
"Chalabati Blues"*
"Sad Beauty Blues"*
"The Nafs"*
"Volcano"*
"Harvard Blues"*
"In Memory of"*
"Blues for Strayhorn"*
"Penny Packer Blues"*
"J&K Blues"*
"Mystery of Love" (Warren)
"Kucheza Blues"*
"Blues for Elma Lewis"*


*Marrakech in the Cool of the Evening*, Verve/Gitanes 521 588-2 (CD),
Marrakech, 28 September 1992

Randy Weston, piano

"In the Cool of the Evening" (Cole)
"Portrait of Billie Holiday"*
"Two Different Ways to Play the Blues"*
"Portrait of Dizzy": "A Night in Tunisia" (Gillespie/Paparelli),

"Woody 'n You" (Gillespie), "Con Alma" (Gillespie), "Tin Tin Deo" (Fuller/Gonzales)
"Lisa Lovely"*
"Uli Shrine"*
"Blues for Elma Lewis"*
"Ballad for T"*
"Valse Triste Valse"*
"Where?"*
"Let's Climb a Hill"*
"The Jitterbug Waltz" (Waller)
"Blues for Five Reasons"*
"Lotus Blossom" (Strayhorn)

*The Splendid Master Gnawa Musicians*, Verve 521 587-2 (CD), Marrakech, 17 September 1992

Randy Weston, piano (3 only); Master Gnawa Musicians (Ali El Mansoum, guembri, percussion, vocals; Molay Abdelaziz, guembri, percussion, vocals; Mohammed Zourhba, guembri, percussion, vocals; Ahmed Boussou, guembri, percussion, vocals; Ahmed Boussou, guembri, percussion, vocals; Abdelouaid Berrady, guembri, percussion, vocals; Mahmoud Gania, guembri, percussion, vocals; M'Barek Ben Outman, percussion, vocals; Abdenabi Oubella, percussion, vocals; Abdellah El Gourd, guembri, percussion, vocals)

"La Voix Erante" (traditional): "Sorie"; "Folinho Rejale"; "Ahayanna Wayi"; "Bokarli Ana"
"Sound Playing" (traditional): "Bermaryho," "Fanyro," "Merkadi," "Yobady," "Ya La La," "Congoba," "Tembara," "Kanerjak Ya Rebi," "Chalabati" (traditional)

*The Spirits of Our Ancestors*, Verve 511 857-2 (2 CDs), New York, 20–22 May 1991

Randy Weston, piano; Idrees Sulieman, trumpet; Dizzy Gillespie, trumpet; Benny Powell, trombone; Talib Kibwe, alto saxophone, flute; Billy Harper, tenor saxophone; Pharoah Sanders, tenor sax, gaita; Dewey Redman, tenor saxophone; Alex Blake, bass; Jamil Nasser, bass; Idris Muhammad, drums; Azzedin Weston, percussion; Big Black, percussion; Yassir Chadly, percussion, karkaba, vocals; Melba Liston, arrangements

"African Village Bedford-Stuyvesant"*
"The Healers"*
"African Cookbook"*
"La Elaha-Ella Allah/Morad Allah" (traditional)
"The Call"
"African Village Bedford-Stuyvesant 2"*
"The Seventh Queen"*
"Blue Moses"*
"African Sunrise"*
"A Prayer for Us All"*


*Well You Needn't*, Verve 841 3132 (CD), Paris, 3 June 1989

Randy Weston, piano; Jamil Nasser, bass; Idris Muhammad, drums, percussion; Eric Asante, percussion

"Well You Needn't" (Monk/McRae)
"Misterioso" (Monk)
"Ruby My Dear" (Monk)
"I Mean You" (Monk)
"Functional" (Monk)
"Off Minor" (Monk)


*Caravan: Portraits of Duke Ellington*, Verve 841-3122 (CD), Paris, 4 June 1989

Randy Weston, piano; Jamil Nasser, bass; Idris Muhammad, drums, percussion; Eric Asante, percussion

"Caravan" (Ellington/Tizol/Mills)
"Heaven" (Ellington)
"Sepia Panorama" (Ellington)
"Limbo Jazz" (Ellington)
"C Jam Blues" (Ellington)
"Chromatic Love Affair" (Ellington)


*The Last Day: Self Portraits*, Verve 841 3142 (CD), Paris, 5 June 1989

Randy Weston, piano; Jamil Nasser, bass; Idris Muhammad, drums, percussion; Eric Asante, percussion

"Portrait of Frank Edward Weston"*
"Berkshire Blues"*

"African Night"*
"Night in Medina"*
"Ganawa in Paris"*
"The Last Day"*


*Blue*, Arch 1750 S-1802 (LP), Seattle, March 1983

Randy Weston, piano

"Penny Packer Blues"*
"Earth Birth"*
"The Last Day"*
"Lagos"*
"Blue in Tunisia"*
"Mystery of Love" (Warren)
"Ellington Tusk"*


*The Healers*, Cora 01 (LP), Pointe-à-Pitre, Guadeloupe, 1980

Randy Weston, piano

"The Healers"*
"Blues Antillais"*
"Blue Moses"*
"Nite in M'Bari"*
"A Prayer for Us All"*
"Nite in Medina"*


*Rhythms and Sounds*, Cora 01 (LP), Vercelli, Italy, 1978

Randy Weston, piano

"Niger Mambo"*
"Portrait of Vivian"*
"Willie's Tune"*
"Hi-Fly"*
"The Man I Love"* (Gershwin)

*Perspective*, Denon YX-7564-ND (CD reissue),
New York, 14 December 1976

    Randy Weston, piano; Vishnu Bill Wood, bass

    "Blues to Be There" (Strayhorn)
    "Body and Soul" (Eyton/Sour/Green/Heyman)
    "Hi-Fly"*
    "Khadesha" (Wood)
    "African Cookbook"*

*Randy Weston Meets Himself*, Pausa 7017 (LP), Milan, 28 January 1976

    Randy Weston, piano

    "Portrait of Tuntemeke"*
    "Buena Cosecha" (Good/Harvest)
    "Out of the Past" (Golson)
    "Monk Steps"*
    "Ode to Om-Kel-Thoum"*
    "The Three Pyramids and the Sphinx"*
    "Sister Gladys"*

*African Nite / Nuit Africain*, Universal 014732-2 (CD reissue),
Paris, 21 September 1975

    Randy Weston, piano

    "Little Niles"*
    "Blues to Senegal"*
    "African Nite"*
    "Samba Bossa"*
    "Jejouka"*
    "Portrait of Miriam Makeba"*
    "Con Alma" (Gillespie)
    "C.W. Blues"*
    "Yubadee"*

*African Rhythms*, Chant du Monde LDX7 4602 (LP), Paris, 4 April 1975

    Randy Weston, piano

    "Lifetime"*
    "Le Cygne du lac d'Annecy"*

"Pretty Strange"*
"Solemn Meditation" (Gil)
"Take Me Back Home Baby Blues"*
"Portrait of Frank Edward Weston"*
"Ruby My Dear" (Monk)
"Night in Mbari"*
"Sound Colors"*
"Seminoz"*


*Blues to Africa*, Freedom 741014 (CD reissue), Zurich, 14 August 1974

Randy Weston, piano

"African Village/Bedford Stuyvesant"*
"Tangier Bay"*
"Blues to Africa"*
"Kasbah Kids"*
"Uhuru Kwanza"*
"The Call"*
"Kucheza Blues"*
"Sahel"*


*Informal Piano Solo*, Hi-Fly 101 (LP), Annecy, France, 11 July 1974

Randy Weston, piano

"Night in Tunisia" (Gillespie/Parelli)
"Willie's Tune"*
"African Lady" (Weston/Hughes)
"Blues for Senegal"*
"How High the Moon" (Hampton/Lewis)
"Kasbah Kids"*
"Hi-Fly"*
"Where"*
"Do Nothin' til You Hear from Me" (Ellington)
"Three Blind Mice" (traditional)


*Carnival Live at Montreux Jazz Festival*, Freedom 741004 (CD reissue), Montreux, Switzerland, 5 July 1974

Randy Weston, piano; Billy Harper, tenor saxophone; Don Moye, drums; Steve Berrios, percussion; William Allen, bass

"Carnival"*
"Introduction"*
"Tribute to Duke Ellington"*
"Introduction"*
"Mystery of Love" (Warren)


*Tanjah*, Verve 527778-2 (CD reissue), New York, 21 May 1973

Randy Weston, piano; Ernie Royal, trumpet, flugelhorn; Ray
Copeland, trumpet, flugelhorn; Jon Faddis, trumpet, flugelhorn;
Al Grey, trombone; Jack Jeffers, baritone trombone; Julius Watkins,
French horn; Norris Turney, alto saxophone, piccolo; Budd Johnson,
tenor saxophone, soprano saxophone, clarinet; Billy Harper, tenor
saxophone; Danny Bank, baritone saxophone, baritone clarinet, flute;
Ron Carter, bass; Rudy Collins, drums; Candido Camero, percussion,
narrator; Omar Clay, percussion; Taiwo Yusve Divall, alto saxophone,
percussion; Earl Williams, percussion; Ahmed-Abdul Malik, oud,
narrator; Delores Ivory Davis, vocals; Melba Liston, arrangements

"Hi-Fly"*
"In Memory Of"*
"Sweet Meat"*
"Jamaica East"*
"Sweet Meat"*
"Tanjah"
"The Last Day"*
"Sweet Meat"*
"Little Niles"*


*Blue Moses*, CTI 6016 (LP), King (Japan CD reissue),
New York, March–April 1972

Randy Weston, piano, electric keyboard; Ron Carter, bass;
Vishnu Bill Wood, bass; Billy Cobham, drums; David Horowitz,
synthesizer; Freddie Hubbard, trumpet; John Frosk, trumpet;
Alan Rubin, trumpet; Marvin Stamm, trumpet; Wayne Andre,
trombone, baritone horn; Garnett Brown, trombone; Paul Faulise,
trombone, bass trombone; Brooks Tillotson, French horn; James
Buffington, French horn; George Marge, English horn, clarinet, flute,
alto flute, bass flute; Hubert Laws, flute, alto flute, bass flute, electric
flute, piccolo; Romeo Penque, English horn, clarinet, flute, alto flute,
bass flute, piccolo; Grover Washington, tenor saxophone; Phil Kraus,

percussion; Airto Moreira, percussion; Azzedin Weston, percussion;
Madame Meddah, vocals

"Ifran"*
"Ganawa-Blue Moses"*
"Night in Medina"*
"Marrakesh Blues"*

*Niles Littleebig*, Comet 027 (LP), Paris, June 1969

Randy Weston, piano; Henry Texier, bass; Art Taylor, drums;
Azzedin Niles Weston, percussion; Reebop Kwaku Baah, percussion

"African Cookbook"*
"A Night in Medina"*
"Jajouka"*
"Marrakech Blues"*
"Con Alma" (Gillespie)
"Afro-Black"*

*Monterey '66*, Polygram 519698 (CD reissue), Monterey, Calif.,
18 September 1966

Randy Weston, piano; Ray Copeland, trumpet, flugelhorn;
Booker Ervin, tenor saxophone; Cecil Payne, baritone saxophone;
Bill Wood, bass; Lennie McBrowne, drums; Big Black, percussion

"Introduction" (Lyons)
"The Call"*
"Afro-Black"*
"Little Niles"*
"Portrait of Vivian"*
"Berkshire Blues"*
"Blues for Strayhorn"*
"African Cookbook"*

*Berkshire Blues*, Black Lion 760205 (CD reissue),
New York, 18 August 1965

Randy Weston, piano; Vishnu Bill Wood, bass; Lennie McBrowne,
drums

"Three Blind Mice" (traditional)
"Perdido" (Tizol)
"Purple Gazelle" (Ellington)
"Berkshire Blues"*
"Lagos"*
"Sweet Meat"*
"Ifran"*

*Blues*, Trip 5033 (LP), New York, 1964–65

Randy Weston, piano; Ray Copeland, trumpet; Frank Haynes, tenor saxophone; Vishnu Bill Wood, bass; Lennie McBrowne, drums; Big Black, percussion

"Blues for Strayhorn"*
"Sad Beauty Blues"*
"Afro Blues"*

*Randy!*, Bakton BRS-1001 (LP), New York, October 1964

*African Cookbook*, Koch 8517 (CD reissue)

"Berkshire Blues"*
"Portrait of Vivian"*
"Willie's Tune"*
"Niger Mambo"*
"African Cookbook"*
"Congolese Children"*
"Blues for Five Reasons"*

*Highlife*, Colpix CP 456 (LP), New York, April 1963 [reissued as part of *Randy Weston Mosaic Select* Mosaic 004 (CD)]

Randy Weston, piano; Ray Copeland, trumpet, flugelhorn; Aaron Bell, tuba; Quentin Jackson, trombone; Julius Watkins, French horn; Booker Ervin, tenor saxophone; Budd Johnson, soprano saxophone, tenor saxophone; Peck Morrison, bass; Charlie Persip, drums; Frankie Dunlop, percussion; Archie Lee, congas; George Young, percussion; Melba Liston, arrangements

"Caban Bamboo Highlife"*
"Niger Mambo"*
"Zulu"*

"In Memory of"*
"Congolese Children"*
"Blues to Africa"*
"Mystery of Love" (Warren)


*Uhuru Afrika*, Roulette 21006 (LP), New York, 1960 [reissued as part of *Randy Weston Mosaic Select* Mosaic 004 (CD)]

Randy Weston, piano; Clark Terry, trumpet, flugelhorn; Benny Bailey, trumpet; Richard Williams, trumpet; Freddie Hubbard, trumpet; Slide Hampton, trombone; Quentin Jackson, trombone; Julius Watkins, French horn; Gigi Gryce, alto saxophone, flute; Yusef Lateef, tenor saxophone, flute, oboe; Sahib Shihab, alto saxophone, baritone saxophone; Budd Johnson, tenor saxophone, clarinet; Jerome Richardson, baritone saxophone, piccolo; Cecil Payne, baritone saxophone; Les Spann, guitar, flute; Kenny Burrell, guitar; George Duvivier, bass; Ron Carter, bass; Max Roach, drums, percussion; Charlie Persip, drums, percussion; Wilbert G. T. Hogan, drums; Candido Camero, percussion; Michael Babatunde Olatunji, percussion; Armando Peraza, percussion; Martha Flowers, vocals; Brock Peters, vocals; Tuntemeke Sanga, narrator; Melba Liston, arrangements

"Uhuru Kwanza"*
"African Lady"*
"Bantu"*
"Kucheza Blues"*


*Live at the Five Spot*, Blue Note LAS98-H2 (LP), New York, 26 October 1959 [reissued as part of *Randy Weston Mosaic Select* Mosaic 004 (CD)]

Randy Weston, piano; Kenny Dorham, trumpet; Coleman Hawkins, tenor saxophone; Wilbur Little, bass; Clifford Jarvis, drums; Roy Haynes, drums; Brock Peters, vocals; Melba Liston, arrangements

"Hi-Fly"*
"Beef Blues Stew"*
"Star-Crossed Lovers" (Strayhorn/Ellington)
"Spot Five Blues"*
"Where"*
"Lisa Lovely"*

*Destry Rides Again*, United Artists UAL 4045 (UAS 5045) (LP),
New York, May 1959

> Randy Weston, piano; Slide Hampton, trombone; Benny Green,
> trombone; Melba Liston, trombone, arrangements; Frank Rehak,
> trombone; Peck Morrison, bass; Elvin Jones, drums; Willie Rodriguez,
> percussion

> "We're Ladies" (Rome)
> "I Know Your Kind" (Rome)
> "Rose Lovejoy of Paradise Alley" (Rome)
> "Antone Would Love You" (Rome)
> "Once I Knew a Fella" (Rome)
> "Every Once in a While" (Rome)
> "Fair Warning" (Rome)
> "Are You Ready Gyp Watson?" (Rome)
> "I Say Hello" (Rome)
> "That Ring on the Finger" (Rome)

*Little Niles*, United Artists UAL 4011/UAS 5011 (LP),
New York, October 1958

> Randy Weston, piano; Ray Copeland, trumpet; Idrees Sulieman,
> trumpet; Melba Liston, trombone, arrangements; Johnny Griffin,
> tenor saxophone; George Joyner (Jamil Nasser), bass; Charlie Persip,
> drums

> "Earth Birth"*
> "Little Susan"*
> "Nice Ice"*
> "Little Niles"*
> "Pam's Waltz"*
> "Let's Climb a Hill"*
> "Babe's Blues"*

*New Faces at Newport*, Metro Jazz E1005 (MM2085) (LP),
Newport, R.I., 5 July 1958

> [one side of LP; other side by Lem Winchester] Randy Weston, piano;
> George Joyner (Jamil Nasser), bass; Wilbert G. T. Hogan, drums

> "Hi-Fly"*
> "Excerpt from Bantu Suite"*
> "Machine Blues"*

*Piano a la Mode*, Jubilee 1060 (LP), New York, spring 1957

> Randy Weston, piano; Peck Morrison, bass; Connie Kay, drums

> "Earth Birth"*
> "Nobody Knows the Trouble I Have Seen" (traditional)
> "Saucer Eyes"*
> "I Got Rhythm" (Gershwin)
> "Gingerbread"*
> "Cocktails for Two" (Coslow/Johnson)
> "Honeysuckle Rose" (Waller/Razaf)
> "FE-Double-U Blues"*


*How High the Moon*, Biograph 147 (CD reissue),
New York, 21–22 November 1956

*The Modern Art of Jazz*, Blue Moon/Dawn 107 (CD reissue),
New York, 21–22 November 1956

> Randy Weston, piano; Ray Copeland, trumpet; Cecil Payne, alto and
> baritone saxophones; Ahmed-Abdul Malik, bass; Wilbert Hogan,
> drums; Willie Jones, drums

> "Loose Wig"*
> "Run Joe" (Jordan/Merrick/Willoughby)
> "A Theme for Teddy"*
> "In a Little Spanish Town" (Lewis/Wayne/Young)
> "Don't Blame Me" (Fields/McHugh)
> "J. K. Blues"*
> "Well You Needn't" (Monk/McRae)
> "How High the Moon" (Hampton/Lewis)
> "Stormy Weather" (Arlen/Koehler)


*Jazz a la Bohemia*, Riverside Original Jazz Classics 1747-2 (CD reissue),
New York, 14 October 1956

> Randy Weston, piano; Cecil Payne, baritone saxophone; Ahmed-
> Abdul Malik, bass; Al Dreares, drums

> "Theme" (Gill)
> "Chessman's Delight"*
> "Hold 'Em Joe" (traditional)
> "It's All Right with Me" (Porter)
> "Just a Riff" (Catlett)

"Once in a While" (Edwards/Green)
"Solemn Meditation" (Gill)
"You Go to My Head" (Coots/Gillespie)
"Solemn Meditation" (Gill)
"Theme" (Gill)


*With These Hands*, Riverside Original Jazz Classics 1883 (CD reissue), Hackensack, N.J., 14–21 March 1956

Randy Weston, piano; Cecil Payne, baritone saxophone; Ahmed-Abdul Malik, bass; Wilbert G.T. Hogan, drums

"I Can't Get Started" (Duke/Gershwin)
"Do Nothin' till You Hear from Me" (Ellington/Russell)
"Lifetime"*
"Little Niles"*
"Serenade in Blue" (Warren/Gordon)
"The Man I Love" (Gershwin/Gershwin)
"These Foolish Things" (Strachey/Link/Marvell)
"This Can't Be Love" (Rodgers/Hart)


*Randy Weston Trio and Solo*, Riverside 12-227-SMJ 6208 (LP), Hackensack, N.J., 25 January 1955, 10 September 1956

Randy Weston, piano; Art Blakey, drums; Sam Gill, bass

"Sweet Sue" (Harris/Young)
"Pam's Waltz"*
"Solemn Meditation" (Gill)
"Again" (Cochran/Newman)
"Softness"*
"Lover" (Hart/Rodgers)


*Get Happy with the Randy Weston Trio*, Riverside Original Jazz Classics 1870 (CD reissue), Hackensack, N.J., 29–31 August 1955

Randy Weston, piano; Sam Gill, bass; Wilbert G. T. Hogan, drums; Ahmed-Abdul Malik, bass

"A Ballad" (Gill)
"Bass Knows"*
"C Jam Blues" (Ellington)
"Dark Eyes" (Salama)

"Fire Down There" (traditional)
"Get Happy" (Arlen/Koehler)
"Twelfth Street Rag" (Bowman)
"Under Blunder"*
Where Are You?" (Adams/McHugh)
"Summer Time" (Gershwin/Heyward)


*The Randy Weston Trio*, Riverside 2515 (LP), New York, 25 January 1955

Randy Weston, piano; Sam Gill, bass; Art Blakey, drums

"Again" (Cochran/Newman)
"Zulu"*
"Pam's Waltz"*
"Solemn Meditation" (Gill)
"If You Could See Me Now" (Dameron)
"Sweet Sue" (Harris/Young)


*Cole Porter in a Modern Mood*, Riverside 2508 (LP),
New York, 27 April 1954

Randy Weston, piano; Sam Gill, bass

"Get Out of Town" (Porter)
"I Get a Kick Out of You" (Porter)
"I Love You" (Porter)
"In the Still of the Night" (Porter)
"Just One of Those Things" (Porter)
"Night and Day" (Porter)
"What Is This Thing Called Love" (Porter)
"I've Got You under My Skin" (Porter)

# AWARDS AND CITATIONS

1994    *DownBeat* Composer of the Year

1995    Five-night tribute, Montreal Jazz Festival

1996    *DownBeat* Composer of the Year

1997    French Order of Arts and Letters

1999    Harvard University residency and tribute concert

1999    *DownBeat* Composer of the Year

2000    "Black Music Star Award" from the Arts Critics and Reviewers
        Association of Ghana

2001    National Endowment for the Arts Jazz Masters Fellowship

2003    New York University residency and tribute concert

2006    Honorary doctorate of music, Brooklyn College

2009    Inducted into the ASCAP "Jazz Wall of Fame"

# INDEX

Page numbers in *italics* refer to illustrations.

RANDY WESTON IS A COMPOSER
AND BANDLEADER.

WILLARD JENKINS IS AN INDEPENDENT CONCERT
AND FESTIVALS PRODUCER AND WRITER.


*Library of Congress Cataloging-in-Publication Data*
Weston, Randy, 1926–
African rhythms : the autobiography of Randy Weston /
composed by Randy Weston ; arranged by Willard Jenkins.
p. cm. — (Refiguring American music)
Includes index.
ISBN 978-0-8223-4784-2 (cloth : alk. paper)
1. Weston, Randy, 1926– —Biography.
2. Jazz musicians—United States—Biography.
3. Composers—United States—Biography.
I. Jenkins, Willard, 1949– II. Title.
III. Series: Refiguring American music.
ML417.W36A3 2010
781.65092—dc22
[B]   2010017148

ISBN 978-0-8223-4798-9 (pbk.: alk. paper)
ISBN 978-0-8223-9310-8 (e-book)

Cover credit: Photograph by Carol Friedman.